T0339443

ECONOMIC REFORMS AND CAPITAL MARKETS IN CENTRAL EUROPE

Transition and Development

Series Editor: Professor Ken Morita
Faculty of Economics, Hiroshima University, Japan

The Transition and Development series aims to provide high quality research books that examine transition and development societies in a broad sense – including countries that have made a decisive break with central planning as well as those in which governments are introducing elements of a market approach to promote development. Books examining countries moving in the opposite direction will also be included. Titles in the series will encompass a range of social science disciplines. As a whole the series will add up to a truly global academic endeavour to grapple with the questions transition and development economies pose.

Also in the series:

Economic Reforms and Capital Markets in Central Europe

KEN MORITA
Hiroshima University, Japan

Routledge
Taylor & Francis Group

LONDON AND NEW YORK

First published 2004 by Ashgate Publishing

Reissued 2018 by Routledge
2 Park Square, Milton Park, Abingdon, Oxon OX14 4RN
605 Third Avenue, New York, NY 10017

First issued in paperback 2021

Routledge is an imprint of the Taylor & Francis Group, an informa business

A Library of Congress record exists under LC control number: 2002043980

Notice:
Product or corporate names may be trademarks or registered trademarks, and are used only for identification and explanation without intent to infringe.

Publisher's Note
The publisher has gone to great lengths to ensure the quality of this reprint but points out that some imperfections in the original copies may be apparent.

Disclaimer
The publisher has made every effort to trace copyright holders and welcomes correspondence from those they have been unable to contact.

ISBN 13: 978-0-815-38869-2 (hbk)
ISBN 13: 978-1-351-15940-1 (ebk)
ISBN 13: 978-1-138-35683-2 (pbk)

DOI: 10.4324/9781351159401

Contents

To Michiyo, Aiko and Takashi

List of Figures

List of Tables

Preface

As the title of this book shows, the author mainly investigates two topics: (1) systemic transition of Central European[1] economies, and (2) the commodity futures market, particularly speculation. The two topics might seem rather different, actually, however, they are closely related as is stated in this book along with J. R. Hicks' assertion.[2] Also in this book the author has tried to consider more deeply (in Chapters one, two, and thirteen) the relations between the two topics. As a matter of fact, there are still many problems to be investigated. Economic reforms in Central Europe were hardly attempted about ten years ago, and the study of the functions of commodity futures markets in Central Europe has just started. In this book, therefore, we will indicate the way in which economic transition and commodity futures markets in Central Europe both work.

This book has three parts. In the first part, we consider commodity exchanges in Central Europe. Our attention is concentrated upon Poland (the Warsaw Commodity Exchange) and Hungary (the Budapest Commodity Exchange); after investigating relationships between centrally planned economies and futures markets and so on, we study the necessity of establishing a commodity exchange for transforming the economic system in Poland, and the function of the commodity futures market in Hungary. As will be seen after reading this book, the Warsaw Commodity Exchange is still of immature and the Budapest Commodity Exchange has had lots of problems for serious consideration (although the Budapest Commodity Exchange is further developed than that in Warsaw).

It seems necessary to investigate what and how serious the risk in the modern international economy is related to capital movements. In particular, important questions to be considered here are the following: what is characteristic risk in the former centrally planned economies and what is characteristic inefficiency related to centrally planned systems. In approaching questions we highlight: (1) risk in transition economies particularly Poland as an example and (2) barriers to foreign direct investment which are important to clarify in terms of the characteristic risks examined as (1) above. These are examined in the second part of the book.

In the third part, we analyze the speculation from which the Budapest Commodity Exchange suffered and which needs to be investigated further. Although it might be doubtful to mention that speculation itself has instability for the market, there has been rather a variety of cases of unstable speculation. If we describe the unstable cases as "excessive speculation", we must study what excessive speculation is and what reasonable policies for regulating against the excessiveness are. To do this, we examine a case study of excessive speculation, and in considering reasonable regulations we study a case involving international agreement for regulating commodity price movements.

That is an outline of three parts in this book. Needless to say, we should continue in a fourth part and fifth part based upon the questions raised in the first three parts of this book. As was mentioned previously, the topics both of economic transition in Central Europe and of speculative behavior in futures markets are now changing, sometimes drastically, which means further considerations will be necessary.

Therefore, each chapter in this book must be scientifically analyzed and carried out successful investigations later on this analysis.

Because this book covers a variety of topics, giving short summaries here in this introduction might be helpful for readers.

The book starts by examining relations between a centrally planned economy and the futures market, pointing out the inefficiency of a centrally planned economy. That might be the first step towards considering commodity futures markets in Central Europe. Then first we inquire about the necessity for and function of commodity exchanges in the Warsaw Commodity Exchange and in the Budapest Commodity Exchange. After that we try to describe the function of the Budapest Commodity Exchange, and after a comparative analysis with the Tokyo Grain Exchange, we conclude that there might be no significant difference between a commodity exchange in Central Europe and a commodity exchange in a developed country, such as Japan. However, it should be recognized that there have been risks, which are characteristic for transition economies. The most typical risks are the factors that hinder capital movement, particularly foreign direct investment into transition economies. In the second part of the book, we examine what the risks are for them. With such an examination, we confirm the typical risk for transition economies is a financial one. The financial risk can have serious effects for large-scale investment, and we can recognize this by statistical analysis that shows that foreign exchange reserves could significantly explain the inflow of foreign direct investment. Based on the above analyses emphasizing the importance of the financial aspect, in the third part of the book we consider speculation and the futures market, focusing our attention in particular upon stability. The short conclusion to the third part shows that, when "excessive speculation" comes into existence, it is extremely difficult to identify at an early stage and to prevent unstable effects for prices, it might be possible to successfully regulate price movements through quantitative regulation with enough commodity stock. Moreover, even if there could be a successful "price stabilization effect", it would also have the effect of expanding the macroeconomic disequilibrium.

Therefore, the view put forward in this book is as follows: for the commodity futures market in transition economies, financial risk still exists, which means that the commodity futures market would be developed by alleviating the financial risk in the transition process. At the same time we can see that it has been difficult for regulation by the authorities against excessive speculation to be successful, and that the best way of dealing with unstable speculation might be to establish a well working infrastructure for the market mechanism.

Hereafter we present a further summary of each chapter.

The purpose of the first chapter is to consider the differences between a centrally planned economy and futures transactions in adjusting disequilibrium (coming from the third and the fourth sources in the Hicksian sense).

As far as the first and second sources of disequilibrium are concerned, it could be eliminated with the functions of futures market and of a centrally planned economy without adjustment of the spot market. In other words, it could be considered that, concerning price expectation adjustment and quantity planning adjustment, a centrally planned economy could have the same function as a market economy. However, a centrally planned economy could not have a flexible mechanism to adjust disequilibrium in the spot market because there could not be flexible spot market adjustment in a centrally planned system. In the same terms as in chapter one, we could say that the difference coming from flexible spot market adjustment between a market economy and a centrally planned economy might be expressed as:

$$a(\mu_x - X_1)(P_f - P_1) \quad \text{or} \quad a\mu_x(P_f - P_1)$$

In chapter two in which we focus our attention upon Poland, we study inflation in Poland in the first section and privatization in the second section. It might not be so easy to recognize relationships between commodity futures markets, macroeconomic transition and structural reform. The purpose of section one is to indicate that important macroeconomic indicators and structural reform would produce the basic necessity for establishing commodity futures markets in Poland. That is to say, high inflation occurred together with a budget deficit to which agricultural expenditure contributed. Prices of agricultural products and the income level of farmers have been closely connected with high inflation in Poland. The huge amount of budget deficit has been one of the sources for speculative money. It would be difficult to say that privatization in Poland has been successful, but the general trend says that they have tried to have an intensive use of agricultural land and this has necessitated more efficient management for the agricultural sector and food processing sector, which seem to be comparative advantage industries. It could be confirmed that there exists necessity both from the supply side (like farmers) and from the demand side (like the food processing industry).

In the Polish economy, however, it has been difficult to eliminate price expectation, and privatization, particularly capital privatization, has been delayed. From the viewpoint of a more active function in the commodity futures market, we could see the necessity for and the possibility of a better functioning commodity exchange. At the same time, however, we could expect that a commodity futures market in Poland would be developed in the near future as part of their transition process.

In chapter three, we describe more about the commodity exchanges in Warsaw and Budapest. Establishing a commodity exchange is undoubtedly connected with the movement toward a market oriented economy. In Hungary the convenience of keeping trade from Chicago might be the main necessity of establishing a commodity exchange, and in Poland (as was shown in chapter two) the main necessities are for a reduction of subsidies to agriculture and for policy adjustment with the EU (European Union). Needless to say, the reform toward a market oriented economy means, in a sense, "Americanization" and "Globalization", which means putting more emphasis upon efficiency and much freer capital movement. In chapter three, we describe developing aspects of the Budapest Commodity Exchange based upon the above considerations. One of the "keywords" which connects the commodity exchanges in Central Europe and economic transition toward a market economy might be "instability". We should discuss in much more detail the way we deal with the instability arising from speculation and capital movements. Chapter three is, therefore, a chapter that raises questions and creates a bridge toward the second and third part of this book.

In chapter four, we discuss the efficiency of commodity exchanges in Central Europe focusing our attention upon the Budapest Commodity Exchange, particularly with a comparative view of the Tokyo Grain Exchange. Although our conclusion might be rather tentative, it is as follows: it might be said that the function of the Budapest Commodity Exchange is no less efficient than of the Tokyo Grain Exchange.

Frankly speaking, however, the turnover of the Budapest Commodity

Exchange (particularly in the sections of livestock and grain) has been fairly small. By expanding the turnover, as in the foreign currency section, efficiency could be increased. This means that joining the EU would be a good opportunity for increasing turnover and for increasing efficiency. At the same time, however, joining the EU indicates more risk in terms of unstable speculation.

To join the enlarged EU might have both positive and negative effects upon: (1) possibility of raising efficiency by increasing market volume, and (2) risk from speculative instability. (Then, are there any effective policies that are more efficient as well as eliminating market instability?) It would be easy for a government or other institutions to have a policy of regulating and intervening in the market by. It would also be easy to expect that unreasonable regulation and intervention would have harmful effects on the market mechanism. The question we should ask is when and how regulation and intervention compatible with economic rationality would be employed. An effective task in approaching the question is undoubtedly what is an effective signal for recognizing disequilibrium between buying and selling. We have made cumulative analyses of the disequilibrium which we usually call "excessive speculation". (In the third part of the book we investigate the question with case studies.)

In the four chapters in the first part, we mainly attempt to recognize necessities and functions of commodity exchanges in Central Europe related to economic reforms in transition countries and also connected with globalization. Although it is difficult to say that the Warsaw Commodity Exchange is now well established, it can be seen that the Budapest Commodity Exchange might not be less efficient than the Tokyo Grain Exchange. However, in terms of its turnover, although this has been growing for the last few years, it has never been enough. Investigating the factors causing lower turnover, particularly from abroad, is the main aim of the second part of the book, mainly focusing our attention upon the transition procedure and foreign direct investment.

The second part consists of four chapters, investigating two topics of economic reform and capital movement. The first two chapters are about economic reform and the second two chapters are about capital movement, in particular foreign direct investment. (The reason we do not separate the four chapters is that they have in common a single question about "risk", basically related to economic transition.)

Chapter five discusses the method and the timing of economic reforms in Poland. The main point of this chapter's discussion is to indicate that structural reform might be more important from the viewpoint of the middle and long term, and thus the reform of government is also very important as well as enterprise efficiency and workers reform in terms of discipline. As is discussed in the second part, where transition economies are concerned, problems of risk are closely related with government behavior. (In a case study of the Philippines, for example, inefficient resource allocation by the government made the capital coefficient much larger and made the potential capacity for economic growth much smaller). The main conclusive points for consideration in chapter five are, therefore, policy changes toward: (1) more growth oriented reform (and a lower unemployment ratio), (2) more radical structural reform, (3) more active policy of protection for infant industries, and above all (4) the necessity of a wiser and stronger strategic political stance on the part of the authority. That is to say, governmental reform which moves from a stability oriented position to a more growth oriented strategic position might be necessary.

Chapter six makes a comparison between the current Polish economic reforms and postwar Japanese economic reforms. It provides a comparative analysis of the postwar Japanese "chukan antei ron" ("gradual reform" in the modern English term) with the radical reform in Poland led by Mr. Balcerowicz. Actually, however, Japan introduced a very radical structural reform by allowing rather high inflation and a low unemployment rate in the postwar Japanese economy. In case of Poland, on the contrary, we cannot see any evidence of "radical" structural reform policy making the Polish economy more competitive and making its income and asset distribution more equal. In that sense, postwar Japanese economic reform of 1946-48, usually described as "gradual reform", might be more radical than the Polish Balcerowicz Program described as "radical reform".

Needless to say, it might not be possible to simply compare experiences of postwar Japanese reforms with current Polish reforms. However, we could undoubtedly mention that for both the Japanese economy and the Polish economy: (1) radical shock therapy for purging inefficiency is necessary, but (2) it is extremely difficult to expect that without structural reform efficiency would improve (they would have high inflation and lots of unemployed workers). Therefore, in order for the Polish economy to be on a higher rate of growth path, radical structural reforms would be necessary. Such a government stance might be closely connected with risks, and where and how they are.

In chapter seven, we focus our attention upon a specific competition, the case of a passenger car production project in the 1980s between the Italian car company (Fiat) and the Japanese car company (Daihatsu) in order to show the decision-making process and the decision-making factor from the viewpoints of the Japanese government and Japanese consortium, and the 1980s Polish situation. And we conclude that we recognize that both the times concerned and, nowadays, the financial factor might be a basic factor for FDI (foreign direct investment) in Central Europe. Two more conclusions in chapter seven are: (1) the main reasons why the Japanese side was inferior to the Italian side in this case were less managerial resources in Japan (Japanese consortium) than in Italy (Fiat) in the case of FDI in Central Europe, and less support from the Japanese government for foreign policies toward Poland than from the Italian government; also (2) (a) as Japanese companies are generally risk averse, transactions will be small when social costs are high, and (b) social costs like imperfect information, higher transaction costs and an immature law system might be (to some extent) eliminated by establishing an international regime, which would make Japan's FDI in Central Europe more active.

Therefore, we could conclude in chapter seven that factors like international relations, managerial resources, risk aversion, and systemic risk are very important in the economic affairs of Central Europe.

In chapter eight, we try to take a general view of closely related factors with inward FDI in Central Europe and capital movements. Through investigation focusing our attention upon Central Europe, particularly the Visegrad three countries of Poland, Hungary and the Czech Republic, we attempt to recognize significantly the correlated factors with capital inflows into Central Europe and to make clear the problems in capital movements in transition economies.

The results we have in chapter eight are: (1) financial factors are extremely important for capital movement into Central Europe, (2) these financial factors might also be recognized to have significant correlations with the growing factors in a macroeconomic sense, and (3), as foreign direct investment has been understood to prevent volatile capital movement, increasing inward foreign direct investment would have a contributing role for successful transition. Therefore we could confirm that as explicitly mentioned in chapter five (as far as the Visegrad three countries are concerned) a more growth oriented policy might be more appropriate for reforming the economy.

As considered in the second part of the book, in the Central European transition economies there have still been risks, particularly of the financial kind. Also the risks might be, needless to say, serious barriers for capital inflow into these economies. The same situation has applied to commodity futures market, of hindering investment into them (and more investigations into the relations between short-term and, middle and long-term capital movement should be done in the future). Thus it seems to us that the risky factors have made the volume of capital markets less and the transactions in capital markets more unstable (when moving capital is risky).

Based upon the above background, in the six chapters of the third part we consider the problems related to government regulation against speculative instability.

In chapter nine, we investigate a case of excessive speculation with the Walter Labys study (although this happened in the middle of the 1970s) focusing our attention on the intervention method, both in cases of spot market intervention and futures market intervention, recognizing for excessive speculation.

In chapter nine we mainly consider that authority can intervene only in the futures market with a short position. We also mention that it is just necessary to clear the short position and leave other things to the market, which means that the authority does not need to have enough stock to absorb the capital inflow or to worry about spot price rise as a result of shortage of stock. That is to say, we would emphasize that an intervention policy in the futures market is undoubtedly effective, because intervention in the spot market might oppose the market mechanism and meanwhile intervention in the futures market might utilize the market mechanism.

In chapter ten we aim to investigate whether or not it is possible to identify excessive speculation at an early stage, and to consider what signal would be appropriate for recognizing the excessiveness.

Considering the characteristics of the topic in this chapter, we investigate a particular case study as a corner market case which happened in the natural rubber market in Japan in 1968.

Based upon the investigation, we have the following results for the above case: (1) it is a case in which they did not operate regulations, and they should have put regulations in motion, and (2) it is a case in which we could identify neither early regulations nor appropriate regulations to deal with a speculator who was not good from the viewpoints of both financial capacity and pricing strategy.

It is also correct, however, to mention that we need more investigations to find the appropriate criteria from an operational point of view.

In order to identify an appropriate and operational regulation, in the chapter eleven, we examine a way of regulation in which through an intergovernmental agreement such as the international commodity agreement authorities try to limit price movement within a particular price range.

In chapter eleven we consider the case of International Wheat Agreement which had a regulation usually recognized as a "multilateral contract scheme". Reconstructing the agreement with price theory suggests that the International Wheat Agreement contributed to the chronic excess supply situation through a destabilizing mechanism built into the agreements of

1953 and 1956, and that the multilateral contract scheme did not really work but rather the "export regulation scheme", which was actually a quantity regulation scheme, worked effectively.

In other words, the function of a multilateral contract scheme which had, to some extent, a market mechanism was quite limited and a mechanism which regulated through quantity worked well.

Such intergovernmental regulation schemes as the International Commodity Agreement have not been more or less successful enough (except in the case of strict quantity regulation). Could we then recognize any *raison d'être* for such intergovernmental regulation policies? In chapter twelve and thirteen, we try to find any *raison d'être* for them by using an interdisciplinary approach of sociology, anthropology and political economy in order to extract the functions "embedded" in such a framework, and to find an appropriate theoretical position for functions of futures markets in an interdisciplinary sense.

In chapter thirteen, investigation from the field of sociology is done. The original issue raised here is McKinnon's proposal which said that, if it were possible to have a futures market with enough distant futures transaction, it would be possible to stabilize income on the one hand and to utilize production factors efficiently with futures market information on the other. By applying functional exigencies and types of exchange put forward by Parsons, Polanyi and Smelser, etc., the McKinnon proposal (utilizing futures market functions) could be interpreted as corresponding to adaptation in terms of functional exigencies and a market type of exchange in terms of types of exchange. As far as international commodity exchange is concerned, this corresponds to goal attainment in terms of functional exigencies and mobilizative type of exchange in terms of types of exchange. Also among international commodity agreement regulation schemes, a scheme which corresponds to goal attainment and to mobilizative types of exchange would be the export regulation scheme. It can be clearly shown that the international commodity agreement has from the origin a functional framework within which to work through quantity regulation.

In chapter thirteen, we study the same issue as in chapter twelve from the viewpoint of political economy, particularly the international regime approach. The focus in our examination is on the correspondence with the nature of benefit coming from regime formation and on change to a regime. In terms of the nature of benefit coming from regime formation, an international commodity agreement corresponds to stabilization effect, and a futures market corresponds to the mitigating uncertainty effect. This means that an international commodity agreement, particularly an export regulation scheme (which seems to be a substantial scheme), could be described as a scheme putting more weight upon stability. If a change of regime comes from a shift in dominance of benefits from regime formation, the tendency of a change of international commodity agreement (toward more research and development, more information collection etc.) could be interpreted as the result of a shift in dominance of benefits from regime formation (toward the effect of decreasing information gathering costs from the stabilization effect). A scheme like that in McKinnon's proposal is therefore shown as coming from attaching more importance to the effect of mitigating uncertainty.

In chapter fourteen, we consider the next question asking which effects were produced in the adjustment process when intergovernmental regulation was successful in a sense that price movement was successfully stabilized through buffer stock operations.

Based upon a model contributed by Carl Van Dyne, we examine the nature of the process to adjust a disturbance which happened initially. We recognize by the analysis that the adjustment process would contribute to expanding the initial disequilibrium. It becomes clear, therefore, that the system of adjustment is unstable. As a result, the current account of a primary commodity producing country would have more deficit and also would have more involuntary stock for the primary commodity.

We could insist therefore that, when destabilizing fluctuation is observed and governmental and/or intergovernmental intervention behavior is successfully implemented, this could introduce disequilibrium factors for the macroeconomic adjustment process.

This is an overview of this book which comprises of three parts made up of fourteen chapters altogether.

At the close of this Preface, I would like to express my gratitude for the financial support of (in alphabetical order) the Japan Commodity Futures Industry Association and Japanese Ministry of Education, Culture, Sports, Science and Technology (Grant-in-Aid for Scientific Research).

Notes

1   It is not easy to define precisely what "Central Europe" is, because it is necessary to carefully examine, for example, historical, ideological, political and cultural factors. In this book, we use the term "Central Europe" to mean the former CMEA six countries, except the former GDR. The main target area of this book, however, is generally limited to Poland, Hungary (and the Czech Republic). Also in this book, as we consider the longer period, we could use the terms Central Europe and Eastern Europe interchangeably if suitable.

2   See, for example, chapter one.

PART I
COMMODITY EXCHANGES IN CENTRAL EUROPE

In Part I, we investigate the commodity futures markets in Central Europe, particularly in Warsaw (Poland) and in Budapest (Hungary). The main issues to be examined are: (1) reasons why it was necessary to establish a commodity futures market in the transition process and (2) the current situation and function of commodity futures markets in Warsaw and Budapest. The second chapter deals with issue (1) and the third and fourth chapters deal with mainly issue (2).

The first chapter provides the basis for the investigations that follow. Needless to say, there have been lots of opinions on the question of why centrally planned economies collapsed. In the first chapter we discuss the interpretation, partly related to the question, that says that inefficiency was mainly caused by incomplete adjustment of disequlibrium occurring as a result of unexpected factors. That is to say, we attempt to rearrange the issue based upon the adjustment mechanism of centrally planned economies from a framework of functions of futures markets.

The second chapter focuses on the Warsaw Commodity Exchange, particularly in connection with budget deficit and agricultural products (pricing). As IMF (International Monetary Fund) policy recommendation and as the purpose of reforms (both radical and gradual) have emphasized, cutting down the budget deficit has been indispensable for a successful transition.

In the third chapter, we mention the current situation of Warsaw and of Budapest, and then indicate problems in examining efficiency.

We have an analysis of the function of the Budapest Commodity Exchange in the fourth chapter. Taking into consideration an evaluation of the efficiency of the Budapest Commodity Exchange, we try to compare the function of the Tokyo Grain Exchange (which is selected as a criterion of judgment in efficiency).

Note that the analyses in the first part of the volume are principally based upon current situations as of the year 1999.

Chapter 1

Futures Markets and Centrally Planned Economies

Introduction

Overall, bad economic performances over a fairly long period in centrally planned economies have mainly resulted from inefficiency, closely connected with economic systems. The question of why centrally planned economies collapsed has prompted lots of opinions and we will try to find better interpretations of the question. From the viewpoint of this volume, at least partially, inefficiency should be interpreted as incomplete adjustment of disequilibrium caused by uncontrollable factors.

The purpose of this chapter is to examine the issue of an adjustment mechanism in centrally planned economies within a framework of futures market functions.

This chapter is divided into four parts. In the first part, we examine the identity of functions against uncertainty in centrally planned systems and forward trading, basically with a contribution by J. R. Hicks (1946). In the second, we examine the identity to eliminate income variance caused by uncontrollable factors mainly with a work by R. McKinnon (1967). In the third, we investigate efficiency of spot market adjustment in commodity exchanges, and in the last part, there is a short conclusion to the chapter.

Forward Trading and Centrally Planned Systems

Four possible causes of disequilibrium were suggested by J. R. Hicks (1946).[1] Here the term disequilibrium means divergence between expected and realized prices, and the divergence comes from inaccurate foresight (which means existence of uncertainty) and causes malinvestment, waste and inefficient production.

According to Hicks, one cause (he said this was perhaps the least important) is produced when different people's price-expectations are inconsistent. Even if all buyers and sellers expect the same price, the total quantity all buyers plan to buy may not equal the total quantity all sellers plan to sell. This is the second cause of disequilibrium, and Hicks said it was perhaps the most interesting cause of all four. Moreover, even if both price expectations and plans are consistent, people may not predict their own wants correctly, or make wrong estimates of the results of technical processes of production. If this arises, they will find that they are unwilling or unable to buy or sell those quantities they had planned to buy or sell. Therefore, realized prices will be different from expected prices. And this is the third cause of disequilibrium due to unforeseen changes in tastes, unforeseen results of technical processes, imperfect foresight of harvest fluctuations and unforeseen political upheavals, etc.

And moreover, even if no disequilibrium in any of the above mentioned three senses exists, nevertheless the most perfect adjustment of resources to wants may not be reached. This is because, when risk and uncertaninty exist, people will generally act not on the price that they expect as most probable, but as if that price had been slightly shifted in an unfavourable direction. In this way the efficiency of the system may be seriously damaged, and this is the fourth cause of disequilibrium (also called imperfect equilibrium).

Those divergences between expected and realized prices due to uncertainties can, in several ways, be eliminated in order to improve the third and fourth causes of disequilibrium mostly found in every economic system, centralized economies or market economies. Even the most perfectly organized economic system cannot avoid causes like harvest fluctuations, inventions, or political upheavals.

The first and second causes can be eliminated in different ways in any economic system. In a completely centralized system the two causes would be removed. (But, as Hicks mentioned, a completely centralized system is a mere figment of the imagination.) And within market economies, a device in which price-expectations and plans can be (at least partially) consistent exists. In market economies, we could have a device for eliminating or reducing the first and second causes of disequilibrium, that is, the device of forward trading. Hicks included, and we also include in this chapter, not only futures market operations, but also dealings given in advance, and all long-term contracts.

Thus, we could say, as economic devices to eliminate the first and second causes of disequilibrium, there are centralized systems in Socialism on the one hand, and forward trading in Capitalism on the other hand. If no causes classified as the third and fourth kinds exist, then, with the device of a perfectly centralized system or forward trading, price-expectations and plans will be consistent, there will be no waste and there will be perfectly efficient production. However, as the third and fourth causes could not be eliminated, disequilibrium caused by them does exist.

In this section, we would like to put the above argument by J. R. Hicks into a little wider perspective of devices to reduce uncertainty. As Hicks mentioned, in the device of forward trading, dealings given in advance and all long-term contracts are included. In those tradings between sellers and buyers, all the terms like trading period, quantities and prices are concluded. As a typical device, we could say that quantities and prices are fixed in advance and are actually traded on each delivery day. The long-term contract, in market economies, is concluded voluntarily between private enterprises. And we usually observe the same device in centralized economies in which centralized authority decides quantities and prices traded in advance, and state enterprises actually transact each delivery day.

In the case of long-term contracts, they need to be mutually reciprocal. Thus, they need time for adjustment to reach mutual reciprocity, and there may be some cases[2] with risk of bargaining stalemates and cost of repeated recontracting and also risk of price fluctuations. The above mentioned cases with risk and cost should be treated as an issue of tension management to reach a long-term contract. In cases where benefits with long-term contracts for stabilization could not cover costs for tension management, there may be possibilities for the buyer and the seller to be vertically integrated. The vertical integration seems to be a typical case. Through integration of the buyer and the seller, several sources are redistributed within the organization, and better information flow could make much less uncertainty. The vertical integration could be observed in market economies with rational reasons. In centralized economies, the same type of transaction could usually be observed between state enterprises under directions from planning authorities, which it redistributes several resources and reduces uncertainty.

In addition to the above, even under market economies, devices to reduce uncertainty through government intervention could exist. When disequilibrium under uncertainty has serious effects against stabilization for the global economy, especially against economies in less developed primary commodity producing countries, both producing and consuming countries may contribute to establishing a fund to stabilize price fluctuations, to stabilize producer's earnings and to secure consumer's imports. They are, perhaps, very important goals for a centralized authority to stabilize producer's earnings, materials for consumers and prices. In other words, such intergovernmental agreement concluded under market economies is a trial to stabilize, even if a market mechanism is partially distorted. The goals in such agreement could be similar to policy goals in centralized economies.

Consequently, the essential framework that Hicks called forward trading means the fairly strict device in which quantities and prices would be predetermined in advance in uncertain situations in order to have coordinated price-expectations and plans. And within the framework, on each day for actual delivery, transactions can be liquidated. Such a framework can be commonly observed both in market economies with private enterprises and in centralized economies with planning authorities.

We recognize the difference between the above mentioned two systems. Since the third and fourth causes of disequilibrium could not be eliminated, both of them should have adjustment schemes to reach equilibrium. The adjustment schemes are not the same in the two systems. To analyze the difference is the main purpose of this chapter, and it will be dealt with in the third section.

In this section, hereinafter, we would like to make Hicks' classification simply embedded in the much wider theoretical framework developed by K. Polanyi et al. (1957, 1977) and N. Smelser (1959), from the viewpoints of anthropology and sociology, in order to correctly arrange economic devices (forward trading and centralized system) in a wider perspective.

Polanyi classified several types of economies into ascendant patterns of integration, which mean movement patterns of economic goods and service. According to Polanyi, there could be three ascendant patterns of integration: (1) exchange, (2) reciprocity, and (3) redistribution. And in each of the three, there are these four characteristics: forms of trade; uses of money; market elements; and types of social structure. Of these, this chapter here focuses upon forms of trade. Polanyi mentioned that forms of trade could be also classified into three types of trade: market trade; gift trade; and administered trade.   According to him, these types of trade are closely linked respectively with the three ascendant patterns of integration. It means that market trade links with exchange, gift trade connects with reciprocity, and administered trade relates to redistribution.

Their simple characteristics are as follows. Market trade means transactions done voluntarily between each economic agent, with market prices as a signal. Gift trade implies transactions based upon reciprocal relations in which economic agents share their value-systems, and with which economic agents can eliminate costs coming out from negotiations. Administered trade means transactions done by government intervention in order to achieve public goals.

In addition to Polanyi's anthropological approach, Smelser analyzed the same problems from a sociological point of view. For the purpose of this chapter, we focus upon only the most adequate portion in Smelser's paper. Smelser raised an interesting question about correspondence between patterns of integration and forms of trade. One of his arguments, especially, was focused upon the link between the categories of administered trade and redistribution.

Although we have no space to examine Smelser's argument against Polanyi's, one point that should be mentioned here is his careful consideration of features of administered trade in comparison with redistribution which leads us to the additional fourth ascendant pattern of integration. Smelser's point of discussion is that redistribution only means for the government to collect wealth and to redistribute it with any changes. The term redistribution, therefore, just means only the direction of movement of wealth, not any function of that movement. In administered trade, however, according to Smelser, any collective social goals like war do exist, and public authority mobilizes resources to achieve those goals. In regard to this aspect Smelser can add the fourth pattern of integration, which is called mobilization.

Instead of a pattern of integration, we would prefer to call it an exchange system, as Smelser did. The four exchange systems (exchange, reciprocity, redistribution and mobilization) are embedded into social structures. Consequently, the devices to reduce uncertainty and disequilibrium that are focused upon in this chapter could vary in accordance with the social structures into which ascendant exchange systems are embedded. One of the most excellent points in Smelser's analysis is that he was successful in finding a correspondence between the four types of exchange and the AGIL scheme by T. Parsons and N. J. Smelser (1956). With the linkage, we can have a clear idea that each ascendant exchange system comes out from the functional ascendancy of the society concerned.[3] Therefore, for instance, when a society puts the function ascendancy into completing some social policy goals, mobilization becomes an ascendant system of exchange.

Here in this section, we have the following concluding remarks in our argument:

(1) Concerning the devices to reduce uncertainty and to adjust disequilibrium, both in market economies and in centralized economies, we could recognize the same function in order to coordinate price-expectations and plans.

(2) However, since ascendant exchange systems vary, we could mention that mobilization (central planning) has been employed in centralized economies and exchange (forward trading) has been employed in market economies.

(3) Consequently, regarding the devices concerned here, we should be careful to recognize that the exchange systems are respectively different, but the function is identical.

Uncertainty and Adjustment Mechanisms

The purpose of this section is to mention that, in case of including the third (and fourth) unavoidable causes of disequilibrium, both forward trading and a centralized system could not eliminate perfectly those sources, and also to examine that, when the third (and fourth) sources could not be eliminated through forward trading or a centralized system, they should have an optimum combination of forward trading (or centralized system) and another device, mainly with arguments by McKinnon.[4]

Although there are many factors in the third cause of disequilibrium, we consider here harvest fluctuations and also suppose an individual farmer as a typical economic agent facing uncertainty. And we assume that income variance is a reasonable measure of risk and uncertainty,[5] and the farmer attempts to minimize income variance.

Also we consider, with McKinnon, to keep the analysis as simple as possible, that an individual farmer's planting decision is made exogenously and he has a fixed production opportunity. And the farmer's output (X) at harvest time can be viewed at planting time as a random variable, and also at planting time, he knows the mean (μ_x) and variance (σ_x^2), which are both fixed. And the actual spot price (P) at harvest time can be viewed at planting time as a random variable with a known mean (μ_p) and variance (σ_p^2). We also assume that X and P have a bivariate normal distribution.

We consider that the farmer sells X_f bushels forward for future delivery at the price P_f in order to reduce his income variance. And we assume that the period over which the farmer can sell forward spans the period over which the major price fluctuations occur. We also suppose that the expected value of P is the future price, that is, $E(P) = P_f$, that means no normal backwardation exists. And finally, for simplicity, we assume that transaction in the futures market is costless.

This farmer's income at harvest time is shown as the revenue by adding the futures market transaction to spot market transaction, that is:

$$Y = P_f X_f + P(X - X_f) = PX + X_f(P_f - P) \tag{1}$$

As his expected income is dependent upon the uncontrolled random variables X and P :

$$E(Y) = E(PX) \tag{2}$$

The farmer chooses the optimal value of X_f in order to minimize the variance of his income. Under the assumption of bivariate normality, we have:

$$
\begin{aligned}
\sigma_y^2 &= E(Y^2) - [E(PX)]^2 \\
&= P_f^2 \sigma_x^2 + \mu_x^2 \sigma_p^2 + 2P_f \mu_x \rho \sigma_x \sigma_p + (1+\rho^2)\sigma_x^2 \sigma_p^2 \\
&\quad - 2X_f P_f \rho \sigma_x \sigma_p - 2X_f \mu_x \sigma_p^2 + X_f^2 \sigma_p^2
\end{aligned}
\tag{3}
$$

where, needless to say, ρ is the coefficient of correlation between X and P.

Differentiating (3) with respect to X_f and equating to zero, we can have X_f^*, the optimal value of the forward sale of X_f:

$$
X_f^* = \rho P_f \frac{\sigma_x}{\sigma_p} + \mu_p
\tag{4}
$$

We can also obtain the minimum income variance σ_y^{*2} by substituting X_f^* for X_f in (3):

$$
\sigma_y^{*2} = (1-\rho^2)P_f^{\,2}\sigma_x^2 + (1+\rho^2)\sigma_x^2 \sigma_p^2
\tag{5}
$$

In equation (5), the term $P_f^2 \sigma_x^2$ means the pure effect output fluctuations, and $\sigma_x^2 \sigma_p^2$ represents the interaction effect between output and price variations. The terms imply that, even if the farmer has the optimal hedge through forward sale X_f^*, a residual income variance still exists, because output fluctuation, which is occurred by the third cause of disequilibrium by Hicks, cannot be eliminated. And, in case of $\rho = 0$, we have:

$$
\sigma_y^{*2} = \sigma_x^2 \left(\sigma_p^2 + P_f^2\right)
\tag{6}
$$

As is shown in the previous section, the third (and fourth) sources like harvest fluctuations cannot be eliminated even in the most perfectly organized economic system. That is clearly represented by non-zero σ_y^{*2}. Consequently, in order to eliminate income variance (which means to eliminate output fluctuations σ_x^2), we should have other devices combined to forward trading or centralized planning.

Concerning devices to eliminate output fluctuations, Mckinnon examined the combined operation of a buffer stock. If actual output becomes less than expected (and average) value, then the difference will be covered by selling from the buffer stock. Conversely, if actual output becomes more than expected (and average) value, then the difference will be eliminated by storing into the buffer stock. With this combination of buffer stock operation, the farmer's output supplied to the market could be completely equalized to the mean value.

We can go to the next step of this discussion, that is, an efficiency of the adjustment devices to eliminate income variance.

McKinnon compared opportunity costs of the buffer stock operation with the buffer fund program, both of which are non-market devices. Anyway, in order to have mean value of the farmer's income[6] $P_f \mu_x$ in every period, McKinnon insisted that a joint buffer stock-forward sale hedge was more efficient than a joint buffer fund-forward sale hedge. He showed this in the following very simple probability model. He supposed that the random variables X and P can be assumed only two values respectively, X_1 and X_2, where $X_1 < X_2$ and both are equally probable, P_1 and P_2, where $P_1 < P_2$ and both are equally probable. And suppose the two variables, X and P are independently distributed $(\rho = 0)$, thus the events (X_1, P_1), (X_2, P_1), (X_1, P_2) and (X_2, P_2) are all equally likely with probability one-fourth. For the farmer, (X_1, P_1) is the least favorable situation, and (X_2, P_2) is the most favorable situation.

The goal of this stabilizing operation is to maintain the following average income in every period, that is:

$$\frac{(X_1 + X_2)}{2} \times \frac{(P_1 + P_2)}{2} = \mu_p \mu_x = P_f \mu_x$$

The problem we face now is to examine the cost of capital investment in order to maintain the average income. And to do this, let us investigate the amount of capital needed in the situation of the worst possible case, just the same as McKinnon did.

In the device of the buffer stock, we assume the farmer would rationally behave as he sells his crop $X_f (= \mu_x)$ forward at the price P_f. However, his actual harvest is in the least favorable situation X_1, which is less than μ_x. Then this farmer has to draw $(\mu_x - X_1)$ units of commodity from the stock at the price P_f. Consequently, the amount that has to be the capital invested in the form of the buffer stock is:

$$P_f\left(\mu_x - X_1\right)$$

And in the case of the buffer fund, the value of output in the worst possible case is simply $P_1 X_1$. However, the farmer sells his crop $X_f(=\mu_x)$ forward at the price P_f. Thus the amount of capital that needs be drawn from the buffer fund to maintain the average income is:

$$\mu_x P_f - P_1 X_1$$

Since $P_f X_1 > P_1 X_1$, as is easily shown:

$$\mu_x P_f - P_1 X_1 > P_f\left(\mu_x - X_1\right)$$

Therefore, McKinnon clearly concluded[7] that, "... capital invested in the buffer stock need be less than capital invested in a buffer fund ...".

Needless to say, the opportunity costs of both cases are the interest charge on the value of the buffer stock and buffer fund. Thus, the opportunity costs compared should be:

$$a\left(\mu_x P_f - P_1 X_1\right) > a P_f\left(\mu_x - X_1\right)$$

Where a is the rate of interest.

Figures 1.1 and 1.2 show the difference graphically. In each figure, the quantity of the output is measured on the vertical axis, and price level on the horizontal axis. As mentioned previously, there are four possible events with equal possibility of one-fourth each, which are shown as points in the figures. The question that McKinnon proposed and we also examine here is to compare the amounts of opportunity costs in order to maintain the average income $P_f \mu_x$ when the farmer is in the least favorable situation, with $P_1 X_1$ value of his output. The opportunity costs are shown as the areas shadowed in each figure. Figure 1.1 is the case of buffer stock, and figure 1.2 is the case of the buffer fund. The area shown as the opportunity cost in the buffer stock case is less than the buffer fund case.[8]

Here in this section, we have the following concluding remarks:

(I) Both a forward trading and a centralized system are impossible to perfectly eliminate output fluctuations occurred by the third and fourth

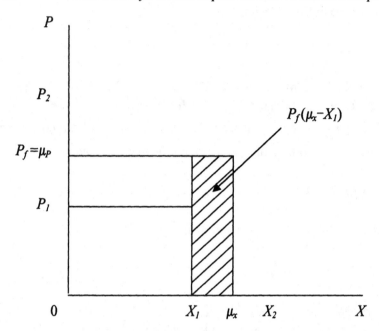

Figure 1.1   Buffer stock case

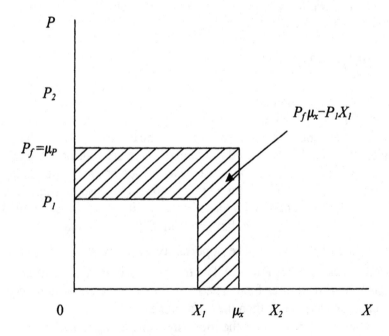

Figure 1.2   Buffer fund case

causes of disequilibrium, therefore, income variance could not become zero.

(II) Consequently, in order to make income variance zero, both market economies and centralized economies should have other devices combined with forward trading and centralized planning.

(III) In considering efficiencies of the joint devices concerned here, since a joint buffer stock and forward sale operation requires less opportunity cost than joint buffer fund and forward sale operation, we could say that the buffer stock is the device with the greater efficiency.

Adjustment Mechanisms and Efficiency

In this section, we focus upon the issue raised in the second half of the previous section, that is, efficiencies of adjustment devices to eliminate fluctuations occurred by the third (and fourth) causes of disequilibrium in the Hicks' sense. As the income variance is a reasonable measure of risk and uncertainty, to eliminate the variance helps to lessen uncertainty. And the adjustment devices for the economy means devices to eliminate the income variance combined with forward trading or a centralized system.

Here we concentrate upon the issue in comparison of opportunity costs to have the average income $P_f \mu_x$ in case of the worst possible situation, in which the revenue from actual output is $P_1 X_1$.

However, from the viewpoint of this paper, argument by McKinnon (and Poole) is not enough, because they did not use full functions of the futures market as adjustment devices. The purpose of this section is to examine just that issue in order to clarify the divergence in efficiencies of adjustment devices between market economies and centralized economies. The devices proposed by McKinnon (and Poole) to eliminate output fluctuations and to have average income $P_f \mu_x$ in every period are confined to non-market devices, the buffer stock and the buffer fund, though there are more functions in the futures market.

We assume just the same as in the previous section, the farmer sells his crop X_f forward at the price P_f, and at the harvest time he faces the least favorable situation.

In this situation, the farmer should have liquidity to settle the forward contract. Nevertheless, he does not need any buffer stock.

We would like to propose, hereinafter, three alternative methods of settling the forward contract:

(1) In the settlement of forward trading, the farmer buys back the whole

amount of the forward sale $P_f\mu_x$ at the futures market and sells the actual crop X_1 at the spot market with the price P_1.

In this first case, (as is previously mentioned, the futures market price equals P_f, which represents the average level), since the forward sale contract $P_f\mu_x$ is bought back with the quantity μ_x at the price P_f, the forward contract can be settled by the buying-back operation. The farmer needs no more operation. And he has the current income P_1X_1 by selling the actual harvest at the spot market.

Consequently, in order to have the average income $P_f\mu_x$, he must have liquidity amounting to $(P_f\mu_x - P_1X_1)$ in order to prepare against the worst possible case. The amount of opportunity cost in this case is the same as the case of the buffer fund mentioned by McKinnon.

Needless to say, the following operation reaches the same result. That is, $(P_f\mu_x - P_1X_1)$ which is prepared in advance in addition to the current income P_1X_1 is paid for buying-back, and the amount $P_f\mu_x$ is received by settling the forward sale contract.

As a result of the above operation, with liquidity $(P_f\mu_x - P_1X_1)$ prepared in advance, the farmer has the average income $P_f\mu_x$.

(2) For liquidation of a forward contract, the portion of X_1 is settled by the actual delivery and the residual portion of $(\mu_x - X_1)$ is settled by buying-back at the futures market price P_f.

In this second case, since the forward sale contract $P_f(\mu_x - X_1)$ is bought back with the residual units $(\mu_x - X_1)$ at the price P_f, the forward contract can be entirely settled. As a result, the farmer has the amount of income P_fX_1 resulting from the sale of the output X_1 at the price P_f.

In order to have the average income $P_f\mu_x$ in this second case, the farmer must have liquidity amounting to $(P_f\mu_x - P_fX_1) = P_f(\mu_x - X_1)$, to prepare for the least favorable situation. The opportunity cost in this case is the same as the case of buffer stock operation mentioned by McKinnon. Nevertheless, the supplier can settle the forward contract by buying-back for the portion $(\mu_x - X_1)$, which cannot be covered by the actual harvest. He does not need to draw from the buffer stock for liquidation as was supposed by McKinnon.

Consequently, as is recognized in the second way, with the spot market adjustment in the commodity exchange, the opportunity cost in case of having liquidity in advance can be just the same as in the case of buffer stock-forward sale operation emphasized by McKinnon. Thus, McKinnon's (and Poole's) argument should be considered as an imperfect result obtained by an insufficient investigation into the functions of a futures market.

Needless to say, we may also suppose that the operation is as follows. The farmer pays $P_f(\mu_x - X_1)$ to settle by buying-back, and he receives the amount $P_f(\mu_x - X_1)$ which equals the amount of forward sale, which subtracts $P_f X_1$ settled by the actual delivery from the contract $P_f \mu_x$. As a result, with preparing the liquidity $P_f(\mu_x - X_1)$, the farmer can have the amount of $P_f \mu_x$ by adding $P_f X_1$ to $P_f(\mu_x - X_1)$.

Here, we can understand why the difference of opportunity costs between the buffer stock case and the buffer fund case results, by referring to the difference between case (1) and case (2). In the first case, although the farmer can sell his output X_1 at the price P_f to settle the contract, he actually sells X_1 at the lower price P_1. In the second case, the farmer sells the actual output X_1 at the higher price P_f as hedged in advance. Consequently, the difference between (1) and (2) does exist. From the viewpoint of this section, the difference reflects the "efficiency" in using the spot market adjustment of the commodity exchange.

Moreover, with just the same assumptions by McKinnon (and Poole), the third way to adjust uncertainty has to be possible.

(3) In the settlement of forward trading, the portion of X_1 is settled by the actual delivery, and the residual portion of $(\mu_x - X_1)$ is settled by buying the crop at the spot market and fulfilling by the additional actual delivery.

In this third case, the amount of liquidity needed for adjustment equals to $P_1(\mu_x - X_1)$, which is less than $P_f(\mu_x - X_1)$ and $(P_f \mu_x - P_1 X_1)$. Besides, by that operation the farmer can get an even profit $(P_f - P_1)$ per unit. Because, on the $(\mu_x - X_1)$ units, he buys at the lower price P_1 and sells at the higher price P_f. With the assumptions supposed by McKinnon (and Poole), this third case has to be possible, because each farmer concerned here can have no effect upon the market price, and also we can assume that the additional demand $(\mu_x - X_1)$ has no effect upon the market price. If the economic agent's adjustment behavior at the spot market has an effect on the market price, the price level will become higher immediately, and the least favorable situation will be eliminated and no problem will exist. The opportunity cost is shown as the area shadowed in figure 1.3, and is easily compared with the shaded areas in figures 1.1 and 1.2.

The third way can be interpreted as a case that, the commodity exchange should be thought of as globally functioning exchanges like the London Metal Exchange (LME) which works to provide the adjustment function for

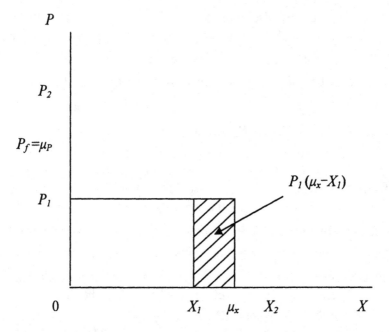

Figure 1.3   Spot market adjustment case

equilibrium,[9] instead of the buffer stock operation by the farmer.

Anyway, with exhaustive investigation of the adjustment functions of futures market, the opportunity costs of the devices mentioned by McKinnon (and Poole) can be arranged within the framework of spot market adjustments in commodity exchanges, and the additional third device should be examined with just the same assumptions.

In this section, we conclude as follows:

(1) the spot market adjustment through commodity exchange needs less capital than non-market devices like the buffer stock and the buffer fund.

(2) Thus, we could say that market economies have devices with greater efficiency and flexibility over centralized economies.

Conclusion

As shown in the previous section, in order to eliminate the income variance which comes from the output variance, it is not necessary to have non-market devices like the buffer stock and the buffer fund. We can have all the functions of the devices within the market mechanism, because the commodity exchange needs less opportunity cost than the non-market devices.

The purpose of this chapter is to examine the difference between the forward trading and the centralized system to adjust disequilibrium occurred by the third (and fourth) causes.

Identifying the function of forward trading and centralized systems to eliminate the first and second causes of disequilibrium could not reach the spot market adjustment. Undoubtedly, under the centralized system, we could suppose that the planning authority can have a plan to make each farmer's income $P_f \mu_x$ in every period and can have non-market devices like the buffer stock and the buffer fund operation for adjustment. However, the planning authority cannot have adjustment systems in which the farmer flexibly adjusts uncertain cases through buying-back, resales and spot market deals in the commodity exchange. In other words, with regard to the function of coordinating price-expectations and coordinating plans, centralized economies have the same functions as market economies. Nevertheless, centralized economies cannot have flexible functions for adjusting disequilibrium through spot market adjustment, because flexible spot market adjustment cannot exist in centralized economies.

Consequently, we could conclude this chapter as follows. Opportunity costs under centralized economies to make each supplier's income the average level in the least favorable situation are, in the case of the buffer stock:

$$aP_f\left(\mu_x - X_1\right)$$

and in case of the buffer fund:

$$a\left(P_f\mu_x - P_1 X_1\right)$$

Nevertheless, the opportunity cost:

$$aP_1\left(\mu_x - X_1\right)$$

can be possible only in case of the spot market adjustment in which functions of the commodity exchange are exhaustively used.

The difference:

$$a(\mu_x - X_1)(P_f - P_1)$$

and:

$$a\mu_x(P_f - P_1)$$

can be interpreted to reflect the difference of efficiencies between market economies with the flexible spot market adjustment and centralized economies without the flexible spot market adjustment.

Notes

1   This section is indebted to John R. Hicks. See J. R. Hicks (1946). (The first edition of the book was in 1939).

2   F. M. Scherer (1970) p.248.

3   For an analysis of correspondence of the frameworks in this section, see Morita (1980).

4   This section is indebted to R. I. Mckinnon (1967). And concerning economic analysis of futures market, see for example, J. Stein (1986).

5   McKinnon did not use the term uncertainty here. And, needless to say, uncertainty and risk are terms with partly different concepts. Hereinafter, however, for simplicity we focus on the common area of the two terms.

6   As McKinnon correctly mentioned, "Once we introduce the possibility of building up or drawing down stocks, one must distinguish cash flow from income. Cash flow minus income is equal to the value of decumulated stocks at current prices," (1967, p. 852). Hereinafter, just for simplicity, we use only the term income with no meaningful loss.

7   McKinnon (1967) p.854.

8   W. Poole criticized the McKinnon's paper, and R. I. McKinnon replied against Poole. However, we have no space here to mention their argument, because the argument was not so crucial for the purpose of this chapter. See Poole (1970) and McKinnon (1971), and regarding some comments about the argument, see Morita (1981).

9   Readers could easily find such cases, for example, in the LME (London Metal Exchange). Also see for example Sakai (1979). A kind of spot market adjustment could actually be observed in (former) USSR and (former) East European countries, which has been called the "second economy", although it has never been so efficient. Concerning the second economy, see, for example, Morita (1986), Bednarski and Kokoszczynski (1988), Los (ed.) (1990), Feige and Ott (eds.) (1999).

Chapter 2

The Necessity of Commodity Futures Markets in Transition Economies

Introduction

The purpose of this chapter is to consider the necessity and prospect of a commodity futures market in Central Europe, particularly in Poland.

It might be necessary to approach these questions from both sides of demand and supply, which seem to be closely related to the transformation procedure. The systemic transformation has involved high inflation from the macroeconomic aspect and privatization from the structural aspect.

In order to correctly understand the necessity of commodity exchange in Poland, we focus our attention here upon the first half of the 1990s.

In the first section of this chapter we have a short look at the high inflation in Poland. The second section investigates the privatization in Poland. The third and final section examines the necessity and prospect of a commodity futures market in Poland based upon the investigation in the previous two sections.

Extreme Inflation in Poland

In Poland we could see extreme inflation in 1989 of 640.0 per cent (annual, CPI - Consumer Price Index) and in 1990 of 585.8 per cent, and a rather moderate rate of 70-30 per cent in 1991-95. (By "inflation", if not otherwise stated, we mean "open inflation" not other types of inflation like "hidden inflation" and "depressed inflation" typically observed in centrally planned economies).

Therefore, we first concentrate upon the extreme inflation of 1989 and 1990. (According to the definition of hyperinflation in the Cagan sense, this is a process of steady price rise in excess of 50 per cent in every consecutive month. Therefore, whether the Polish case was hyperinflation or not is controversial. However, here we use the term hyperinflation, an extreme inflation etc., with no exact definition.)[1]

A critical factor of the 1989-90 extreme inflation that differentiated it from the later periods' moderate inflation in the vicinity of 70-30 per cent was, needless to say, money supply. Growth rates of money supply (the so-called point-to-point growth rate) in 1989 and 1990 were 510 per cent and 520 per cent respectively. However, in 1991-95, the rates decreased to 50-35 per cent (see Table 2.1).

What caused the extreme inflation in Poland in 1989-90? Four factors might be indicated as the main causes: (1) real wage increase of 14.4 per cent in 1988 and 9.0 per cent in 1989; (2) increase of state budget spending typically observed in purchase prices of agricultural products; (3) for repaying the huge amount of foreign debt, Poland had to get a trade surplus which was converted into domestic money supply; (4) a government price policy mainly adjusted to shock therapy package.[2]

Table 2.1   Sources of money supply in Poland: 1990-95

	Growth rate of money supply (%)	Source of money supply (%)			
		Net foreign reserves	Govern-ment sector	Loans to non-financial sector	others
1990.12	513.6	39.0	− 4.8	62.0	3.8
1991.12	47.6	25.3	7.9	69.0	− 2.2
1992.12	45.3	31.2	44.2	59.1	− 34.6
1993.12	35.8	33.6	53.6	58.3	− 45.6
1994.12	39.3	35.6	52.3	53.8	− 41.7
1995.12	34.8	48.2	40.1	54.0	− 42.3

Source: WERI (Annual, '94/'95)

It goes without saying that the price liberalization policy helped the inflation. In 1989 we found an official price list with 22 items, which was cut down to only six items in July 1990 (1. heating, warm water; 2. medicines; 3. services of public health care institutions; 4. gas, electricity; 5. spirits and derived beverage; 6. personal contribution to health service). Apart from the above six items, there were other items subject to official regulation such as house rental charges, postal and telecommunication fees, rail fares, intercity bus fares.[3]

However, as previously mentioned, the price liberalization policy might not be a main cause of this period's extreme inflation. Actually, as Kolodko indicated, "at the beginning of 1990, 14 percent of retail prices (in value terms) were still directly set by the state. In addition, about 10 percent of prices were subject to a kind of indirect state control."[4] Rather, first of all, factors for the 1989-90 inflation was the state's corrective behavior for cost movements. As was reported (in Kolodko[5]) the retail price for coal rose as much as seven times overnight and the electric power price twofold.

How about interest rates? As far as real interest rates are concerned, different from 1989, in 1990 real interest rates were not consecutively negative if not always positive. In 1989 the negative real interest rates have made households consume more, but since 1990 the gradual rise of real interest rates attracted more saving. What made the situation complicated was a kind of interesting speculation about an inflationary effect such as people's commodity searching behavior; a rise in interest rates led people to expect a coming recession with production decline, and people preferred commodity to money.[6]

As far as the exchange rate is concerned, from 1 January 1990 a zloty exchange rate was set to be 9,500 for one US$ and the internal convertibility was introduced. As the rate in December 1989 was about 5,500 zloty, it meant around 73 per cent depreciation. The exchange rate of 9,500 zloty for one US$ introduced by the shock therapy method has never been seen as the equilibrium exchange rate. The majority's view about the equilibrium rate of the zloty for US$ seemed to be in the vicinity of 8,000, and if 8,000 was an equilibrium, the 9,500 zloty rate showed 15 per cent overshooting. The 9,500 exchange rate was kept until March 1991 and the "undervalued" exchange rate was reflected to be a trade surplus of 2,214 million US$ in convertible currency. The 585.8 per cent annual inflation rate in 1990 with the stable exchange rate, as a matter of fact, might produce a kind of "corrective inflation" which reduced a trade surplus to 51 million US$ in 1991.

Since 1991, three-digit annual inflation dropped to become two-digit moderate inflation in Poland as the crucial factors mentioned above partly disappeared. Needless to say, structural reform has never been implemented to a great enough extent and "almost two-thirds of the production of all goods still comes from monopolists".[7] So, in Poland in 1994 30 per cent inflation still persisted which was related to "cost-driven" and "inflationary overhang" factors.[8]

An important aspect for this chapter is to clarify one of the major causes of the Polish inflation, which was closely related to the budget expenditure policy and pricing policy for agricultural products.

The Polish Way of Privatization[9]

Polish Experience of Privatization

After the post-communist countries started to transform their economies to market oriented ones, one of the most serious targets for their transformation has undoubtedly been privatization. However, most privatization processes in the post-communist countries have been delayed and have never been so successful. The purpose of this section is to have a short look at the current situation and problems of the Polish privatization experiences.

The Polish ways of privatization can be classified into three types: (1) capital privatization; (2) direct privatization; (3) liquidation. Capital privatization is a way of first transforming state owned companies into companies wholly owned by the state Treasury and then the Treasury selling the shares to investors to privatize them.   Direct privatization is, as the name indicates, a process of directly privatizing the company's ownership by (1) mainly leasing the company's assets; (2) selling the whole company or a part of the company's assets; or (3) using the company's assets for other companies. Liquidation is most unpopular because the procedure requires the winding up of a state owned company.

Usually we would divide companies into the above three types as follows: large state owned companies with a good financial situation into capital privatization; small and medium sized companies whose financial situation is good into direct privatization; small and medium sized companies with a bad financial condition into liquidation. However, as far as the sector is concerned, there is no big difference between the three types. Most of them concentrate on the industrial sector.

As is often mentioned, the second type of privatization, particularly leasing, has been popular because direct privatization is a most peaceful way for workers.   In the six years from 1990 to 1995, altogether 1,610 company privatizations were completed in Poland, of which ten per cent were capital privatizations, 65 per cent were direct privatizations and 25 per cent liquidations (see table 2.2).

The Mass Privatization Program in Poland has been subject to serious delays. After more than five years from the reform, Poland started the National Investment Funds Project in 1995. The scheme has 15 national investment funds and 512 companies, which is about the same number as Lipton and Sachs mentioned: "If most of the top 500 firms can be privatized, then an important part of the industrial sector, measured by employment, sale, and net income, will have been privatized" (Sachs

(1994), pp. 301-302). However, it is difficult to say that the Polish Mass Privatization Program has performed well. We think that it is too early to evaluate the policy method, but several reasons are sometimes given to criticize the program: (1) late implementation; (2) excess intricacy; (3) centralization and red tape; (4) covering by the program of the enterprises which so far have failed to adjust to the changing environment; and (5) small interest shown by foreign capital etc. (see Karpinska-Mizielinska and Smuga (1996), p.161).

Table 2.2 Ownership transformation in 1990-95: by section of national economy and privatization method

	Total (%)	Capital privatization (%)	Direct privatization (%)	Liquidation (%)
Total	100.0	100.0	100.0	100.0
Agriculture	10.3	0.6	6.3	20.6
Industry	70.8	94.6	67.1	57.3
Services	18.9	4.8	26.6	22.1

Source: Karpinska-Mizielinska and Smuga (1996).

Some Problems in the Polish Privatization

Not only for Poland but also for all the transition economies, the main goals of privatization would be twofold: (1) at the microeconomic level, to search entrepreneurs and to let them manage companies (needless to say, in order fully to implement the roles it is necessary to develop capital markets - for direct finance, and to have efficient banks - for indirect finance); (2) at the macroeconomic level, to dismantle a distorted production structure towards a more efficient one.

It goes without saying that the distorted production structure means an overgrown industry and underdeveloped service sector.   As Winiecki correctly mentioned (1988, chap. 3), the distorted structure was coming from over-substitution of imports and the autarkic bias for centrally planned companies (both of them are, needless to say, the legacy of the centrally planned system). Statistically speaking, we could easily find evidence of the distortion. Table 2.3 shows the overgrowth of industry in Poland compared with Greece and Spain.

Table 2.3 Distribution of output by sector

(%, 1987)

	Poland	Greece	Portugal	Spain
Agriculture	13	13	9	5
Industry	61	30	40	37
Service	26	57	51	58

Source: Sachs (1994).

To reform the economy more efficiently, therefore, they need to dismantle the overgrown industry and to foster the service sector.

If we now evaluate the results of privatization in Poland, two main problems should be referred to. To be sure, as Balcerowicz mentioned, there is "the declining share of industry (including construction) from 52.3 per cent of the GDP (Gross Domestic Product) in 1988 to 46.6 per cent in 1991" (1995, p.332). However, since 1992 the share of industry in GDP has been growing by 8.8 per cent, although agriculture was declining by 0.8 per cent and service declining by 8.0 per cent. Since 1992, industry has grown more instead of declining as far as the GDP structure is concerned.

The second problem is about the microeconomic level shown by table 2.4 and table 2.5. Table 2.4 means the ratios of total costs to total revenues and in 1991-94 cost input in per cent in the private sector was more than in the public sector (the public sector was more efficient than the private sector). Table 2.5 shows the ratio of gross profit to total costs. It indicates, except in 1992, that the ratios of profit to costs in the public sector were higher than in the private sector (and the public sector was more profitable than the private sector).

With the above two statistics concerning the overgrown industrial sector and increased efficiency of the public sector, it is difficult to argue that until 1994-95 the Polish privatization policy had a good result.

What should be done next for Privatization?

Privatization is a policy tool to raise the economic efficiency through dismantling an inefficient structure. According to a study investigating reasons for privatized companies' good performance (see Karpinska-Mizielinska and Smuga (1996)), they are: (1) the quality of managerial staff; (2) low conflict rate in the enterprise; (3) good adjustability to changing external conditions etc. The study suggests that privatization does not seem to have a critical effect upon a company's performance. In other words, whether it is state owned or not, profitable management makes companies improve.

Table 2.4   Cost input in per cent

	1991	1992	1993	1994
All economic entities	94.0	96.8	96.1	95.7
Public sector	93.7	96.0	94.9	94.7
Private sector	97.8	99.0	98.5	97.4

Source: GUS (Annual), Bednarski (1995).

Table 2.5   Profitability in per cent

	1991	1992	1993	1994
All economic entities	4.8	2.2	2.9	4.2
Public sector		3.6	3.9	5.5
Private sector		6.0	1.1	2.1

Source: See Table 2.4.

Based upon the viewpoints of the Polish experience, we could understand important factors such as these described below. First, support for a newly established company, particularly in the tertiary sector. Second, as was mentioned previously, private companies are less efficient than public ones. Among several factors is one of the most serious elements for the inefficiency of private sector a lack of capital which makes the scale of companies too small and makes efficient management difficult. Although as is often suggested the low profitability of private companies is partly because they do not want to report their true profits, it is hard to scientifically confirm. The factor of capital shortage is still critical. Third, as indicated later, a goal of privatization is to free a government from supporting inefficient state owned companies. Generally, a soft budget scheme for enough capital would not be a good policy. Instead of the soft budget scheme, an infant industry approach should be taken, which needs some criteria to select some preferred industries. According to Karpinska-Mizielinska and Smuga (1996, p.167): "Capital privatization is to cover the following branches: the manufacture of tobacco, chemicals, pharmaceuticals, foodstuffs and beverages, machinery and equipment, building material; trade and the banking sector." The criteria seem to be the price of shares and terms of payment, the export oriented nature of investment etc. Apart from the above criteria from the viewpoint of the overgrown industrial sector, appropriate industries for capital privatization by the Polish government would be the comparative advantage industries like foodstuffs and beverages, machinery and equipment, and the trade sector.

Referring to the Polish experience of privatization, therefore, we would emphasize that the necessary conditions for successful privatization are more active governmental support toward establishing new private companies and improving potential comparative advantage industries.

The Necessity and Prospect for a Commodity Futures Market in Poland

In the first and second sections, we considered high inflation and privatization in Poland. Both policies have been the crucial measures for Polish economic transformation. Also, as discussed, the inflationary situation has been reduced to a two-digit number. The unemployment rate, however, has increased to around 15 per cent. The main reason for the "stagflationary" circumstances is undoubtedly due to a monopolistic industrial structure that is the "legacy" of the centrally planned system. It would be easy to expect that because of the delay in the planned privatization, in which the capital privatization share is only ten per cent, a dismantling policy against large-scale inefficient state owned companies has never been easy to implement. The National Investment Fund Project started in 1995 finally, after a long political negotiation upon the NIF problems, converged in a rather less radical form.

What has happened concerning the commodity futures market?

In the discussion on inflation in the first section, we pointed to the government purchase program of agricultural products as a major cause of the budget deficit increase. At the time of the suppression of the high inflation, actually, we could recognize the budget deficit reduction.

In connection with the privatization we indicated in the second section, that during 1991-95 the share of the agricultural sector became smaller by 0.8 per cent in the industrial structure.

Taking into consideration the above mentioned situation, we might say as a temporary result of the Polish economic transformation that this resulted in: (1) a reduction of agricultural producers' income level; and (2) a drastic movement toward inequality of income and wealth.

Agriculture and its related products industry has seemed to be a comparative advantage industry for Poland. Actually it is one of the most important industries in economic relations with the EU. It is, therefore, strategically crucial strategy for Poland to have an adequate agricultural policy from the viewpoint of any market oriented scheme. The most important agricultural products for Poland now are wheat, rye, pork and milk, as these four products are the main sources of farmers' income.

The current pricing mechanism for the important products is as follows. First, the Polish Agency of Agricultural Market (hereafter, PAAM) purchases agricultural products from farmers. At a floor level the purchase price the PAAM buys from farmers is determined by a committee that is organized with ten ministries (including Ministry of Finance, Ministry of Industry, Ministry of Agriculture, Fair Trade Committee etc.), representatives of the Peasant Party, representatives of farmers. The floor price is proposed by a president of PAAM to a cabinet meeting, in which the floor price is formally determined. As an actual authority would be a president of PAAM, it is rather easy to understand that some political pressures put on the PAAM mainly by the Ministry of Finance and the Ministry of Agriculture in connection with subsidies for farmers and government expenditure. A market mechanism for searching a long-term equilibrium price is necessary to avoid such political pressures.

What would the PAAM do in a sale of agricultural products? Reasons for establishing the Warsaw Commodity Exchange (which is closely connected with PAAM and is supported by the Chicago Board of Trade, the Poznan Commodity Exchange established by PAAM, the Agriculture Exchange in Poznan, which cooperated with PAAM, and is financially supported by Switzerland) mainly come from needing to have a mechanism to reach an equilibrium selling price for agricultural products that PAAM has held.

It goes without saying that reasons are also found in agricultural producers who are on the supply side and from the food processing industry which is on the demand side.

A drastic change in Polish agriculture, which came about through the economic reform, was a change of agricultural land area. Before the reform, it was not permitted to have more than 100 hectare of agricultural land, and the average area of agricultural land was about six to eight hectares (as shown in table 2.6). Through the systemic transformation, this regulation was removed to become more liberal. As a result, it produced big farmers who have huge areas of agricultural land (they reported one case of a farmer having 4,500 hectares of agricultural land). Their interest has seemed to be focusing upon a rational decision on what and how much they would plan to grow based on as much information as possible.

The food processing industry has been in the same situation. Under the centrally planned system, a food processing factory did not need to take into consideration its cost of production. It could not go bankrupt under the system. On the contrary, however, the new transformation has made food processing factories bankrupt if their performance has been significantly poor. As was mentioned in the second section, it is rather difficult to say that the market mechanism in Poland has been well established. As a general tendency, however, we could recognize the way toward that direction. Privatization in Poland has made it necessary for the food processing industry to hedge the buying price.

We mentioned in the first section that the high inflation in Poland, which was a three-digit number at its peak, was fundamentally due to a monopolistic market structure and excess money supply. Super normal profit produced by an excessive supply of money and a monopolistic structure has led to more inequality in income and wealth distribution. It is mentioned rather often that the stock markets of the four Central European countries (Poland, Hungary, Czech Republic and Slovak Republic) have growing stock price indices and also the ratios of stock price with revenue have been relatively low. We could expect that there has still been enough potential "speculative money" that would search for more expected profit.

It could be indicated, therefore, that in Poland, related to inflation and privatization, the following three factors would be important from the viewpoint of this chapter: (1) a movement searching for the equilibrium price, eliminating political pressure; (2) a necessity for hedging against uncertainty concerned with agricultural products from both sides of demand and supply; and (3) an existence of speculative capital being able to respond to the hedging necessity.

Conclusion

This chapter has looked at inflation (first section) and privatization (second section) and the necessity for a commodity futures market (third section). The main purpose of this chapter is to describe the inflationary situation and the privatization which seem not to be closely related to commodity markets and are actually part of the case for a commodity futures market.

Inflation, which has mainly been caused by budget expenditure, has been closely tied to prices of agricultural products and farmers' income levels, and also has become one of the major causes of potential capital for speculation.

Privatization, which has never been implemented enough in Poland, has roughly produced an important tendency toward more intensive use of agricultural land and a stronger food processing industry, which is expected to have a comparative advantage and to be more efficient.

Table 2.6 Agrarian structure of the peasant-owned sector 1950-90 and forecast to 2020

(hectare, %)

Farm Size in Hectares	1950	1990	2000	2020
1-2	15.0	17.7	17.6	16.7
2-5	35.9	35.1	33.3	25.7
5-7	17.3	14.9	14.3	13.3
7-10	18.0	14.9	13.8	12.6
10-15	8.9	11.3	11.7	12.7
15 and more	4.9	6.1	9.3	19.0
Total	100.0	100.0	100.0	100.0
Average Size in Hectares	5.3	6.3	7.6	8.1
Share of Land in Farms of over 10 Hectares	33.5	42.7	42.4	47.4

Source: WERI (1994) p.230.

As examined in the first and second section, in Poland the inflationary potential has been still tough and the privatization procedures has been more delayed than expected. From the viewpoint of a more active function in the commodity futures market, Poland has great potential which has not actually been reached yet.

We could therefore have the prospect of a commodity futures market in Poland.

Notes

1 See Kolodko (1992), p.76, footnote 2.
2 For example, Kolodko (1992) and Lavigne (1995).
3 Sajkiewicz (1995), pp.55-56.
4 Kolodko (1992), p.81.
5 Kolodko (1992), p.82.
6 Kolodko (1992), p.97.
7 Bozyk (1999), p.31.
8 WERI (Annual, '94/'95), pp.81- 82.
9 This section draws from the two excellent works on privatization, which are Bednarski (1995) and Karpinska-Mizielinska and Smuga (1996).

Chapter 3

Current Situation of the Commodity Exchanges in Central Europe [1]

Introduction

It might be the "Perestroika" led by former USSR leader Mr. Mikhail Gorbachov that started the first wave of radical transition, which was the middle 1980s. Also various Central European countries began the transition toward market oriented economies after 1989. In 1989 the Budapest Commodity Exchange was actually established. The purpose of this chapter is to examine briefly rather unfamiliar institutions for most readers, Commodity Exchanges in Central Europe, particularly focusing on the Budapest Commodity Exchange and the Warsaw Commodity Exchange. However, at the same time, the backdrop to such an investigation is indispensably "globalization". At the end of this chapter we refer to the relations between Commodity Exchanges in Central Europe and globalization and present issues to be investigated. (See also chapter eight on the same topic of capital movements.)

In this chapter, we first have a short look at the Warsaw Commodity Exchange and the Budapest Commodity Exchange (in the first section), and in the second section we analyze the function of the Budapest Commodity Exchange (which was better established in the 1990s than the Warsaw Commodity Exchange), and in the third section, we conclude the chapter, by focusing on globalization and issues to be examined in the future.

The Warsaw Commodity Exchange and Budapest Commodity Exchange: A Brief Exposition

In 1999, the Warsaw Commodity Exchange had 25 employees altogether, particularly younger generation specialists of around 35 years old working for such sections as marketing, analysis, etc. However, as far as the Warsaw Commodity Exchange is concerned, it would be difficult to acknowledge that the Exchange has worked actively. Transactions have been limited to

Polish citizens and foreign legal persons and individual persons have not been allowed to participate. In 1999, public relations and providing information about the Warsaw Commodity Exchange were approved only in the Polish language, whose regulation was totally different from the Budapest Commodity Exchange.

In 1999, the Commodity Exchange Act was discussed at the economic committee (whose members were ministers of each ministry), and (the then) deputy prime minister and finance minister, Mr. Leszek Balcerowicz, was the chairman of the committee. It was expected that the Act would be signed and the situation on the Warsaw Commodity Exchange became similar to that of the Budapest Commodity Exchange. (The Act was signed on 26 October 2000, see "1099 Ustawa z dnia 26 pazdzienika 2000r. o gieldach towarowych (1099 Act of 26 October 2000 on commodity exchange)".)

Futures transactions were started on January 1999. US$, German Mark and wheat were then traded and pork was added later. Actually, however, futures transactions of wheat and pork were almost nothing and futures transactions were limited to currencies.

As far as spot transaction was concerned, the exchange was active. For example, (in 1999) at the spot transaction of frozen pork on Thursday from 11:00 am for around one hour, seven to eight dealers communicating with exporters were on the purchasing side and traded by auction with the suppliers from the Polish Agency of Agricultural Market based upon a floor price already established by the Agency. The Polish Agency of Agricultural Market purchased pork meat from Polish producers with a monopsony position, and they sold it by auction. Usually, it was backwardation for the Agency because the price level was set up for exporters to be advantageous in export to Western European countries.

Therefore, the situation is that the Exchange did not work as a market of futures transactions. (With regard to the Poznan Commodity Exchange, they arranged wheat futures transactions in which, however, there were almost no transaction.)

It has to be said from the above situation that it was undoubtedly too early to talk about statistical information and market activity. (Needless to say, however, after the situation is better organized so that it is similar to the exchanges in the US, Western Europe and Japan, some organizations lose their vested interest. There might be politically difficult situation needed to accomplish it.)

Another difficulty for a commodity futures market is how to spread the education of commodity futures transactions. It is easy to understand that, if the market mechanism has never been recognized enough among citizens, to spread education about the futures transaction and make it active would be a hard job. However, it could not be avoided. The theoretical aspect could be taught at the university social science faculties. As far as the practical aspect is concerned, the Exchange has a specific job and to be a dealer it is necessary to have the education and to pass the examination. (To be sure, the difficult issues of management might not be so serious and, taking into consideration the present situation of the Warsaw Commodity Exchange, it would be rather normal.)

As mentioned earlier, the Budapest Commodity Exchange is organized much better than the Warsaw Commodity Exchange. (In Hungary, there was only one commodity exchange.) However, because of its far reaching function compared with the Warsaw Commodity Exchange, the Budapest Commodity Exchange suffered as a result of the "Russian crisis" in 1998. The main transaction commodity in the futures market in Budapest was currencies (Euro, US$, German Mark, British Pound, Swiss Franc, Japanese Yen, etc., whose main transactions were Euro and US$) which shared 96.54 per cent of the total volume of transactions. When the effect of the Russian crisis (that is, capital outflow) reached Budapest, the transaction volume was radically decreased. The volume of trade in grain was slightly increased but in livestock (pork) there was little business, but the serious effect of the radical decrease of currency transaction attacked the all the transactions in the Budapest Commodity Exchange. This reduced the number of employees in the Budapest Commodity Exchange fall from 22 at the end of 1998 to 15 in November 1999. Also there has been undoubtedly globalization as a result of integration with the Budapest Stock Exchange and new legislation toward electronic transaction have been researched. (The average age of the 15 employees was around 30 and they seem to be young and active.)

Compared with the Warsaw Commodity Exchange (in which almost all transactions were in spot and the quotation was determined by auction like the frozen pork example above), most transactions in the Budapest Commodity Exchange were in futures. For example in 1999 the share of spot transactions in Budapest was only 0.06 per cent. The commodities traded there were classified into three as mentioned above, currency, grain and livestock. The transaction of grain and livestock was done by floor trade, and currency transaction was done by floor trade in the morning session and by electronic trade in the afternoon session. (Futures transaction was covered for eight months futures delivery.) As far as the transaction of grain and livestock were concerned, there was no regulation, however, concerning currency transaction there was regulation only for Hungarian citizens (and foreign legal persons jointly undertaken with a

Hungarian corporation).

The reason why the present Budapest Commodity Exchange was established in 1989 and mainly traded in grain was not for the same reason as in the Warsaw Commodity Exchange (as was explained in chapter two), that is, directly connected with the budget deficit. It mainly came from the necessity for reasonable convenience requested by companies related with Hungary that wished to trade in Budapest in addition to other markets in the world. It was quite reasonable from the viewpoint of economic rationality to be available for 24-hour trading. Because of the rationality, (as of the year 1999) 100 legal persons including 10 large scale companies participated in grain trade. (In the Budapest Commodity Exchange they have a regulation of price movement limit.)

As in Warsaw, in Budapest they have tried out several ideas for letting Hungarian citizens learn how to trade in commodity futures markets. Although it is true that the Hungarian history of economic reforms is longer than the Polish, the transition towards market oriented mechanisms in Hungary might have no significant difference from Poland. It would therefore be correct to say that education for commodity futures markets has also been a hard job. In addition to a course in commodity futures transactions at the four universities, such as Budapest University of Economics, the person in charge of the Budapest Commodity Exchange has contributed at higher schools in Hungary to spread the concept of commodity futures transaction. (In addition to the formal position on problems and management, the details have to be examined particularly from the viewpoint of legal regulation in the future.)

Commodity Exchange in Central Europe and Efficiency Market Hypothesis: The Case of Hungary

What do we understand about the present function of commodity futures markets in Central Europe? More detailed consideration will be attempted in the fourth chapter, and here we indicate difficulties and examine what these mean.

There is a theory of efficient market hypothesis, which assumes that when a price at a market is determined with all available information, the market is considered to be "efficient". According to Komiya and Suda (1983) who summarize the theory appropriately, it is as follows: "Assuming a set of all available information relating to asset evaluation concerned at $(t-1)$period to be ϕ_{t-1}, and we assume also a price of a certain asset at t period determined based upon the ϕ_{t-1} to be P_t. That could be recognized as the correct price of the asset determined by the correct information. On the other hand, assuming a set of actual information in asset evaluation at $(t-1)$ period to be ϕ_{t-1}^m, and also we assume a price of the asset at t period determined by the information set of ϕ_{t-1}^m to be P_t^m. Needless to say, ϕ_{t-1}^m is a partial set of ϕ_{t-1}. Efficiency market hypothesis could be defined therefore as a proposition that ϕ_{t-1}^m equals to ϕ_{t-1}, and thus P_t^m which is held at actual asset market equals to P_t which is recognized as the correct price." (p.134)

We usually assume, according to Fama (1970), three kinds of "efficiency": "weak efficiency", "semi-strong efficiency" and "strong efficiency", as follows.[2]

"Weak efficiency" results when price movements are totally independent of prior price movements.

Therefore, analyzing historical price patterns would not be beneficial in yielding any substantial profit.

Prices only take into account all new and relevant information on economic activity.

With "semi-strong efficiency", the market is efficient in the sense that prices adjust instantaneously and without bias to newly published information. At this point it is useless for investors to try to take advantage of published data for profit maximization. There exists no advantage in trying to gain insight into which commodities may be 'mispriced' according to fundamental analysis, for everyone within the market has access to the same available information.

At the level of "strong efficiency", market prices reflect not only published information, but information not yet readily available to the general public. For example, an insider trying to maximize profit by trying to capitalize on his or her awareness of an ensuring event would have no edge over the average investor. This is due to prices already factoring in that information which is not yet accessible to all market participants.

According to the above explanation, the easiest proposition to hold that P_t^m equals to P_t is called "strong efficiency", the second is "semi-strong efficiency", and the last is "weak efficiency". That is to say, price series being independent from prior price movement is described as "weak form efficiency", and if prices are adjusted instantaneously so that no investors can move into an advantageous position within the market, this is described as "semi-strong efficiency". When all the information is not yet readily available to the general public (that is, even insiders not in an advantageous position), this would be described as "strong efficiency".

Therefore, the investigation of "weak form efficiency" is done from price predictability from prior price movement. According to Gordon and Rittenberg examination of "semi-strong efficiency" can be "tested by looking at the speed at which new information is incorporated into" commodities' prices. Also "testing of the strong form requires comparing the performance of 'insiders,' ... to the performance of the market." (p. 8).

There have been many arguments concerning efficient market hypothesis. For example, E. F. Fama, who has argued most enthusiastically for the hypothesis mentioned, has said as follows. Assuming that all the market participants have the same perfect information and the same foresight with regard to the price in the future is not realistic, such simplification might be necessary to improve understanding of phenomena in the real world.[3] On the contrary, however, (concerning the foreign exchange market) there could be the following argument: "We would not recognize that by examining the efficient market hypothesis and by statistical testing of it our understanding could be improved and we could have some useful insights into functions of the market. ... Neither rejecting nor accepting any null-hypothesis for efficient market hypothesis provides any significant effect for market behavior and for policy options."[4]

Anyway, it would be reasonable that most tests, whether or not the market was efficient, were based upon the weak form efficiency. As far as the commodity futures markets are concerned, we have had a variety of research testing independence of time series price data (if independent, it means efficient in the weak form sense). For example, Praetz (1976) suggested that, of the nine case studies, four were independent, four neutral (or a little dependent) and one rejected the independency. (Needless to say, several analytical tools were applied to test the independency and dependency in price movements).

With the development of analytical tools many tests have been tried. For example, in such journals as *Applied Economics* and *Applied Financial Economics*, many arguments on analytical tools etc.[5] and on the efficiency of the London Metal Exchange etc.[6] have been actively discussed.

The purpose of this chapter is neither to examine the tests on efficiency nor to explicitly describe our position (pros or cons) with regard to the efficient market hypothesis, but to investigate commodity futures markets in Central Europe with efficient market hypothesis as the key. We have chosen to examine the Budapest Commodity Exchange because (as mentioned earlier) its information is better organized information than other commodity exchanges in Central Europe. Here in this chapter we describe a short statistical test on a commodity in the Budapest Commodity Exchange and have an interpretation of it.

A tested commodity is the EUROPE Live Hog I. The reason why we have selected this commodity is that it has interesting features to be considered and it provides the appropriate case in studying the relationship of commodity futures markets with the European Union (EU). (However, as pointed out earlier, in the Budapest Commodity Exchange in addition to livestock including the EUROPE Live Hog I, currencies and grains have been traded in the futures market and the traded percentage of currencies has been overwhelmingly large. At present in 1999, clear features recognized in the EUROPE Live Hog I were limited to livestock. Analyses of other commodities can be attempted later and the research in the next chapter is a part of this.) From the annual report of the Budapest Commodity Exchange, we can pick up futures price series data for 80 trading days in the August delivery month of 1997 and of 108 trading days in the December delivery month of 1997. We have the auto-regression analysis of the futures price series data to test its random walk. If the futures price series data show randomness (impossible to forecast price levels from prior price movements), the market concerned is evaluated as efficient in the weak form sense. The estimation was done with,

$$L_{(t+1)} = a_{(0)} + a_{(1)}L_{(t-1)} + a_{(2)}L_{(t-2)} + a_{(3)}L_{(t-3)} + e_{(t+1)}$$

Here $L_{(t)} = \log(f_{(t)}) - \log(f_{(t-1)})$, in which $f_{(t)}$ shows the futures price series.[7] As the unit root was recognized in the selected futures price series data, we have the above difference form. The table 3.1 indicates that none of $a_{(0)}$, $a_{(1)}$, $a_{(2)}$, $a_{(3)}$ has significant difference from zero. It is understood that the selected futures price series data might be impossible to forecast and the market concerned would be evaluated as efficient (in the weak form sense).

If we evaluate according to the efficient market hypothesis, we would see that the EUROPE Live Hog I market is efficient.

What does it mean that the EUROPE Live Hog I market is efficient? (Just for convenience) we can cut out the long tables, but the trade volume of EUROPE Live Hog I in the August delivery month of 1997 and in the December delivery month of 1997 in the Annual Report of the Budapest Commodity Exchange was as follows. Of the 80 trading days in the August delivery month trade volume was only recorded for 20 days (small volumes), and of 108 trading days in the December delivery month trade volume was only recorded for 10 days (also very small volumes). It might be difficult to evaluate that this market could be recognized as efficient from the results of the analysis with the futures price series data. Actually (according to the opinion of an official of the Budapest Commodity Exchange) it was said that participants in the EUROPE Live Hog I market were few and the participants were not very interested in trading itself but in future prospects after Hungary joins EU (although this is only one interpretation).[8] As far as the EUROPE Live Hog I market in the August delivery month of 1997 and in the December delivery month of 1997 in the Budapest Commodity Exchange are concerned, it would be doubtful to evaluate that based upon the weak form efficiency; the futures price series data were independent and the markets concerned were efficient.

Table 3.1   Result of auto-regression analysis

	August delivery month	December delivery month
$a_{(0)}$	0.000152 (0.163726)	- 0.000184 (- 0.368442)
$a_{(1)}$	- 0.016176 (- 0.130198)	0.049301 (0.534141)
$a_{(2)}$	0.053211 (0.409538)	0.141306 (1.481255)
$a_{(3)}$	0.067749 (0.554307)	0.148012 (1.633511)
R^2	0.009455	0.079805

* The figures in parentheses are the *t*-values.

From the above analysis we can conclude the following. As far as the EUROPE Live Hog I market in the August and the December delivery months of 1997 in the Budapest Commodity Exchange are concerned:[9] (1) it would be necessary to develop analytical tools to further analyze efficiency; and (2) concerning the current situation of the EUROPE Live Hog I market (in the August and the December delivery months of 1997), we have to point out that the markets would be fairly dependent upon domestic policy in Hungary and on international affairs.

Conclusion: Commodity Exchanges in Central Europe and Globalization

We have briefly looked at the Commodity Exchanges in Central Europe, the Warsaw Commodity Exchange and the Budapest Commodity Exchange in particular. As pointed out earlier, establishing commodity futures markets was undoubtedly a step toward opening the economy to international markets.

In Hungary, the *raison d'être* has been the convenience for investors of trading for 24 hours and in Poland the *raison d'être* of it has been: (1) cutting down the budget for agriculture; and (2) policy adjustment with a view to joining the EU. (Needless to say, the agriculture issue in Central Europe has been one of the hardest issues of the international political economy to deal with in negotiations for joining the EU).

The transition towards a market oriented economy has meant, at the same time, "globalization" and "Americanization" which means putting more emphasis on efficiency and being exposed to more flexible international short-term capital movements.

The issue concerning commodity futures markets and globalization is, in other words, that economic policies in Central European transition economies have had to become compatible with the road to globalization. This has been closely connected with difficult domestic problems and difficult issues in the international political economy. (The latter issue, in particular with regard to joining the EU, should be insisted upon in other volumes and papers.)

In Budapest, as stated in the first section and as we will see in chapter four, the performance until 1998 and in 1999 (the first quarter) was totally different. For example, in 1997 there was 91.78 per cent of the total volume of currencies, 8.18 per cent of grains, and in 1998 96.54 per cent of the total volume of currencies, 3.44 per cent grains. Of the total volume in 1999 (the first quarter), currencies had an 84.65 per cent share and grains had a 15.28 per cent share. In comparison with the shares in 1998, estimating the percentage figures for the first half of 1999 (based on results for the first quarter) results would be 35.4 per cent in grains, 24.8 per cent in livestock and 6.9 per cent in currencies. Total trading volume in the first half in 1999 in the Budapest Commodity Exchange reached only 7.9 per cent (not 25 per cent). If simply extrapolating the situation, the total volume in 1999 would show only 32 per cent of that in 1998. According to *Futures Industry* (February 1997, p.17), the annual trading volume of the Budapest Commodity Exchange in 1996 ranked in 22nd position.

It is worth mentioning particularly the growth rate which was around 288 per cent compared with 1995's ranking of 36th. The extremely high growth rate of nearly 300 per cent was noticeably different from other futures markets and it made the Budapest Commodity Exchange well known in the world. (The growth rates of trading volume in the same year in other major futures markets were for example, 3.3 per cent in the Chicago Board of Trade, 2.8 per cent in the London Metal Exchange, minus 7.7 per cent in the Tokyo Stock Exchange. However, according to statistics from the Budapest Commodity Exchange itself, the growth rate of annual trading volume in the same year was 423.4 per cent, which was contributed to by 388.9 per cent grains, 18.2 per cent livestock and 517.4 per cent currencies.) The main contribution to such extreme growth was undoubtedly a high rate of growth of currencies transaction.

It was also currencies transactions which caused the big fall of trading volume in 1999 (in the first quarter) in the Budapest Commodity Exchange. Undoubtedly the main reason for the big fall was the capital outflow coming from the Russian crisis. It could also be said, by the same token, that it came from capital globalization. In just two or three years the Budapest Commodity Exchange experienced both an extreme increase and a big fall.

Therefore, as far as the commodity futures markets in Central Europe are concerned, one of the clearest features of globalization has been "instability". (Incidentally, the growth rate of trading volume in the Peking Commodity Exchange notably decreased to minus 42.8 per cent in 1996 and minus 76.7 per cent in 1997.)

However, there could be much discussion about whether or not the "instability" is a negative factor. We will attempt to investigate this issue in other cases, but here I would like to draw attention to the existence of serious issues such as this.

Notes

1   As was suggested in introductory text to the Part I and in the previous chapters, economic, social and political situations in transition countries are still changing. This chapter was written based upon the situation in November 1999.
2   Concerning the explanation that follows, see Gordon and Rittenberg (1995), pp.7-8.
3   See Komiya and Suda (1983).
4   Komiya and Suda (1983), p.140 and also see Schiller (1991), p.8.
5   See for example Gilbert (1986).
6   See Sephton and Cochrane (1991), Serletis and Scowcroft (1991) etc.
7   This estimation equation was used by, for example, Kiminami and Kiminami (1995). Although the estimation equation is a little different from the equation in the chapter four, in this chapter we use the same equation as in Kiminami and Kiminami (1995).
8   Even when trading volume was zero, why could the lowest, the highest and the closing price be moved? There could be various interpretations but we will not go into this here.
9   (Except the EUROPE Live Hog I) Efficiency analysis of several commodities will be attempted from different viewpoints in the next chapter. Needless to say, it has been necessary to develop more effective analytical tools and to examine the meanings of efficiency analysis.

Chapter 4

The Functions of Commodity Exchange in Central Europe

Introduction

The Central European transition economies have had around ten years in transformation to market oriented from central planning. As in chapter three, we investigate here the commodity futures market in Central Europe, in particular in Hungary. As indicated by J. R. Hicks (1946) and also examined in this book, the futures market and central planning are opposite institutions in terms of limiting risks. The futures market, in that sense, might be a symbolic institution for market oriented transition.

The Budapest Commodity Exchange (hereafter in this chapter, BCE) in Hungary was established in 1989, which was much earlier than other Commodity Exchanges in the transition economies concerned. Thus, we can focus our attention upon BCE by analyzing its efficiency. As mentioned in chapter three, we partly investigated the efficiency of BCE, in which connection we mentioned the result of the futures price series of Live Hog I in the context of which "Efficient Market Hypothesis" (hereafter in this chapter, EMH) approach might have some problems. In chapter four, we try to consider more the efficiency of BCE with other commodities in the grain section (corn, milling wheat, feed barley and sunflower seed) and in the financial section (US\$ and DEM[1]), not including the livestock section (because of the problems mentioned in the previous chapter). Of the six commodities, we basically analyze four markets (December 1995, July 1996, July 1997 and December 1997, but if the commodity does not have the market, we have the nearest monthly market, and two more markets of corn, July 1995 and December 1996) and we can test the efficiency in the weak efficiency sense of the EMH. In the first section, we have a short overview of the BCE and the Tokyo Grain Exchange (hereafter, TGE). In the second section, we try to do the efficiency test in the weak efficiency sense of BCE, and for comparing the efficiency of BCE, we try also to have the same test with four commodities at TGE, which are corn, raw sugar, US soybean and red beans, and four markets (in the same months as for BCE) of the four commodities, as well as the two more months of corn in TGE for the same months as BCE corn markets. Also in the second section, we compare the efficiency of BCE and TGE with the nonparametric test. In the third section, we have a short coverage of the efficiency and stability of BCE along with the EU enlargement.

An Overview of the Budapest Commodity Exchange and the Tokyo Grain Exchange

Here in this chapter we focus our attention upon BCE as a futures market in Central Europe, because BCE has been the first well-established futures market in that region. We also look at TGE to compare the efficiency with BCE, since TGE has been one of the best exchanges in terms of a well-organized information system.

In this section, we have a short overview of BCE and TGE based upon their annual reports etc. (although some overlap with the third chapter).

For the year 1999, BCE has the three sections: currently trading financial section (DEM, US$, ECU, JPY, ITL, GBP, CHF, CZK, short-term interest rate, three-month BUBOR - Budapest inter Bank Offered Rate - one-month BUBOR), grain section (Euro Wheat, Milling Wheat, Corn, Feed Wheat, Feed Barley, Sunflower Seed and Wheat Flower) and livestock section (Live Hog I, Live Hog II, Live Hog III), and also the option trading of Euro Wheat, Milling Wheat and Corn. According to *Future Industry* (February, 1998), BCE was ranked in the top 22nd position of the world futures markets on turnover in 1996 and 1997.

The short history of BCE is as follows. We can go back to the 1850s. In 1854 the Pest Lloyd Company established the Grain Hall with the purpose of concentrating Hungarian grain trading in one place. From here, we go to the modern history of BCE, in 1989 when Commodity Exchange Ltd. beginning, with an equity capital of HUF 1.9 million, was established to provide the opportunity for market participants to trade corn and milling wheat contracts. The purpose was to establish a non-profit institute, which could provide all the conditions required for the operation of an exchange. In 1990 Commodity Exchange Ltd. was restructured into BCE.

By the end of 1991, the livestock section was opened, and BCE wanted to ensure the safety of production and sales. And in 1992, BCE decided to eventually operate three sections, so a resolution was passed for the establishment of the financial section. In 1993, with the opening of the financial section, dynamic progress was made in BCE enabling it to open a new 1,000 square meter computerized trading floor which was well-equipped with telecommunication lines. Also in October 1993 three different organizations, the National Bank of Hungary, the Budapest Stock Exchange and the BCE, established the Central Depository and Clearing House Inc. (KELER Rt.) guaranteeing all transactions concluded both on the Budapest Stock Exchange and the BCE.

In April of 1994 the Act on Commodity Exchange and Commodity Exchange Transactions (Act XXXIX of 1994) was passed by Parliament. Also in 1999 Commodity Exchange Ltd. ceased to exist and, as its legal successor, BCE was established.

1995 was an outstanding year for BCE. The turnover indicated a sharp increase and the total volume of trade in 1995 was a fourfold increase compared to 1994, with most prominent progress experienced in the financial section. Also in 1996, BCE's turnover grew fivefold during the year and BCE was ranked 22nd in the list of the top world futures exchanges.

TGE is one of the leading commodity futures exchanges in Asia, which is a non-profit membership organization trading red beans, corn, raw sugar, US soybean, arabica coffee and robusta coffee futures. Options on US soybeans, raw sugar, and corn futures are also being traded. According to *Futures Industry* (February 1998), TGE's turnover in 1997 ranked the top tenth position in the international futures markets.

As is well known, the birth of futures trading in Japan can be traced back to 1730 when rice futures were traded at the Dojima Rice Market. This was in response to the requests by rice traders who were asked by clans to commercialize rice produced on their territories. From 1870 rice futures were traded at the location of the present exchange. And in 1893 the Exchange Law was enacted to modernize the exchange, giving birth to exchanges dealing in cotton, sugar and raw silk in addition to rice. However, in the event of the Second World War, trading on all commodity exchanges in Japan was suspended. Following the war, a new Commodity Exchange Law was promulgated and instituted in 1950.

Two years later, TGE was established in the premises of the original Exchange. In 1987 the building that is standing today was erected to provide space for future expansion to meet anticipated growth. In April 1988 the conventional session trading of hand signals that had taken place on the floor was replaced with Japan's first fully computerized trading system.

On 1 October 1993 TGE merged with the Tokyo Sugar Exchange in order to provide market participants with greater access. Following the trend to centralized trading, TGE merged with the Hokkaido Grain Exchange on 1 April 1995.

The Efficiency of the Budapest Commodity Exchange and

Efficiency Test

In this section, first we consider for BCE the four markets (December 1995, July 1996, July 1997 and December 1997) of the six commodities (corn, milling wheat, feed barley and sunflower seed in the grain section, and US dollar and DEM in the financial section), and also two more markets (July 1995 and December 1996) of corn, which means altogether 28 markets. However, we exclude commodities in the livestock section because (as mentioned in the previous chapter) their trade volumes were abnormally small. The estimation was done with the following equation,

$$L_{(t)} = a_{(0)} + a_{(1)}L_{(t-1)} + a_{(2)}L_{(t-2)} + a_{(3)}L_{(t-3)} + e_{(t)}$$

Here, $L_{(t)} = \log(f_{(t)}) - \log(f_{(t-1)})$ and $f_{(t)}$ means the futures market price series. As we recognize the unit root in each price series, we have the difference. (As we could not recognize the unit root in the futures market price series of the corn market of July 1997, we would have instead $L_{(t)} = \log(f_{(t)})$ being without the difference). We can recognize a coefficient as not significantly different from zero if its t-value is less than 2.0. (If t-value is less than 1.5, not less than 2.0, though the number of markets with a random walk becomes less, the result of this section is unchanged).

The markets in which we can recognize a random walk in the price series are as follows: two markets of four US$ markets (December 1995 and June 1997), one of four DEM markets (June 1996), one of six corn markets (July 1995) and one of four feed barley markets (December 1995). In the other 21 markets (which mean two US$ markets, three DEM markets, five corn markets, four milling wheat markets, three feed barley markets and four sunflower seed markets) there might not be considered to be a "random walk" because there could be coefficients in them which might be significantly different from zero. (Table 4.1 to 4.5 show the efficient market cases.)

In TGE, they now have six commodities futures transactions and option trade. In this chapter we analyze four commodities (because their historical price data is comparable with BCE commodities and is available): corn, raw sugar, US soybean and red beans. Of the four commodities, we have four markets for each and two more of corn (altogether 18 markets) with about the same months to investigate.

With the same estimation as in BCE, the markets estimated as random walk are the following seven: July 1997 and November 1997 for corn,

August 1996 for US soybean and all four markets for red beans, November 1995, June 1996, June 1997 and November 1997. The other 11 markets (four of corn, three of US soybean and all the four of raw sugar) might not be thought as efficient because coefficients could be observed in them that are significantly different from zero. Table 4.6 to 4.12 present the results of efficient TGE cases.

A Comparative view of the Budapest Commodity Exchange and Tokyo Grain Exchange

As was mentioned previously, five markets of four commodities in BCE and seven markets of three commodities in TGE were recognized as efficient (in the weak efficiency sense). We focus our attention here upon the efficiency of BCE based on the above investigation. What can we say about the efficiency of BCE?

Table 4.1   BCE US$: December 1995

$a_{(0)}$	- 0.0000114 (-0.039299)
$a_{(1)}$	0.050767 (0.776676)
$a_{(2)}$	- 0.026689 (- 0.408194)
$a_{(3)}$	0.012970 (0.200781)
$a_{(4)}$	- 0.030065 (- 0.465675)
R^2	- 0.012948

*The figures in parentheses are the t-values.

   As was discussed in the previous chapter, we could conceive as efficient a futures price series data with a random walk test even if the market has a very small trade volume.[2] However, actually, a commodity such as US$ in the financial section of BCE is very active in terms of transactions, as a

Table 4.2   BCE US$: June 1995

$a_{(0)}$	0.000192 (1.036989)
$a_{(1)}$	0.102351 (1.618770)
$a_{(2)}$	0.099016 (1.558209)
$a_{(3)}$	- 0.029193 (-0.459341)
$a_{(4)}$	- 0.005160 (-0.081214)
R^2	0.006414

*The figures in parentheses are the t-values.

Table 4.3   BCE German mark: June 1996

$a_{(0)}$	- 0.000354 (- 1.760153)
$a_{(1)}$	0.004721 (0.066737)
$a_{(2)}$	- 0.046728 (- 0.651747)
$a_{(3)}$	0.061944 (0.868889)
$a_{(4)}$	- 0.031265 (- 0.443974)
R^2	- 0.013297

*The figures in parentheses are the t-values.

Table 4.4   BCE corn: July 1995

$a_{(0)}$	0.001450 (1.138297)
$a_{(1)}$	- 0.034223 (- 0.171725)
$a_{(2)}$	0.365367 (1.867213)
$a_{(3)}$	0.085023 (0.428556)
$a_{(4)}$	- 0.112245 (- 0.681125)
R^2	- 0.007878

*The figures in parentheses are the t-values.

Table 4.5   BCE feed barley: December 1995

$a_{(0)}$	0.002695 (1.557593)
$a_{(1)}$	0.329676 (1.946474)
$a_{(2)}$	0.088995 (0.504609)
$a_{(3)}$	0.172357 (0.977279)
$a_{(4)}$	- 0.113595 (- 0.67069)
R^2	0.087880

*The figures in parentheses are the t-values.

Table 4.6   TGE corn: July 1997

$a_{(0)}$	- 0.001170 (- 1.137672)
$a_{(1)}$	- 0.032825 (- 0.496449)
$a_{(2)}$	- 0.096927 (- 1.466735)
$a_{(3)}$	- 0.072398 (- 1.096059)
$a_{(4)}$	0.047841 (0.721989)
R^2	0.001123

*The figures in parentheses are the *t*-values.

Table 4.7   TGE corn: November 1997

$a_{(0)}$	0.000862 (0.788226)
$a_{(1)}$	- 0.030940 (- 0.474127)
$a_{(2)}$	0.033972 (0.516494)
$a_{(3)}$	- 0.022221 (- 0.338901)
$a_{(4)}$	- 0.057286 (- 0.874267)
R^2	- 0.01133

*The figures in parentheses are the t-values.

Table 4.8   TGE US soybean: August 1996

$a_{(0)}$	0.001255 (1.220354)
$a_{(1)}$	- 0.034627 (- 0.531489)
$a_{(2)}$	- 0.056297 (- 0.869079)
$a_{(3)}$	0.011318 (0.174282)
$a_{(4)}$	- 0.049005 (- 0.755471)
R^2	- 0.010112

*The figures in parentheses are the t-values.

Table 4.9   TGE red beans: November 1995

$a_{(0)}$	- 0.003430 (- 1.943926)
$a_{(1)}$	0.062169 (0.669494)
$a_{(2)}$	0.088491 (0.950429)
$a_{(3)}$	- 0.012390 (-0.132047)
$a_{(4)}$	- 0.005381 (- 0.57992)
R^2	- 0.021696

*The figures in parentheses are the t-values.

Table 4.10   TGE red beans: June 1996

$a_{(0)}$	0.001060 (0.828132)
$a_{(1)}$	0.099812 (1.068546)
$a_{(2)}$	- 0.049959 (- 0.533284)
$a_{(3)}$	0.070822 (0.756202)
$a_{(4)}$	0.058154 (0.633886)
R^2	- 0.013751

*The figures in parentheses are the t-values.

Table 4.11   TGE red beans: June 1997

$a_{(0)}$	- 0.001182 (- 1.005304)
$a_{(1)}$	- 0.035524 (- 0.375223)
$a_{(2)}$	- 0.049732 (- 0.537777)
$a_{(3)}$	0.153376 (1.644078)
$a_{(4)}$	0.104206 (1.112167)
R^2	0.002289

*The figures in parentheses are the t-values.

Table 4.12   TGE red beans: November 1997

$a_{(0)}$	0.000803 (0.387004)
$a_{(1)}$	0.122066 (1.223608)
$a_{(2)}$	0.119808 (1.187067)
$a_{(3)}$	0.105793 (1.050513)
$a_{(4)}$	- 0.175960 (- 1.734833)
R^2	0.027971

*The figures in parentheses are the t-values.

result of which we could rather easily find a random walk. Also in a red beans market in TGE, we could easily recognize them as efficient. Thus, it might be said that a market with much trade volume and with a well-organized information system might become more efficient easily, which automatically means that the weak efficiency test of EMH could be, to some extent, useful.

In this section, we try to consider whether a comparative investigation of BCE with TGE (as the two "populations") shows any significant difference between the two. Our consideration focuses upon a study of whether or not there could be any significant difference in efficiency of the futures market price series between BCE and TGE. In such a study, we usually have a Chi-square test (χ^2 test) to recognize a difference in efficiency. Both populations of BCE and TGE seem to satisfy the minimum condition to apply the test, which requires that all cells have numbers greater than five, which we can easily calculate. (Although we omit here the calculation) the result is 2.07, which means it is outside the rejection region at the 0.05 level. Therefore, it might be argued that, at the 0.05 level, we can not recognize a significant difference in efficiency between BCE and TGE.

It might be safer to have two more tests in addition to the Chi-square test for both populations: (1) a nonparametric test to recognize a significant difference between just the commodities in the grain section; and (2) a nonparametric test to study a significant difference between the same commodity (corn) in BCE and TGE. In such nonparametric tests, however, as the sample sizes are too small, we have the calculation with the Yates correction.

First, we have a test with 18 markets of four commodities (in the grain section: corn, feed barley, milling wheat and sunflower seed) in BCE and 18 markets of four commodities (corn, raw sugar, US soybean and red beans) in TGE. (Here again we omit the calculation) the result is 2.370, which shows it outside the rejection region at the 0.05 level. It indicates that we could not recognize a significant difference in efficiency between the grain sections in BCE and TGE.

Second, we also have the same test with six markets of corn in BCE and six markets of corn in TGE. (Here again we omit the calculation) the result is 0.412, which clearly means it is outside the rejection region at the 0.05 level. It says, like the previous calculation, that we could not recognize a significant difference in efficiency between the corn market in the BCE and TGE. (With another calculation, we did not recognize significant correlation with regression analysis between the corn market prices in BCE and the corn market prices in TGE. We also carried out tests with the above two, not using the Yates correction, but by the direct calculation of probability and had the same results.)

Therefore, we would argue here that, based upon the above analysis, it might not be said that BCE is less efficient than TGE.

Actually, it would not be easy to say whether or not the futures market price series in BCE shows efficiency in the weak efficiency sense of EMH, as was mentioned in the previous chapter. The purpose of this chapter, therefore, is to have a comparative view of efficiency in BCE compared with TGE, which was ranked tenth position in the world futures markets in 1997 with a well-established information system. With the purpose and the investigation in this chapter, and based upon the above data and statistics, we could argue here that it might not be said that BCE is less efficient than TGE.

Implications for the EU Enlargement

As was (temporarily) emphasized in the above, "it might not be said that BCE is less efficient than TGE".

Straightforwardly, however, trade volume in BCE (the grain section and livestock section in particular) is still rather small compared with the international futures markets. It also means that with increasing trade volume like the commodities in the financial section in BCE, it could probably become more efficient. In that sense, the EU enlargement would give a good opportunity for BCE to increase efficiency through growing trade volume.

On the other hand, joining the EU (which means joining the global financial market) might introduce short-term instability, which could lead to a rapid decrease of trade volume and reductions in staff numbers, as the 1998-99 experience in the financial section of BCE shows. Actually, as was mentioned in the chapter three, BCE trade performances in 1998 and in 1999 were completely different. (The distribution of 1997 turnover was 91.78 per cent in the financial section, 8.18 per cent in the grain section and 0.04 per cent in the livestock section, and the same distribution for 1998 was 96.54 per cent in the financial section, 3.44 per cent in the grain section and 0.02 per cent in the livestock section. The distribution in turnover for the first quarter in 1999 was 84.65 per cent in the financial section, 15.28 per cent in the grain section and 0.06 per cent in the livestock section.) As the total turnover of the first quarter in 1999 was only 7.9 per cent of the 1998 total, the first quarter's distribution for each section in 1999 was 6.9 per cent (in the financial section), 35.4 per cent (in the grain section) and 24.8 per cent (in the livestock section) of each performance in 1998. Therefore, we can easily say that the rapid increase in turnover at BCE was mainly coming from the extreme increase of turnover in the financial section, and that the rapid decrease of turnover in BCE was chiefly due to the extreme decrease in turnover in the financial section. We can recognize that also in the employment situation in BCE, which showed (as was indicated in chapter three) that the number of staff in BCE decreased to 15 in November 1999, from 22 in December 1998. The above-mentioned rapid change was closely related with the short-term capital movements in the global market, which might be called "mad money".[3] Joining more closely to the global market through EU enlargement might more easily introduce such an unstable financial situation.

Therefore, joining the EU would have the two opposite effects: (1) a possibility of raising efficiency by increasing trade volume; and (2) a possibility of raising instability by short-term capital movements.

Are there any effective policies against instability whilst keeping efficiency?

The indispensable task in approaching the above question is to find an effective way of saying there is an exact situation of "market balance" (based upon selling and buying) and to find the "speculative index", which was analyzed many years ago and referred to as "excessive speculation". Unfortunately, however, it is necessary to mention that the study has been developed enough based upon the increase of derivative operations, flexible international short-term capital movement, etc. The analyses of "market balance", "speculative index" and "excessive speculation" might be the next step for intensive investigation, some of which analysis is attempted in the third part of this book.

Conclusion

The aim of this chapter was to have some idea of the efficiency of BCE, as one of the symbolic tests of Hungarian economic transformation into a market oriented system. Because a statistical analysis of efficiency test has not been sufficiently developed, we have a way in this chapter to compare efficiency results of TGE, which has been one of the best markets with a well-organized information system. The efficiency test in both markets is done with an auto-regression model and then the results are compared with nonparametric tests (Chi-square test and Yates correction) to see whether there might be any significant difference in efficiency between BCE and TGE.

With the above investigation, it might be argued that BCE is no less efficient than TGE.

We can say here that, by increasing the trade volume and by increasing a number of market participants, BCE might become more efficient, other things being equal. By joining the EU, BCE would be moving in the direction of more efficiency with more trade volume. However, we could also indicate that, by joining the enlarged EU, BCE would become an easier target for international short-term capital movements. It would be necessary, therefore, to have appropriate policies against instability due to short-term capital movement with investigation of the "market balance" and "excessive speculation", etc.

Notes

1   As of the year 2002, they have Euro transactions into which European currencies have been integrated.
2   As mentioned in chapter three, we will not investigate the issue in this chapter.
3   See Strange (1998). Also see chapter eight of this book.

PART II
ECONOMIC REFORMS AND CAPITAL MOVEMENTS IN CENTRAL EUROPE

In the second part of the book, we will focus our attention upon issues of economic reforms and capital movements in Central Europe. As far as the contemporary environment in flexible capital movement is concerned, examining what kind risks have existed is indispensable. We have to consider what the characteristic features of risk in post-communist economies and what the characteristic natures of inefficiency in transition economies are. Also concerning risk of hindering capital movement to Central Europe, we can approach this with FDI cases.

The chapter five considers such questions as what are the main tasks for economic reform in Central Europe and also focuses on the correct viewpoints of the way forward in transition.

In the chapter six we try to clarify Polish economic reforms compared with the experience of postwar Japanese economic reforms

In the chapter seven, we attempt to clarify the nature of risk closely connected with the (negative) legacy of the communist regime by considering a foreign direct investment (FDI) case between Poland and Japan which occurred in the 1980s.

In the chapter eight, take into consideration the topics in the third part of the book, I will examine factors correlated with FDI focusing upon the Visegrad three countries (Poland, Hungary and the Czech Republic). Also I will try to investigate some problems with capital movement based upon FDI investigations.

We will also do the same here as in the first part of the book, which means that the analyses in the second part were principally based upon the period concerned.

Chapter 5

Political Economy of Reforms

Introduction

The Koizumi cabinet in Japan, which started in April 2001, has struggled in reforming the Japanese economy. Its major task has been undoubtedly in its priority between structural reform and expansion policy. We have heard rather often US and Western European journals such as the *Economist* saying that it would be indispensable for rebuilding the Japanese economy to have a much looser monetary policy toward more expansion of the Japanese economy. Such an argument would be understood as attaching more importance to a growth oriented policy. As a matter of fact, in the middle of August 2001, The Bank of Japan announced a more quantitative monetary policy.

The arguments concerning which oriented policy, restructuring or growth, might become a target for serious discussion when deep-rooted reform becomes necessary.

We had similar arguments about the ways of reform (restructuring or growth) in postwar Japan and in postwar (West) Germany which were usually understood to be the "gradual way" in Japan and to be the "radical way" in (West) Germany. Also since 1989-90, in Central and East European countries, they have tried to transform their economic system. It has been said the economic transition movement was the "greatest reconstructuring job in history".[1] This chapter and the next have the purpose of investigating this, mainly focusing attention upon the Polish experience of reform in the middle 1990s[2] compared with postwar Japanese experience (needless to say there are some overlapping portions in the fifth and the sixth chapters). This chapter is approached in a rather practical way and the next chapter in a rather analytical way.

Patterns of Economic Reforms

In the transformation from a centrally planned economy to a market oriented economy, needless to say (here we do not discuss the definition), there are some patterns. Usually economists have assumed the two patterns of a "radical reform" and a "gradual reform" and with their distinctive features they have applied the patterns to actual transition economies. That approach has been so limited that we have such appropriate wording as "hidden shock therapy".[3]

However, unless we are very specific about a problem, arguing whether a reform is "radical" or not does not seem to be so meaningful. A more important way of approaching it is looking at what policy goals a transition economy has. Also we should ask what benefit and what costs the transition economy would have in completing the policy goals, and if the policy has been appropriate or not.

We think it is necessary to investigate reforms from the above viewpoints.

As regards the Polish case, when the "Balcerowicz Program" was introduced in 1990, it was necessary to have a shock therapy method to absorb the inflationary overhang. As far as the shock therapy to eliminate the inflationary overhang is concerned, we can evaluate the policy to be rather effective.

The Balcerowicz Program was, however, never limited to fighting inflation. As the National Bank of Poland Annual Report said,[4] the goals of the program were: (1) disinflation; (2) the eradication of shortages; (3) a sound national currency; (4) privatization and structural reform. It covered not only the financial area but also almost all areas of main economic activities. It is extremely difficult to classify the policy into a mainly targeted sphere. The reason the program was a shock therapy was because it was introduced at a single stroke on 1 January 1990 to fight for price liberalization, raising interest rates, deep depreciation of the zloty exchange rate, tax reform, cutting subsidies, etc. In other words, they tried to transform at a stroke (within one to two years) an economic mechanism in which all the prices of the commodity (and service) market, capital market, foreign exchange market, and (by privatization) labor market could be determined by demand and supply. Needless to say, if the market mechanism works reasonably, resource allocation and income distribution would be well accomplished through the market. Because Hungary was thought to have a well-functioning market infrastructure by way of her many years economic reform since 1968, it was not assumed Hungary headed a very short-term drastic reform. Now, however, it is well known by the actual economic performance that the Hungarian reform method might not have been appropriate. The Hungarian economic structure has never been, even in her more than 20 years' effort in economic reform under the communist regime, restructured enough and compatible with a market mechanism. Actually the argument about ways of reform was not only theoretically, but also practically, confused. According to our understanding, the shock therapy "in Central and Eastern Europe" should be limited to a short-term policy only to eliminate an inflationary overhang and hyper (or high) inflation (hereinafter we would say it is hyperinflation).

Going back to the Polish case, what is it about the purge of economic inefficiency? The purpose of the shock therapy is basically to make hyperinflation disappear and to have a fundamental infrastructure for efficient economic working. With the "soft budget" it is difficult to purge economic inefficiency and to attract capital inflow. This indicates that measuring the economic inefficiency by the budget deficit (to GDP-Gross Domestic Product) and capital inflow is not meaningless.

However, economic efficiency is essentially gained by competitive structure and competitive behavior in the market (and efficient resource allocation by government). Actually there could be an economy with a rather monopolistic market structure which decreases its budget deficit (as per cent of GDP) and increases capital inflow. (It goes without saying that such an economy could not work efficiently.) As of the middle of 1990s, the Polish economic situation was just the same as mentioned above. Actually, almost two-thirds of the production of all goods came from monopolists.[5] Therefore, measuring the economic efficiency with a budget deficit and a capital inflow is neither always wrong nor always correct. As far as the Polish case was concerned, it would be extremely dangerous. (In that sense, the viewpoint of considering reforms focusing the attention upon only financial aspects as the IMF does might be fairly dangerous.)

Concerning the postwar Japanese experience, we could say that the radical method called the Dodge Program introduced in 1949 was the basis for a more efficient economy. However, by the Korean War which started about one year after the program, the policy effects had never been implemented enough. This suggested that from the Japanese historical experience we could not directly confirm the effectiveness of shock therapy. With the Japanese experience, we would argue that factors for the postwar economic recovery and high speed economic growth were the following four: (1) accumulated experience of market mechanism up to the prewar period; (2) radical structural reforms during 1946-50 like zaibatsu dissolution, agricultural land reform, law for the elimination of excessive concentration of economic power, anti-monopoly law; (3) Ishibashi fiscal policy putting more weight on employment; and (4) a priority production system intensively allocated resources into the coal and steel industry. Although it is not easy to measure the effectiveness of those policies, it is easy to say that the Dodge Program was not the main basis for the economic recovery and high speed economic growth in postwar Japan.

In other words, the postwar Japanese economy had worked along the line of recovery oriented and growth oriented reform policies apart from very short periods of tight monetary policy in 1946 and 1949. Alternatively speaking, we could say that even with deep intervention of a government, competitive private structure can make rather rapid economic growth, if the intervention is not be very distorted.

In short, for the postwar economic recovery and high speed economic growth in Japan, shock therapy was not a crucial method. More important policies were: (1) employment absorbing growing money policy by Ishibashi fiscal policy; and (2) very radical structural reform policies.

When we classify the postwar Japanese way of reform, we can say it was a "growth oriented reform". It was different from a "stability oriented reform" which puts more emphasis on the short-term equilibrium mainly through a shock method. (Regardless of the initial systemic difference) Poland seemed to prefer the latter way. Hungary and the Czech Republic also classified it as "stability oriented reform". It seems to be a very important point.

For a shock method, an extremely radical and at-a-single-stroke structural change should be the heart of the reform. Although Japanese postwar reform has usually been classified as a gradual method,[6] its structural change was very radical. In the Polish case, even though it has been positioned as a radical method, structural change like privatization has been very slow. For us, in Poland, a radical way is not correctly understood, because it seems that in Poland the word "radical" equally means *"laissez faire"*, which seems to indicate that no intervention by government is the radical way, and that the less intervention, the more radical is reform.

For a radical structural reform, needless to say, active government policy is indispensable. Particularly for transition economies to reform from a centrally planned and state-owned monopolistic production system to a market competitive system, government intervention should be the first of all activities. The market mechanism should not become the substitute for the government intervention policy. Therefore, under the name of "radical" and *"laissez faire"*, the delayed attitude for structural reform is nothing less than a government's default.

Taking into account the above considerations, the usual classification of radicalism and gradualism is not only effective to practically solve problems but also (as mentioned later) gives a ground of "excuse" for a government. We understand that the more appropriate classification of reforms is "growth oriented vs. stability oriented" in place of "radical reform vs. gradual reform".

Cost-Push-Inflation without Structural Reforms

Polish inflation until 1989 was a demand-pull type inflation coming from the inflationary overhang, usually under a shortage economy. However, after the shock therapy was introduced, in the first quarter of 1990, Poland had the first excess supply situation since the Second World War, which had never existed during the days of the planned economy. Also Polish inflation after 1990 has been interpreted as a cost-push type inflation for which the energy price increase mainly contributed.

What is important is that an inflation eliminated by a shock therapy would be limited to the demand-pull type inflation. That very type of inflation, as the National Bank of Poland reported,[7] basically disappeared some months after the shock therapy.

There are several factors for the cost-push-inflation. However, the basis of it in Poland would have an effect on: (1) monopolistic and inefficient production structures in which producers can easily transfer their production costs to the sales price; and (2) poorly-disciplined managers and workers without the incentive for cost reduction (needless to say, they are the negative "legacy" of the centrally planned system). To reform them toward competitive and efficient structure and well-disciplined managers and workers requires many years and a wise and powerful government.

Therefore, once again, one can emphasize that some months' shock therapy to eliminate the demand-pull type inflation was effective, but more than five years of the shock method would not be appropriate. Moreover, the structural reform has been delayed for many years.

What has been the result? A higher rate of unemployment, a continuous decrease of the real standard of living (and a terrible decrease in some rural areas), greater inequality of income and asset distribution that happened quite rapidly.

In Hungary, the Czech Republic and the Slovak Republic, they have also been suffering from inflation, unemployment, a real decrease of living standard, inequality of income and asset distribution as the result of their reform policies, even though they might be less serious than Poland's (as of the middle of 1990s).

Focusing our attention upon the period after elimination of the demand-pull type inflation, we undoubtedly arrive at a question about appropriateness of reform policies employed by the transition economies. For the success of the Balcerowicz Program, it was absolutely necessary to completely "finish" the structural change of production within one or two years (not more than two years) as well as eliminating the hyperinflation. (It is not necessary to repeat that such very short-term transformation plans as the 500 days Shatalin Plan in Russia and the Balcerowicz Program in Poland could not succeed in such a short time). What we should mention here is that when it became impossible for them to implement the short-term drastic reform (at the latest before the third year started), the shock method should have been changed to a growth oriented policy. (However, structural reforms should be done in as radical a way as possible - even if they are, it would undoubtedly be a 10-20 year political fight.)

As was previously mentioned, there could be some patterns of reforms. Also as mentioned earlier, some years after the shock therapy, a theory of selecting a way of reform should be changed from the "radicalism vs. gradualism" to the "growth oriented reform vs. stability oriented reform". In any way, the structural reform should be implemented in as radical a way as possible. It means that a selection of a "radical way vs. gradual way" says almost nothing.

What factors differentiated the growth oriented reform from the stability oriented reform?

The Dodge Program in postwar Japan did not have the full effect because of the Korean War. However, there has never been any doubt about the Dodge effect of purging inefficiency from the Japanese economy. The chief reasons for it came from the accumulated experience of the market economy in the prewar period and the drastic structural reforms after the Second World War. Therefore, a full success of a shock therapy seems to be dependent upon the fundamental infrastructure for accepting a market force. However, Central and Eastern Europe, and Russia were under the centrally planned scheme for 50-70 years until 1990.

A crucial difference for the transition economies lies in the infrastructure. We need to speculate about the production structure working for 50-70 years in Central and Eastern Europe, and Russia when the shock therapy was planned, implemented and kept or changed. As is usually expressed, it had led to the "overgrown of the manufacturing sector under the planned economy".[8] Dismantling the overgrown production structure undoubtedly needs many years and a huge amount of money.

Therefore, it would be reasonable that with the distorted production structure, after the demand-pull-inflation was basically eliminated through the shock method of the Balcerowicz Program, the liberalization of prices has made an (upward flexible and downward rigid) price structure compatible with the monopolistic production structure.

Under the above mechanism, the level reached through demand and supply adjustment is the "monopolistic equilibrium" position, not the "competitive equilibrium" position. The economic situation is still rather inefficient.

A short conclusion to this section is as follows. If the economy has competitive structures, a choice between the growth oriented and the stability oriented totally depends upon the preference of the economy on inflation, growth rate, environment problems, etc. However, for an economy which has distorted production structures like Central and Eastern Europe, and Russia, a stability oriented reform would be dangerous. Because a cost-push-inflation would be stark in that economy, it would not be easy to decrease the rate of unemployment, and a market expansion would be unlikely. There seems to be only one way for those distorted economies: the growth oriented way. They should reform their distortion as soon and radically as possible with the maximum growth possibility (to absorb workers) - even then more than ten years might be necessary.

To change to the growth oriented from the stability oriented, what would be necessary? Suggestions will be made in the next section.

Toward the Growth Oriented Reform

Arguing a topic of "radicalism vs. gradualism" is, (as previously mentioned), mostly leading to vague conclusions not to helpful results. Nuti and Portes (1993) is an example. Needless to say, one agrees with some of their assertions. According to them, shock therapy is essential since otherwise there would be a danger of the transformation process being dragged back as a result of dilution of the new rules of operation of the economy. For instance, temporary maintenance of subsidies might result in a lack of interest in improving productivity and discontinuance of the restructuring of production. On the other hand, gradualism is essential in construction of the new institutional system, which is of its nature a longer-term process. However, for them, gradualism is nothing other than a gentler version of shock therapy.[9]

Also, we often come across such arguments as theirs; the differences between gradualism and shock therapy are small since, on the one hand, the possibilities of implementing gradual changes are limited, on the other, there are areas of the economy in which big bang style therapy is not feasible.

It has been a fact that both Poland preferring the radical method and Hungary selecting the gradual method had serious negative growth rates, high inflation and huge number of unemployed workers. In that sense, the differences between them are surely small.

Emphasizing the point of small differences might not only be making problems vague but also very dangerous. The small differences discussion has given the governments concerned: (1) a convenient "excuse" and (2) a dubious attitude, both of which are dangerous when there is an urgent necessity for radical structural reforms. As a matter of fact, the Polish radical reform seems equal to a structural reform without active government activities.

For more than five years Polish radical reform, with a basically unchanged distorted planned economy, has paid a huge amount of costs, particularly in serious unemployment and regional problems. Actually as a means of systemic transformation shock therapy could not be considered so much without the prospect of external subsidy of the reforms (as with the Balcerowicz Program). However, as the Dodge Program of postwar Japan vividly showed, shock therapy is, essentially, a hard way to become free from domestic and external subsidy and to move towards being an unaided independent nation. It means that shock therapy with the prospect of external subsidy (like the Balcerowicz Program) sounds very strange.

What governments in the process of systemic transformation in Central Europe should make a serious action first of all is to dismantle the centrally planned production structure and move toward improving the efficient production structure and lessen the unemployment cost by labor movement. Up to now at least we cannot recognize any government (in transition economies) which has taken such policies as mentioned above. Mainly because, according to our understanding, their transformations have been in line with stability oriented reform. By stability reform, the actual basic structure of production (regardless of the ownership) would be unchanged, the unemployment rate would be stark being in the vicinity of 15 per cent, the inflation rate would still be in 20-30 per cent, and the real Gross National Product (GNP) growth rate would be stable at around five per cent.

What we wish to propose in this chapter is that, in Poland, as well as reforms of enterprises and workers, government which could not aggressively transform the old regime should be radically reformed. The accumulated budget deficit in 1995 was about 60 per cent to GDP and it means the Polish government is not a "cheap" government. The government is still a very important player in Poland. We think that some lessons from market oriented developing economies are useful. For instance, in the Philippine economy which works in a market oriented manner, resource allocation by the government has been so distorted (therefore their capital coefficient has never been small) and its economic growth rate is rather low.[10] Government's more useful resource allocation should be an urgent priority in Poland.

Taking the postwar Japanese experience too much into consideration is too risky for Poland if it works to have the right economic policy, because the differences both of systemic and international environment have been too big. Therefore, through the above economic investigations, chiefly regarding the reform patterns (not directly from the postwar Japanese experience), we can propose the following alternative line of policy prescription.

With regard to economic policy in Poland, priority should be given to the following: (1) reduction of its around 15 per cent unemployment rate; and (2) transformation of its still distorted production structure to a more competitive comparative advantageous structure. For Poland to do this we think it is necessary for there to be an increased supply of money (in order to change to growth oriented reform) and more efficient and selective allocation of the investment resources toward (explicit and implicit) comparative advantageous industries. (Concerning the infant industry discussion, we have never had a completely satisfactory theory. See chapter six.) What we feel is necessary in Poland, before the structural theory and practice, is the government's active behavior toward structural reform.

Experiences in most countries show that government intervention has continued even after becoming unnecessary, which is often exhibited as an accumulated budget deficit. However, it does not indicate that all government interventions are dangerous. There could be some reasonable and necessary interventions. Particularly, inefficiency brought about by a planning authority should be dismantled through government policy. It might not be the right job for the market.

The conclusion of our argument is as follows. Necessity of government activities toward: (1) growth oriented reform; (2) radical structural change; (3) active protection for infant industries; (4) powerful implementation of a wise policy for a development strategy. Government should not be silent on stability oriented reforms.

Notes

1　Summers, Lawrence, ("The Transition", The World Bank, August 1994, p.2) cited from Zloch-Christy (1996), p.1.
2　This chapter is based upon the joint paper of Morita and Bozyk (1997) with necessary additions to Morita's part of it.
3　Bakos (1994), p.1191.
4　National Bank of Poland (1990).
5　Bozyk (1999), p.31.
6　See Morita (1994b) and (1995).
7　See National Bank of Poland (1990).
8　See Winiecki (1988).

9   See Bozyk (1999), pp.32-33.
10 Morita (1994c).

Chapter 6

Polish Economic Reforms in the Japanese Historical Perspective

Introduction

It has been suggested that there are no superior strategies for the Central European transition because "There is no significant difference in the output decline of the countries implementing shock and gradual treatment. ... one can't say that countries in favor of a gradual approach (such as Hungary and the Ukraine) are more successful than those preferring shock treatment."[1]

This chapter sheds some indirect light on this controversy by showing that the policies adopted in Poland and other transition states were neither sufficiently stringent nor pro-competitive to have generated the efficiency gains achieved by the Japanese with their mixed use of shock therapy and gradualism.

High-speed Economic Growth in Postwar Japan

The standard authority on postwar Japanese economic reform and growth is Komiya (1975b and 1975c). According to these sources, Japan's average annual growth rate of real GNP over the decade 1950-60 was 9.5 per cent, higher than that experienced by most other industrialized countries including West Germany at 7.7 per cent, Italy at 6.0 per cent, France at 4.2 per cent, Canada at 3.7 per cent, the US at 3.3 per cent, and the UK at 2.8 per cent. This superior performance was propelled by high rates of savings and investment. The ratios of gross domestic saving to GNP in the industrialized countries during the decade 1950-60 were as follows: Japan 29.9 per cent, West Germany 26.0 per cent, Italy 20.5 per cent, France 18.4 per cent, Canada 22.5 per cent, the US 18.3 per cent, and the UK 15.5 per cent. The ratio of gross domestic investment to GNP during the same decade were Japan 28.9 per cent, West Germany 23.3 per cent, Italy 21.0 per cent, France 18.4 per cent, Canada 24.4 per cent, the US 17.6 per cent, and the UK 15.7 per cent.

Postwar Japanese marginal capital coefficients were also low, implying a very high efficiency of the newly-invested capital. The crucial factors in achieving this were as follows: (1) labor-intensive industries had a majority share of industry as a whole; (2) postwar labor conversion from the military sector and excess labor in rural areas made the prices of labor relatively cheap; (3) Japan rapidly transferred and diffused foreign technology; (4) market structures were mostly competitive; and (5) the distribution of income and assets became more equal, facilitating the achievement of economies of scale.

These supply side opportunities were complemented by the high rates of domestic savings which obviated the need for foreign investment. Why did people save so much? Savings shares in the decade 1950-60 were as follows: private savings 37 per cent, depreciation allowances 26 per cent, government net saving 21 per cent, and corporate net saving 16 per cent. Private savings obviously played the major role. Government and corporate net savings as shares of GNP were actually lower in Japan than in other industrialized countries, as were depreciation allowances. But the ratio of private savings to GNP was much higher: 10.9 per cent, compared with West Germany's 8.7 per cent, Canada's 5.2 per cent, France's 4.3 per cent, the US's 5.2 per cent, and the UK's 1.9 per cent. This high propensity is attributable to the unincorporated business sector. Although the exact propensity to save varied from year to year, figures for 1955 show that the ratio of saving in the unincorporated business sector was 25 per cent before the tax (the ratio of the agricultural sector was ten per cent and the employee sector's was eight per cent). About 38 per cent of the unincorporated business sector's saving was accumulated as investment in new business equipment. The ratio of their transient to overall income was higher than that of employees, who seemed to save money largely as a precaution.

Postwar Japanese Economic Reforms

Radical Stabilization versus Gradual Stabilization

Japan lost 25 per cent of its capital stock during the Second World War and had more than ten million jobless workers (more than 30 per cent of the total labor force) in late 1945, most of whom were transferred from the military sector. This is comparable in some respects with the Central European and Russian economies, which have experienced 40-50 per cent declines in real GNP since 1990, with unemployment rates of 15-16 per cent or higher.

However, in Japan the unemployment rate had already decreased to 1.1 per cent, by 1947, with real GNP growth rate reaching 8.6 per cent, enabling per capita real GNP to recover to 55.3 per cent of the 1934-36 level (by 1949 the recovery had reached 68 per cent) (see table 6.1).

As far as the Engel coefficient is concerned, this was 67.8 in 1946 and 60.1 in 1949, both higher than the 32.5 recorded for 1931. (Engel coefficients for Poland for various labor categories were: employee 52.3, farmer 51.8 and pensioner 57.9 in 1990; employee 39.2, farmer 51.8 and pensioner 43.8 in 1993). How was full employment restored so quickly? The main reason seems to be the inflationary "Ishibashi fiscal policy" of the first Yoshida cabinet, begun in May 1946, which caused prices to rise by 364.5 per cent in 1946 and 195.9 per cent in 1947, despite the Emergency Financial Measures Ordinance of 16 February 1946 introduced by the Shidehara cabinet. Under this program, all deposits were frozen. Old currency greater than five yen could not be circulated and only 100 yen could be changed into the new currency by each individual. Money circulation decreased by 50 per cent following these measures, and cash plus non-frozen deposits diminished by 70 per cent. Moreover, on 3 March 1946, a new property tax (with rates between 25 and 90 per cent) was imposed, and was expected to absorb 9.2 per cent of nominal GNP in 1946.[2]

The Ishibashi policy lingered on until 1949, when it was replaced by the shock therapy of the Dodge Program, aimed at improving economic efficiency. Although employment was already 21 per cent above the level of 1930, production was still only 39 per cent of the 1930 level. Also, the money supply had drastically increased from 173 billion yen in February 1947 to 413 billion in February 1948, and the trade balance was in huge deficit, with exports covering only 30 per cent of imports.

Faced with excess money expansion, low labor productivity and low exportability, Dodge imposed a tight policy, forcing firms and workers to be self-sufficient and reducing Japanese dependence on US assistance, which reached five per cent of Japanese GNP in the years 1946-49. These goals were accomplished by eliminating the budget deficit, terminating loans issued by the Reconstruction Finance Bank, establishing the US Aid Counterpart Fund Special Account, and setting a unified exchange rate. Reconstruction Finance Bank loans were unsterilized, and stopping them automatically decreased the money supply. The US Aid Counterpart Fund Special Account promoted efficiency by ending the practice of using US Aid commodities receipts to subsidize firms and institutions. Multiple exchange rates also provided hidden subsidies through the undervaluation of yen exports and the overvaluation of yen imports.

Table 6.1 Economic indicators of Japanese economic performance

Year	Real GNP growth rate (%)	Inflation (WPI, %)	Unemploy-ment rate (%)	Gross capital (1934-36=100)	Trade balance (US$ million)
1946		364.5	4.0	120.4	- 238
1947	8.6	195.9	1.1	124.8	- 267
1948	12.7	165.6	0.7	129.9	- 285
1949	2.1	63.3	1.0	135.0	- 195
1950	11.0	18.2	1.2	139.8	34
1951	13.0	38.8	1.1	145.4	- 291

Source: Ministry of Finance (1978), Morita (1993b).

This sharp policy change provoked a debate over the comparative merits of shock therapy and gradualism, that is, "one-shot radical stabilization versus intermediate gradual stabilization". The shock therapists insisted that radical monetary reform was the elixir of sustainable rapid growth, while the gradualists emphasized improved resource allocation through a policy such as the "priority production system".[3]

The specifics of the gradualist proposals are interesting, because they showed a shared concern with the shock therapists for monetary stabilization, but added a greater concern for industrial policy. The program called for the absorption of the monetary overhang within six months, followed during the succeeding year by a full-scale, staged deflationary initiative, supplemented over the next three-four years with a concerted development program.

Structural Reforms

The key feature of the Japanese reform strategy was the elimination of anti-competitive barriers to efficiency including: (1) deconcentration policies, such as the dissolution of the Zaibatsu, the Law for the Elimination of Excessive Concentration of Economic Power, and the Anti-Monopoly Law; and (2) Agricultural Land Reform Policies which led to a more equitable distribution of income and assets.

It is very difficult to prove scientifically the relationship between deconcentration policies and competitive market structures.[4] However, we could say there have been some connections between the two. According to Nakamura, these policies worked: "In most industries, the concentration ratio particularly of the largest three companies was lowered. And it helped to make the conditions for keen competition which was the feature for postwar Japanese industries" (Nakamura (1978), p.153). Comparing the concentration ratio in 1937 with those in 1950, the ratios of the largest three firms in particular sectors of industry were reduced as follows: in the pulp industry, from 65.2 per cent to 39.5 per cent; in the caustic soda industry, from 55.1 per cent to 33.8 per cent; in the marine transportation industry from 29.8 per cent to 18.1 per cent.

The agricultural land reform policies - the redistribution of land ownership rights from landlords to tillers - were drastic. They were decided by the General Headquarters of the Supreme Commanders for the Allied Powers (GHQ) and approved in the Diet on 11 October 1946. They caused the share of tenanted land to decrease dramatically from 46 per cent in 1941 to just 13 per cent in 1949. During the period of high rates of inflation, agricultural land values decreased. "In 1939 the price of 1 tan [= 0.099 hectares] of good paddy land was equivalent to over 3,000 packs of cigarettes or 31 tons of coal. In 1948, however, it was equivalent to only 13 packs of cigarettes or 0.24 tons of coal" (Kawagoe (1993), p.195), facilitating peasant ownership.

The results of three efforts were successful, although it might not always seem so because of the high concentration ratios in many Japanese industries. For example, according to the World Bank (1993), the concentration ratio of the largest three companies in Japan in 1980 was 56 per cent (average across sectors), far higher than in Taiwan, the US, Brazil and Argentina. None the less, competition among firms in the same industry has been keen and contributed significantly to Japan's postwar economic growth. Apparently, there was the potential for competitive new entry firms.

This suggests that the post-communist transition states might be well advised to pay attention to their industrial policy, especially since some of them continue to resist effective monetary stabilization\ Pro-competitive programs, following the Japanese example, would obviously be desirable, as might more directive policies of the sort championed by the Ministry of International Trade and Industry (MITI) as long as they promote infant industries capable of being - or becoming - competitive without entrenching other, inefficient firms. MITI attempted to master this juggling act by applying (1) an income elasticity test; and (2) a productivity test,[5] which will suffice when they happen to correspond with the more demanding Mill and Bastable criteria.

According to Bastable, infant industry assistance is justified when the (present value of) social benefit exceeds (present value of) social cost. The cost has two components:[6] (1) tariffs normally reduce consumption; and (2) the opportunity costs of importable substitutes are too high. These aspects can be illustrated with the aid of figure 6.1.[7] The horizontal axis plots quantities, the vertical axis prices, showing the international price level p_w and domestic price level p_d. The equilibrium quantities corresponding to p_w and p_d are q_w and q_d respectively.

The first social cost, a decrease of consumer surplus, is indicated in figure 6.1 as the area of the triangle BAC, because with decreased consumption, from $0q_w$ to $0q_d$, consumer surplus decreases by BAC. And the second social cost, due to distorted resource allocation, is shown by rectangle $p_w p_d AB$ because, given the cost of domestic importables, the quantity $0q_d$ defines the import opportunity cost rectangle $0 p_d A q_d$. Deducting the import payment $0 p_w B q_d$ from the cost $0 p_d A q_d$ results in a net allocational inefficiency loss indicated by $p_w p_d AB$.

The total social cost attributable to government protection is the trapezoid $p_w p_d AC$.

Infant industry subsidies are justified if the total (present value of) social benefit exceeds the total (present value of) social cost. This may occur when (1) the domestic price level p_d falls towards the international price level p_w; and/or (2) q_d rapidly approaches q_w. The (1) may hold when productivity is increasing sharply and the (2) when demand is elastic. Both these conditions are considered to have held in the postwar Japanese case and could apply selectively in Central Europe.

Polish Economic Reforms: The Situation after the Balcerowicz Program

Poland began experimenting with shock therapy on 1 January 1990, when it

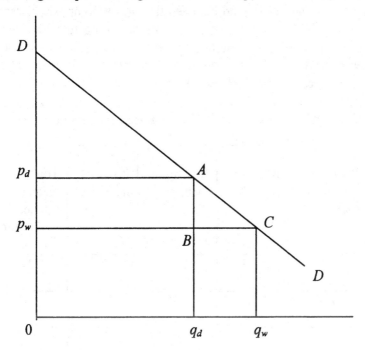

Figure 6.1   Social cost (1)

adopted the Balcerowicz Program. The goals of the program, influenced by the IMF and World Bank were: (1) disinflation; (2) the eradication of shortages; (3) a sound national currency; (4) privatization and structural reform. "From January to March in 1990, a 50 per cent decrease of the money stock in real terms took place" and the program led "to the appearance of excess supply and its development for the first time in 45 years".[8] But these gains were accompanied by unexpectedly severe depression.

Several years later the debate over the wisdom of the Balcerowicz Program continued. The real GNP growth rate turned positive after 1992 and inflation followed at a moderate 30-40 per cent annually, evaluated from the standpoint of other transition economies. However, inflation was hardly negligible and the unemployment rate was approaching 15-16 per cent by the middle of the decade. The inflationary overhang persists. Queuing for goods in short supply was eliminated by raising prices to clear the market.[9]

The evidence on privatization and structural reform was likewise mixed. The main purpose of the Balcerowicz Program was to purge the economy of its inefficiency. Few in Poland believed this was accomplished, despite the evidence in table 6.2 showing a rising rate of aggregate growth in the vicinity of five per cent per annum and industrial production expanding (from -11.9 per cent in 1991 compared with the previous year) to 3.9 per cent in 1992, 6.2 per cent in 1993 and 11.9 per cent in 1994.

Table 6.2 Economic indicators of Polish economic performance

Year	Real GNP growth rate (%)	Inflation (CPI, %)	Unemploy-ment rate (%)	Invest-ment (YtoY,%)	Trade balance (in c.c.) US$million
1990	- 11.6	585.8	6.1	- 10.0	2,214
1991	- 7.6	70.3	11.8	- 4.0	51
1992	2.6	43.0	13.6	0.7	512
1993	3.8	35.3	16.4	1.0	- 2,293
1994	5.0	32.2	16.0		- 836

Source: Morita (1999), WERI (Annual).

Skepticism, however, is in order because real monthly income in Poland was shrinking, the income and assets distribution were extremely inegalitarian[10], and official statistics were suspect. For example, the official unemployment rate in Poland stood at about 15 per cent in the mid-1990s, but if involuntary pensioners were counted the number of unemployed workers increased to 11.5 million and the effective unemployment rate to 40 per cent.[11] Also, monopolistic market structures remained entrenched, particularly in large-scale manufacturing industries, and privatization was half-hearted, amounting to only ten per cent of the potential in the industrial sector in the mid-1990s.

To sum up, institutional reform was feeble and income and assets redistribution perverse. For this reason, it was hard to believe that Poland's growth path of over five per cent a year would prove to be sustainable.

Polish Economic Reform in Japanese Historical Perspective

The Polish and Japanese postwar transition strategies had elements in common. Both used shock therapy (such as the Dodge Program in Japan - though it was finished quickly because of the start of Korean War - and such as the Balcerowicz Program in Poland) to dampen inflation and spur efficiency, bolstered by structural reforms. The differences, however, are equally stark. In addition to variations in timing, Poland's shock therapy was less stringently implemented and its structural reforms were limited. As a consequence, inflation remained pronounced and efficiency gains were meager, casting doubt on Poland's long-term modernization potential.

The Japanese example demonstrates that Poland might have done much better with a firmer stabilization program, and stronger pro-competitive policies. The same conclusion holds for a gradual strategy since we have seen in the Japanese case that this did not preclude monetary stabilization. The central lesson of this comparison, therefore, is that neither shock therapy nor gradualism mean much if the underlying policies do not do enough to create competitively efficient markets.

Notes

1 Stanley Fisher, early 1993, cited by Kiss (1993), p.69.
2 See Kousai (1995), p.20.
3 Such an assertion, insisting on the importance of industrial policy, is sometimes maintained by Central European economists who are quite knowledgeable about the Japanese economy. See, for example, Bakos (1994).
4 See, for example, Miwa (1993).
5 Concerning the tests, see Komiya (1984).
6 See Grubel (1966).
7 If we adhere strictly to the MITI criterion on elasticity, figure 6.A should be used in place of figure 6.1, implying that, as the income level increases, the demand curve shifts from DD to $D'D'$, and a more elastic demand gives rise to a more rapid demand increase towards q_w starting q_d. Readers should re-read figure 6.1 in the text, not as describing a movement from A to C along the same demand curve DD, but as a demand curve shift from DD to $D'D'$ and then moving from A to C.
8 National Bank of Poland (1990), p.7.
9 According to Kornai (1993), the same thing occurred in Hungary.

10   See, for example, Bozyk (1992) and WERI (Auunal, 1994).
11   See, for example, Bozyk (1995).

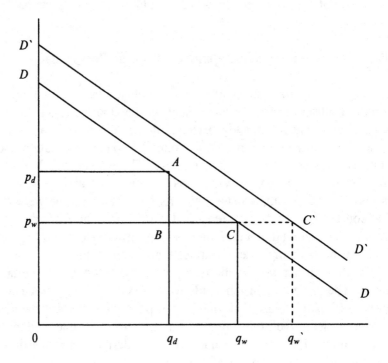

Figure 6.A   Social cost (2)

Chapter 7

An Economic Analysis of the Daihatsu-FSO Case

Introduction

The main purpose of this chapter is to examine Japan's stagnating presence in Central European countries related to risk in the host countries. The so-called "Daihatsu-FSO Case", a planned project for medium-sized automobile production between FSO (Fabryka Samochodow Osobowych - a Polish passenger car company) and foreign automobile companies, will be analyzed particularly. Throughout the 1980s, Japanese Daihatsu and other Japanese companies have been in keen competition to get a contract for the project with the Polish FSO.

During the course of this competition process, the Japanese consortium played second fiddle to the Italian competitor, although it was said that compared to the Italians the Japanese offered both a better credit policy and a superior technology transfer policy.

This chapter focuses on the reasons for European superiority over Japan in such competitions[1] in order to investigate the stagnant presence of Japan's foreign direct investment in Central European countries.

Facts

The Stagnant Presence of Japan's Foreign Direct Investment in Central European Countries

Although Japan's foreign direct investment has reduced since its 1990 peak of US$ 48.0 billion in the flow base (about 21 per cent of the world total), the flow amount of Japan's foreign direct investment in 1991 equaled US$ 30.7 billion (a reduction of 36 per cent from the previous year), which represented the largest single position (around 18 per cent) in the global total amount in the flow base. In the 1991 stock base Japan accumulated US$ 231.8 billion which represented about 15 per cent of the world total and put them in the second position after the US (US$ 450.2 billion and 29 per cent).

As for Japan's foreign direct investment in Central European countries, until the end of 1991, the stock value amounted to US$ five million in Poland, US$ 221 million in Hungary, US$ nine million in Romania, US$ one million in Bulgaria. Of the total stock value of Japan's foreign direct investment, the ratios were 0.002 per cent (Poland), 0.1 per cent (Hungary), 0.004 per cent (Romania) and 0.0004 per cent (Bulgaria).[2]

Needless to say, Hungary has received almost all of Japan's foreign direct investment in Central European countries. In 1990 and 1991 Hungary received US$ 29 million and US$ 181 million respectively in international direct investment from Japan. The dramatic increase principally came from the Magyar Suzuki case (automobile production of the Japanese Suzuki Motor Corporation with a Hungarian partner).[3]

According to statistics from the Polish Agency for Foreign Investments (PAIZ) in Poland, the overall equity and loans value of 100 major foreign investors in Poland as of 1992 equaled US$ 1.79 billion (although the overall investment commitments value of the same major investors was equal to US$ 41.4 billion), of which US$ 1.6 million (or only a 0.089 per cent share) represented Japanese investment held by three major Japanese investors. According to data from the Japanese government, at the end of 1992, there were approximately 9,000 internal direct investors in Poland with an overall equity and loans value of US$ 1.7 billion.[4] Japanese direct investments in Poland equaled only 19 with a value of about US$ 4.5 million, or a 0.21-0.26 per cent share.

Although the statistics vary from one source to another, whichever statistic is used, the Japanese position in foreign direct investment in Poland is quite small. In the sections that follow, we will try to explain why.

The Daihatsu-FSO Case

A summary of the essential facts of this case study are as follows. It is easy to speculate about confidential information regarding the tough negotiations which extended over many years. This discussion will rely on information coming from several journals published in West Europe and Japan.

From 1982 FSO was in the process of modernization. In 1983 it began discussions with foreign car producers, mainly in an effort to lead economic development in Poland. It considered 16 foreign automobile companies as potential partners. Japanese candidates included Japanese Daihatsu, which offered its proposal to the company through Itochu (a Japanese general trading company) which exported FSO automobiles to third countries, as well as Sumitomo (another Japanese general trading company), which imported Daihatsu passenger cars into Poland. Daihatsu, Itochu and Sumitomo joined together to form a consortium.

The first article to announce this project in Western European journals was, as far as the author can find, in *East-West* (27 March 1984). According to this article, Poland was considering a new model passenger car to be manufactured in cooperation with a Western automobile company. The new model would be a five-seater, 1200cc engine vehicle, manufactured at the rate of some 120,000 units per year with 25 per cent of output allocated for export. It was also announced that the total cost of this project would be about 300 billion zlotys.

However, in 1985, an article in *Business Eastern Europe* (12 April) said that the launch of the project had been delayed, mainly due to Polish economic problems and the lack of Western company interest.

A fairly long article under the title "Development Plans for Polish Car Industry" in *East-West* (26 September 1985) reported on a talk given by Mr. Jan Raczko, technical director of FSO, which indicated that it was expected that a contract with a Western partner would be signed before the end of 1985. An article in *East European Markets* (18 October 1985) mentioned that the various Western candidates were Daihatsu, Nissan, Toyota, Fiat, Renault and Seat. This article said that Daihatsu was favored to be the winner because of its diesel engine with considerable fuel economy.

According to Japanese sources, Japanese interest in this project had become stronger as a result of linking the Japanese consortium, through MITI, with the Japan-Poland Economic Committee this had been initiated by the committee's chairman, Mr.Toshikuni Yahiro, president of Mitsui (a Japanese general trading company), which had joined the above mentioned consortium. On 28 May 1986, a document from the Minister of Metallurgy and Machinery Industry in Poland, Mr. Janusz Maciejewicz, requesting cooperation with a Japanese automobile company, was received by Mr.Yahiro.

In 1986, *East-West* (11 September), in the article "Daihatsu in Poland", announced that Daihatsu was likely to make a final decision by the end of the summer in 1986 about the assembly of cars in Poland. And, an article in *Ostwesthandel* (29 October 1986) entitled "Polen: Lizenzverhandlungen mit Daihatsu und Fiat", mentioned that Mr. Edward Pietrzak, FSO general director, had said at a press conference in Warsaw on 25 October 1986 that the terms of a financial offer would play a role in the negotiations.

On 27 November 1986 the FSO Worker's Council announced their analysis of the case and supported Daihatsu, claiming that Daihatsu was offering a more advanced type of car and better financial conditions, including lower licensing costs, more favorable terms of loan repayment and better conditions for the export of cars made in Poland (*East-West*, 24 February 1987). The same article also mentioned the interesting opinion that *the Polish authorities apparently favored Fiat* (emphasis added), but that their decision was made more difficult because the FSO Workers Council supported the Japanese offer.

The first article that we could find mentioning difficult points in Daihatsu's offer to Poland, was in *East-West* (19 December 1986). This article said that Poland claimed that Daihatsu had demanded a very strict system of quality control, which was not enforceable in Poland.

Prime Minister Mr. Yasuhiro Nakasone visited Poland on 16 and 17 January 1987, and his visit had an influence upon these negotiations. (Before his visit to Poland, a program on Polish National TV took the position that the visit was expected to be important to Poland in selecting its partner.) In his talks with the First Party Secretary, Mr. Wojciech Jaruzelski, and the Prime Minister, Mr. Zbigniew Messner, Mr. Nakasone did not commit to giving Poland official financial help to promote Daihatsu cooperation with FSO. However, it was said that the mere fact that the summit talks included this very project, initiated mainly by private companies, was significant and gave rise to optimistic expectations.

Another influential visit concerning the project was that of Mr. Jaruzelski to Japan on 28 June and 2 July 1987. This followed his visit to Italy. According to a Japanese source of information, in the summit talks, the First Party Secretary announced a plan for allocating the medium-sized car production project to Daihatsu and the small-sized production project to Fiat. In addition, Mr. Jaruzelski mentioned that he had not accepted any request from Italy on this project and that he had rejected an Italian proposal for setting up a committee of third party countries to mediate in the tough negotiations. The Japanese stance on giving official financial credit to Poland did not change. It seems to the author that the leaders' visit (including Mr. Jaruzelski's visit to Italy) helped to strongly promote Japan's economic relations with Poland. This resulted in a very pessimistic statement from Mr. Govanni Agnelli (the president of Fiat). In his statement, Mr. Agnelli said that Fiat apparently had lost a contract to Daihatsu in a bid to build a modern car plant in Poland and that the Japanese had offered superior technology and better financial terms. (*International Herald Tribune* and *Financial Times*, 1 July 1987, *East-West*, 6 July 1987, *Business Eastern Europe*, 13 July 1987, etc.).

It was said that, in his talks with Mr. Jaruzelski in Japan, Mr. Nakasone noted that he positively appreciated the Japanese consortium's willingness to consider a "bridging loan", i.e., a loan on a private basis, to fill in the time lag before being given financial credit on a government basis. The Japanese consortium, however, did not actually consider the bridging loan enthusiastically.

The Japanese consortium was also in sharp conflict with MITI concerning whether or not MITI would give a definite written promise of export insurance for the project. We could assess the inner negotiations in Japan as follows: MITI thought that the private companies had to take the risk that the business would be profitable; the consortium, on the contrary, thought that official financial support for this project was a small burden for the Japanese government budget compared to the expected benefits.

On 20 August 1987, an article in *Radio Free Europe Research* (RFER) said that Daihatsu would produce a medium-sized car in Poland. In the same article, RFER specifically announced the following three points: (1) the Polish government had exploited the competition to obtain progressively better terms for its own automobile industry, that explained the lengthy period to complete the agreement; (2) the adaptation of Japanese work methods and style to Poland might be a problem; (3) while the Japanese were steadily pursuing the Polish contract, the article stated that they did not seem particularly enthusiastic about investing on such a large scale in Poland. In any event, RFER recognized that the Japanese were in a strong position to win the contract.

According to information coming from a Japanese source, in mid-October 1987, officials of the Polish Ministry of Foreign Affairs and Polish Ministry of Foreign Trade expressed the opinion, in a diplomatic sense, that Daihatsu would win against Fiat.

On 13 November 1987, in an article entitled "Daihatsu decision expected soon", *East European Markets* announced that, as of the summer of 1987, Poland thought Daihatsu was offering better technological and trade terms than Fiat. However, the same article also mentioned that the Japanese companies were unable to come up with the necessary financing, and said that the already completed Polish agreement with Fiat for the FSM (Fabryka Samochodow Malolitrazowych - a Polish small-sized passenger car company) small-car plant gave the edge to Fiat. In addition, it reported that the Italian government had given Fiat the go-ahead to purchase one million cars from this agreement, on condition that the machinery and equipment for FSO and FSM came from Italy.

On 29 January 1988, an article titled "FSO looks ahead" in *East European Markets* announced that Mr. Edward Pietrzek said he thought the long-running negotiations with Fiat and Daihatsu on the future of the plant were coming to an end.

While these negotiations were proceeding, Poland was engaged in multilateral and bilateral negotiation of its outstanding debt. Although the rescheduling negotiation in the Paris Club reached agreement, bilateral negotiations between Poland and Japan were far from complete at the beginning of 1988. Around this time the Japanese side apparently recognized Fiat's strong activity favoring "roll back".

On 6 August 1988, bilateral negotiations between Poland and Japan concerning the third and the fourth rescheduling plans finally resulted in an agreement to set interest rates at 6.5 per cent (in Japanese yen) and 7.95 per cent (in US$). Objectively viewed, this constituted a Japanese concession. It was thought that after many years of tough negotiation the most serious obstacle for successful talks between the two parties had been eliminated.

Just after reaching the agreement, however, on 19 August, Mr. Tomohiro Eguchi, the president of Daihatsu, declared his pessimistic expectation concerning the keen competition with Fiat at a press conference (*Nihon Keizai Shimbun*, 20 August 1988). Mr. Eguchi actually visited Poland at the end of July, 1988, and we could readily speculate that some high ranking Polish officials who favored Fiat told him in confidence of their decision with regard to the project.

On 8 September 1988, also just after the successful agreement on the rescheduling talks, the Polish government requested that the Japanese government start renegotiation of interest rates in the first and second rescheduling plan (around nine to ten per cent), which was already complete. Needless to say, the Japanese Ministry of Finance immediately rejected this unprecedented request.

Only five days after this request by Poland, on 13 September, Mr. Pietrzek announced that Fiat was the winner of the contract. (*Zycie Warszawy*, 14 September 1988, *Rzeczpospolita*, 15 September 1988, *Ostwesthandel*, 19 September 1988).

However, on 6 December 1988, after the reshuffle of the Polish cabinet, Mr. Jerzy Urban, the Polish government spokesman, announced a new Polish decision. This decision, led by Mr. Mieczyslaw Wilczek, the new Minister of Industry, was to stop medium-sized passenger car production. At the same time Mr. Pietrzek resigned FSO president.

Since the drastic Polish change towards a market economy began in 1990, the outcome of this project has remained uncertain, but with European superiority. Based on the facts above, we can see some points crucial for explaining the reasons for Italian superiority over Japan up to the end of the 1980s, even though Mr. Agnelli had officially recognized Fiat's loss in 1987. These could be viewed in a conceptual framework relating to foreign direct investment.

This chapter intends to interpret the reasons for European superiority from the above viewpoint and to speculate about risk related to the foreign direct investment in Central European countries in the light of these findings.

Interpretation

The case described here concerned could be considered as economic behavior relating to the export and import of technology and materials for manufacturing passenger cars. However, I wish to emphasize the aspects of foreign direct investment observed in this case, using one of the official definitions of foreign direct investment in Japan, i.e., "long-term credit not accompanied by equity ownership is included in outward direct investment, if a certain close relationship exists between the lender and the borrower."[5]

The above definition is, I think, rather easily applied to the described case here and should be interpreted as Japan's foreign direct investment.

In addition, the historically close relations between Poland and Italy in the fields of economy, culture, diplomatic relations, etc., seem to have played a crucial role in Fiat's success over Daihatsu. This means that this case should not be interpreted as involving only export-import behavior between the two parties. Rather, it should be viewed in terms of foreign direct investment behavior and several other factors not involving export-import behavior.

Polish experts have emphasized several beneficial factors which would make foreign investment in Poland attractive. Some of these are as follows (mainly quoted from *Polityka*, 10 June 1989, and based on the situation in 1989): (1) Poland is the biggest country in Central Europe (area: 312,000 sq. km; population: 38 million; income: the per capita national income amounts to US$ 2000 to 2500) and has the biggest market; (2) Poland is in a very good geographical situation in that Warsaw lies halfway between Moscow and Paris, and Stockholm and Budapest; in other words Warsaw lies between the East and West as well as the North and South of the continent; (3) Poland has a very well developed railroad network with one third of the 27,000 km of railway line electrified; the density of the railroad network in Poland is greater than in France, Great Britain or Italy; (4) Poland has 250,000 km of roads, including 150,000 km with an asphalt surface; (5) Planes belonging to 35 airline companies land at Warsaw airport, while the Polish Airline LOT provides regular flights to and from 40 countries; (6) the merchant marine consists of 250 cargo vessels with a combined capacity of over four million dwt; the Polish Baltic ports have a handling capacity of over 50 million tons a year; (7) Poland has substantial mineral resources, compared to other European countries; (8) Poland has a large and skilled labor force; (9) in addition to the above advantages, direct investment in Poland provides a production base to spread business over other West and Central European countries.

Among these benefits, the last was considered the most advantageous by Daihatsu because, according to the plan, some 120,000 passenger cars would be manufactured in Poland, of which 25 per cent would be allocated to West European markets.

Meanwhile, because Fiat played a major role in the Polish automobile industry for many years, it would have been a very serious blow to Fiat, if Daihatsu had been a winner. For Poland, the main purposes of negotiating with foreign automobile companies had been: (1) needless to say, to modernize its outdated automobile industry; and (2) to attract foreign capital in order to develop its economy. Some Polish experts particularly stressed the beneficial point that Poland had a large and skilled labor force in comparison with labor costs (see item (8) in the list above), as the most attractive advantage for foreign investors.

Considered on the basis of the facts mentioned in the previous section, we can conclude that Poland attached great importance to capital inflow as well as to the traditional diplomatic relations with West European countries. We could also speculate that one of the important issues which caused the keen competition between Fiat and Daihatsu was the West European market, taking into account both the global automobile market and EU economic integration.

There was a big difference concerning the unity between government and company on the Japanese side as compared with the Italian rival. The Italian government and Fiat had formed a strong united front against the Japanese rival to block the rival presence in the European market. The Japanese side, on the contrary, experienced the differences between the government and the companies, and between the Japanese Embassy in Poland and the Ministry of Foreign Affairs in Japan.

It seems to the author that the Japanese Ministry of Foreign Affairs held to the view that close and stable diplomatic relations between Japan and West European countries such as Italy and France was more important than relations with Central European countries such as Poland. From the Japanese Ministry of Foreign Affairs point of view, in a diplomatic sense, giving priority to the West was plausible. From the consortium point of view, in a business sense, their behavior in adopting a very cautious attitude toward joining the big scale project was also plausible.

Regarding the behavior of the Japanese side, I would like to explicitly mention three points in the next section to interpret the facts in the previous section.

Characteristics of Japan's Foreign Direct Investment

The first point concerns the characteristics of Japan's foreign direct investment. As mentioned previously, in 1991, Japan had the largest position of all countries in foreign direct investment measured on flow base. However, Japan's position in the direct investment field was never strong. The flow was decreasing in 1991 compared with in 1990 principally because the profit rate in the manufacturing sector was lower than both the profit rate from domestic investment by Japanese companies and foreign investment by other countries' companies. It was easily shown that the dramatic increase in Japan's foreign direct investment in the 1980s was coming from: (1) appreciation of the Japanese yen; and (2) avoidance of trade conflict, not from superiority of "managerial resources" in the global market.

Along with Komiya (1988), we note the following characteristics of Japan's foreign direct investment. First, Japan was the latest-comer in the field of foreign direct investment, and is still in its early stage of development as a direct investor country. Many statistics indicate the fact that Japan was far from a state of maturity as a direct investor country, for example, in an international comparison of the ratio of the outstanding value of foreign direct investment to GNP, Japan's ratio was the lowest among the major investor countries such as the US, UK, and (West) Germany. Second, the Japanese share of manufacturing industries in foreign direct investment is substantially smaller than the shares of the US, UK, and (West) Germany. Third, in the regional breakdown of Japan's foreign direct investment the shares of developing countries used to be relatively large in comparison with foreign direct investment by other major developed countries. Fourth, as mentioned above in connection with the discussion of the recent decrease of Japan's foreign direct investment, the profitability of Japan's foreign direct investment was lower than the profit rate in Japan. In addition, the profit rate earned by Japanese-owned subsidiaries in the US manufacturing sector was much lower than the average rate earned by all foreign-owned subsidiaries in the same sector.

The fact that there are very few examples of Japanese-owned large-scale and well-established subsidiaries in foreign countries is closely connected with these characteristics.

With "Komiya's assertion" in this field, the above facts and characteristics are well explained as being based on the fact that Japanese companies have not yet accumulated the "managerial resources" necessary for running factories abroad as efficiently as those at home. In this regard, "managerial resources" simply means the "organizational knowhow and expertise necessary to run a firm efficiently".[6] In other words, it is the ability to make profit by correctly accepting and excluding factors (which are economic, cultural, political, sociological, etc.) that cannot be separated from host countries. In order to accumulate such scarce resources, it probably takes many years. This is especially so in the case of running subsidiaries in Central European countries which still have rather different economic adjustment mechanisms. Accordingly, running factories in such countries as efficiently as in the home country seems to be extremely difficult. Italian Fiat, as mentioned previously, has a long tradition of working with Central European countries. This experience is rare among Western companies.

Therefore, taking into account these general characteristics of Japanese foreign direct investment, namely the lack of managerial resources, makes it easer to understand the differences between Fiat and Daihatsu when it comes to accumulating managerial resources within the Central European region.

Characteristics of Risky Foreign Direct Investment

In the previous section, we used foreign direct investment theory to interpret the case with which we are concerned here. In addition to general theory, this case has a specific important factor which must be taken into account, that is, the huge amount of foreign debt in Poland. As mentioned in the facts of this case, better financial terms were a crucial point in the tough negotiations.

Also, the lack of accumulated managerial resources mentioned earlier seems to make Japanese companies in general more risk averse in foreign direct investment. Issues raised in the previous sections are, therefore, deemed to be more appropriate to Japan's foreign direct investment behavior.

In the light of certain aspects of specific factors here, I think we can correctly interpret the reason for the long negotiation period. As we saw earlier, Polish experts often emphasize that the most attractive point about Poland for foreign investors is the existence of a large and skilled labor force compared with labor costs. If Poland were free from its foreign debt, Poland would, as Polish experts emphasize, be a very attractive country for foreign investors. However, foreign investors are not free from the risk that arises from the huge amount of Polish debt and this makes them believe that Poland is a very risky country. Therefore, we should investigate the distinctive features of risky direct investment along the lines used by Frey (1984).

Frey (1984) statistically examines political and economic determinants of foreign direct investment in 54 cases involving less developed high-risk countries, comparing four competing models. He concludes that the "politico-economic" model he presents performs relatively best with respect to goodness of fit. In his investigation, 11 economic and political determinants are statistically considered and the standardized regression coefficients are calculated. Among the 11 determinants, the most influential economic determinants are real per capita GNP and the balance of payments. Frey writes that "the higher the per capita income and the lower the balance of payments deficit, the more foreign direct investment is attracted".[7] Two very interesting findings in Frey's research, which impact on the subject of this chapter and the points emphasized by Polish experts, are as follows: (1) "Among the less important economic influences are the growth of GNP and *the worker's skill level*" (emphasis added); and (2) "Among the political determinants, the amount of bilateral aid coming from Western countries has the strongest stimulating effect".[8]

The research described above was done with data in 1979, but I think the findings are correctly applicable to interpret even the latest cases and, needless to say, the case herein concerned. First of all, as mentioned earlier, Poland has a large and skilled labor force with cheap labor costs, a factor that has been emphasized by some experts in Poland. However, as long as Poland is a risky country for foreign investors, the determinant of the workers' skill level has a less important influence. I think this finding explains the huge difference in viewpoint between the Polish side and the foreign automobile companies, which led to the lengthy and tough negotiations. In addition to that, the Polish level of skilled labor was far from adequate from the viewpoint of Daihatsu and Fiat, especially by Daihatsu. The workers' skill level in Poland has not only a negative effect on foreign direct investment, but also might deter such investment (even if the level of the Polish workers' skill is higher than exists in most developing countries).

The dominating negative influence of the balance of payments problem, that is, the huge amount of foreign debt closely connected with the amount of bilateral aid from Western countries, plays a crucial role in this case. Therefore, the difference between the lack of unity on the Japanese side and the existence of unity on the Italian side (mentioned earlier) should also be considered a crucial factor in the winning of the contract with Poland. This is because official aid plays a very important role for private companies investing directly into risky countries.

Towards Establishing An International Regime

As mentioned previously, in the case described here, uncertainty and risk, closely related to the lack of accumulated managerial resources in Japanese companies and the difference between Japan and Italy in terms of government and company unity, played important roles. In this section, we approach and examine the issue solely on the basis of the international regime theory.

This section focuses upon more rational political economic aspects designed to make the extremely weak economic presence of Japan in Central European countries stronger.

Concerning the stagnant presence of Japan's foreign direct investment in Central European countries, it seems that social costs have played crucial roles hindering capital movement. The main cost factors come, I think, from: (1) lack of a clear legal framework establishing liability for actions; (2) information imperfections; (3) positive transaction costs. Needless to say, the above three cost factors, understood to be market failures, are conditions relatedly indicated by Coase (1960). By inverting the Coase theorem,[9] this means that if at least one of them exists, international regimes are of value in facilitating agreements among governments.

I think it is useful to examine the international regime to overcome serious cost factors. Generally speaking, where there are orderly, stable and active relations between countries, social scientists usually describe the situation as a "regime". Such a regime has certain features.

According to Keohane (1983), to reach the concept of an international regime, we have to distinguish "harmony", "cooperation" and "discord". That means that if each actor's policies (pursued without regard for the interests of others) are perceived by others as facilitating the attainment of their goals, no communication is necessary and no influence need be exercised, that is, no international regime is necessary. On the other hand, if each actor's policies are regarded by others as hindering the attainment of their goals, and if their policies are adjustable and become significantly more compatible with one another, cooperation takes place. (If their policies are not adjustable, or incompatible even in adjustable cases, discord ensures.) As Keohane correctly indicates,[10] a major function of regimes is to facilitate the achievement of specific cooperative agreements among governments.

In accordance with Keohane (1984) and Krasner (1983b), we define international regimes as sets of implicit or explicit principles, norms, rules and decision-making procedures around which actor's expectations converge in a given area of international relations. Also, we agree with Keohane that international regimes should be comprehended chiefly as arrangements motivated by self-interest. We should emphasize, at the same time, that because international regimes reflect patterns of cooperation over a long time, regimes can produce shared interests for actors, as institutionalists maintain.

In focusing upon economic interests which take into consideration economic relations between Japan and Central European countries, generally speaking, the following four factors are understood to be shared interests: (1) decreasing uncertainty; (2) decreasing the costs of collecting information; (3) making relations more stable; and (4) decreasing transaction costs.[11]

Considering the application of international regime theory to more orderly, stable and active economic relations, we should particularly emphasize that Japan and Central European countries have just embarked on an attempt to establish such a regime. Japan has never had any common principles, norms, rules, or decision-making procedures with Central European countries. This was clearly reflected in the Daihatsu-FSO case mentioned in the previous section.

Therefore, we indicate that the stagnating presence of Japan's foreign direct investment in Central European countries has been, after all, due to the non-existence of a regime producing the shared interests.

Also as many experts correctly stated,[12] the Japanese business community is more risk averse than the American and West European business community. That means Japanese (more risk averse) companies will make fewer agreements under potential market failure conditions than less risk averse companies, and Japanese companies will make fewer agreements than they would under conditions of perfect information. And, needless to say, cost factors coming from market failure conditions make the economic mechanism inefficient through moral hazard and adverse selection.

Therefore, eliminating asymmetric information, decreasing transaction costs, making a clear legal framework and having more certainty through establishing an international regime can produce a more efficient mechanism and make risk averse companies more active.

Conclusion

The two main conclusions arising from the above investigation are as follows:

(1) In the automobile production project discussed in this chapter, the main reasons that the Japanese consortium played second fiddle to Italian Fiat were, first, the difference of accumulated managerial resources between the two competitors, particularly in the field of investing directly to Central European countries and, second, the difference of attitudes and policies toward Central European countries between the Japanese government and the Italian government.

(2) Concerning Japan's stagnated economic presence in Central European countries, in addition to the factors, mentioned above, we could point out the following two closely related factors: (a) because Japanese companies are more risk averse when they have limited information and they make fewer transactions with partners than less risk averse countries, Japan's, Japan's foreign direct investment in Central European countries has stagnated, and, therefore, (b) as risks for Japanese companies mainly come from market failure conditions like asymmetric information, lack of a clear legal framework, and positive transaction costs, only through establishing an international regime and thus decreasing the cost factors can capital movement from Japan to Central European countries become more active.

Notes

1   Since October 1993, as a matter of fact, Italian Fiat has been concentrating upon producing small-sized automobiles in cooperation with FSM. In the field of medium-sized automobile production with FSO, GM (Europe) has the biggest advantage and after that Korean Daewoo. Our attention is mainly focused on the period from the beginning till the end of 1980s when Japanese players joined the competition.
2   Statistics of the former Czechoslovakia was not available.
3   See Bakos (1992).
4   Needless to say, this amount was less than the US\$ 1.79 billion from 100 major investors included in data from the Polish Agency for Foreign Investments (PAIZ).
5   See Komiya (1988), p. 222.
6   See Komiya (1988), p. 261.
7   See Frey (1984), p. 83.
8   See Frey (1984), p. 83.
9   See Keohane (1983).
10 See Keohane (1983), p. 62.
11 See, for example, Morita (1993a).
12 See, for example, Bakos (1992), Morita and Rosefielde (1994).

Chapter 8

Inward FDI and Capital Movements in Central Europe

Introduction

The purpose of this chapter is to consider capital movement based upon the inward flow of foreign direct investment (FDI) into Central Europe. Needless to say, when capital moves to foreign companies, we usually define it as FDI if the share of the total stock value exceeds ten per cent (if less than ten per cent, it is defined as portfolio investment or as indirect investment). Investment with a stock value of more than ten per cent results in management participation.

This tells us that we have never had any definite criteria to judge FDI or portfolio investment when capital moves through stock gain. Therefore, when we take into consideration risks that accompany capital movement, it might be hard to approach the nature of risk in respective cases separately. It is harder when we investigate capital movements in Central Europe.

In line with the purpose of this book, in this chapter we confirm that various issues related to capital movements are closely connected with a framework of international economic relations, taking into consideration both FDI and portfolio investment.

This chapter therefore has the roles of investigating how to approach the inward FDI in Central Europe particularly with reference to Poland as seen in the earlier chapters within a framework of international economic relations, and how to introduce a kind of insurance function accompanied by international economic relations. The chapter therefore provides a bridge to the chapters that follow by dealing with the issue of capital movement.

We proceed as follows. In the next section, we first sketch the general picture of FDI inflows to the Central European transition economies during the 1990s. In the second section we investigate some closely correlated factors mainly in the case of Central European countries. In the third section, based upon the investigations of Strange (1998) etc., we attempt to find a reasonable position on capital movements from the perspective of international economic relations.

Trends of Inward FDI in Central Europe[1]

The opening up of Central European economies in the post-communist period of transition to a market-based economy have presented new opportunities for foreign investors. In most cases, however, the barriers posed by the uncertain conditions of the transition have caused potential investors to adopt a cautious stance. Over the 1990s, therefore, FDI flows to the economies of this area have varied greatly, but on the whole have been much slower to develop than anticipated.

By the end of 1998, the ten transition economies included in table 8.1 had received cumulative inflows estimated at more than 50 billion dollars. The bulk of this (almost 78 per cent, according to the European Bank for Reconstruction and Development-EBRD-estimates) came after 1993, in the second half of the first decade of transition.

A brief explanation of the discrepancies in FDI statistics for the area is necessary at this point. The most comprehensive, reliable and readily available data are for equity capital investments through the balance of payments, and are reported by the IMF. Other, more statistically problematic, components of total FDI inflows are contributions in kind, reinvested earnings and intra-company loans. Data on these vary among countries in terms of availability and reliability, and this is the major cause of variation in the comparative estimates of international organizations. Nevertheless, principal sources tend to corroborate broad trends and relative magnitudes.

FDI has not been evenly spread across the Central European economies. In the 1990s, three countries in Central Europe, the Czech Republic, Hungary, Poland have been the major destinations of FDI flows to the region. According to the EBRD (table 8.1), the three Central European countries received about 78 per cent of the 53 US$ billion in cumulative FDI inflows to the ten transition economies over the period 1989-98 that it records.

As table 8.1 indicates, FDI flows to Central Europe rapidly grew after the second half of 1990s. From 1994 to the end of 1990s the Visegrad three countries' annual FDI flows expanded to 11.6 US$ billion from 2.4 US$ billion. As far as the cumulated amount of inward FDI to the three countries is concerned, it grew around four times. Particularly in 1997 and 1998 the inward FDI to the three countries grew and, in 1998 it expanded more than twice. However, as table 8.1 clearly shows, the remarkable increase of inward FDI to the Visegrad countries at the end of the 1990s was contributed to by the inward FDI into Poland and the Czech Republic. (Hungary received much more FDI in the first half of the 1990s than other

Central European countries. Taking into consideration the economic size, the received amount of FDI in Hungary was extremely high. As table 8.2 indicates, per capita inward FDI in Hungary reached more than four times that in Poland).

As is well known, most inward FDI to Central Europe has come from the EU and US. It can be seen, however, that home countries of inward FDI in the Visegrad countries varied from one to another. In particular, as table 8.3 points out, the difference between Poland and Hungary was significant, which meant that Poland received FDI from rather more variety of sources, but Hungary received a greater percentage from EU countries.

FDI in Central Europe and Foreign Exchange Reserves

As was mentioned previously, three countries (Poland, Hungary and the Czech Republic) received 78 per cent of the cumulative FDI inflows to the ten transition economies in 1989-98. Also, from the end of 1994 to the end of 1998, total annual inflows to the three countries rose drastically (from 2.4 US$ billion to 11.6 US$ billion).

First, we try to find correlation coefficients between FDI and several economic variables in eight Central European countries (except Albania and Macedonia in table 8.1 and table 8.2). Then as the eight sample size is rather small, (we could have the same data from the *Business Central Europe Database*) 13 countries including Russia, Ukraine, Lithuania, Ratvia, Estonia are selected as samples of cross-section data for a regression analysis for the three years of 1992, 1995 and 1998. Needless to say, it would be better to have time series analysis with more than 15-20 samples for each Central European country. However, because the transition attempt of each country started in 1989, or the beginning of the 1990s, unfortunately, it might be too early to examine exact time series analyses for transition economies. This could be attempted several years later and here we could investigate as suggested above with a correlation coefficient and regression analysis with 13 cross section data, including the five former USSR countries for having rather rough perspectives.

(FDI of capital market as the independent variable) several economic variables, taking into consideration Frey's analysis (1984) and the current situation of transition economies, including GDP growth rate and average wage rate expressing the goods market and the labor market are picked up as dependent variables. In addition, we choose the budget balance (as per cent of GDP) as a policy variable and foreign exchange reserves as indicating the risk level of transition host countries. (FDI inflow means the increase of foreign exchange reserves, but we examine here whether a size of foreign exchange reserves has played a major role as a determinant of FDI).[2]

The correlation coefficients between FDI in eight Central European countries and the above four variables are shown in table 8.4.

Table 8.4 indicates some variables as significantly correlated with FDI, and, generally speaking, in most countries average wage rate and foreign exchange reserves would seem to be significant. (Average wage rate indicates positive significant correlation in most countries, which means that there is more income if the average wage rate is higher.)

Table 8.1   Stock of FDI in Central Europe, 1989-98

		(US$ million)
Country	1993	1998
Albania	85	423
Bulgaria	138	1,323
Croatia	228	1,997
Czech Republic	1,535	9,997
Macedonia	–	242
Hungary	7,302	16,459
Poland	981	15,056
Romania	708	4,510
Slovak Republic	374	1,762
Slovenia	39	1,192
Total	11,390	52,971

Source: EBRD (1999), p.79.

Then we can carry out a regression analysis with cross-section data from 13 countries in 1992, 1995 and 1998. The estimation equation is for each year as follows,

$$x_1 = a_1 + a_2 x_2 + a_3 x_3 + a_4 x_4 + a_5 x_5 + e$$

Here x_1, x_2, x_3, x_4, x_5 indicates FDI inflow (flow, US$ million), GDP growth rate (per cent), budget balance (as per cent of GDP), average wage rate (US$), foreign exchange reserves (US$ million). The result of the regression analysis for each year is shown in tables 8.5, 8.6 and 8.7.

Table 8.2   FDI stocks and flows to Central Europe

	Cumulative FDI inflows per capita (US$, 1998)	FDI Stock as % of GDP (1997)	FDI inflow as % of gross fixed capital formation (1997)
Albania	132	14.7	—
Bulgaria	159	9.4	44.0
Croatia	444	7.5	10.4
Czech Republic	967	22.8	8.1
Macedonia	121	1.7	3.0
Hungary	1,627	34.7	20.5
Poland	389	11.6	17.1
Romania	200	10.4	18.4
Slovak Republic	326	8.2	2.4
Slovenia	596	12.1	7.5

Source: Column 1, as in Table 8.1; columns 2 and 3, data from UN (1999).

According to the results of the regression analysis, in 1992 no variable was significant. Both in 1995 and in 1998 only foreign exchange reserves were seen to be significant.

FDI and Capital Movements

As shown in the second section, for inward FDI in Central Europe (and Russia, Ukraine, Lithuania, Latvia, Estonia) only foreign exchange reserves were significant. As seen in chapter seven, this might derive from risk which has occurred because of a rather in-built system in the former socialist regime and has been accompanied by foreign debt. It also suggests a close relationship of inward FDI in Central Europe with globalization, particularly with more flexible capital movements.

In this section, we first try to find significant factors of correlation coefficient with foreign exchange reserves for the three Visegrad countries (Poland, Hungary and the Czech Republic). Table 8.8 shows the correlation coefficients.

Table 8.3   Stock of FDI by country of origin (%)

Source	Hungary (end 1996)	Poland (end 1998)
European Union (of which):	71.2	59.2
Germany	23.8	18.8
Austria	14.5	2.8
France	7.8	8.8
Netherlands	9.5	7.0
UK	5.8	7.1
Italy	3.8	7.5
Other (of which):	28.8	40.8
US	17.1	18.0
Switzerland	2.3	2.4
Japan	1.6	0.7
South Korea	0.8	5.2
Russia	0.8	3.5

Source: National statistics.

Table 8.4   Correlation coefficient with inward FDI

	GDP growth rate (%)	Budget balance (% of GDP)	Average wage rate (US$)	Foreign exchange reserves (US$ million)
Poland	0.6558*	0.2050	0.9771 *	0.9765 *
Hungary	0.2130	- 0.3257	0.5354	0.6991 *
Czech	0.2800	- 0.1281	0.7638 *	0.8086 *
Slovakia	0.5468	0.1485	0.7215 *	0.3588
Bulgaria	0.4030	0.6285	- 0.0988	0.9188 *
Romania	- 0.1000	- 0.3596	0.5592	0.7226 *
Slovenia	0.4240	0.0933	0.2128	0.0080
Croachia	0.2503	0.3676	0.7711 *	0.8362 *

Source: Business Central Europe and author's calculation.

* Significant at the 0.05 level.

Table 8.5   Result of regression analysis in 1992

a_1	141.6061	(0.369428)
a_2	5.788119	(0.375631)
a_3	-1.203006	(-0.061557)
a_4	0.136811	(0.153110)
a_5	161.0644	(2.081893)
R^2	0.173179	

The figures in parentheses are the *t*-values.

* Significant at the 0.05 level.

Table 8.6   Result of regression analysis in 1995

a_1	- 908.7	(-0.85575)
a_2	57.34501	(0.854535)
a_3	- 174.853	(-0.97873)
a_4	0.850096	(0.551798)
a_5	196.8064	(4.630791) *
R^2	0.600601	

The figures in parentheses are the *t*-values.

* Significant at the 0.05 level.

Therefore, (excluding FDI here) in Poland the current account balance, average wage rate and foreign debt are correlated significantly; in Hungary GDP growth rate, average wage rate, industrial production growth rate, foreign debt are correlated significantly; and in the Czech Republic the average wage rate, industrial production growth rate and foreign debt are correlated significantly. It is easily seen that foreign debt (and current account balance in Poland) is a variable closely correlated with foreign exchange reserves. Then, what do GDP growth rate, average wage rate and industrial production growth rate explain?

Situations with which growth related variables are significantly correlated seem to indicate a positive evaluation for (host countries') domestic market expansion. It seems to be remarkable that foreign investors have put more positive weight on market expansion than the unemployment rate, inflation and budget deficit per cent of GDP, etc. Such results of the investigation with the correlation coefficient are consistent with the determinants of market seeking in Central Europe as many investigations have clearly shown. This confirmation is what we indicate first here.

Table 8.7   Result of regression analysis in 1998

a_1	334.5291	(0.635599)
a_2	12.01204	(0.1595)
a_3	-47.7967	(-0.2685)
a_4	-0.59913	(-0.52577)
a_5	193.523	(5.333405) *
R^2	0.726959	

The figures in parentheses are the t-values.

* Significant at the 0.05 level.

As examined in the previous section, a significant variable (in regression analysis) with inward FDI in Central Europe (and Russia, Ukraine, Lithuania, Latvia, Estonia) was foreign exchange reserves. It would confirm that monetary factors related with inward FDI are important. It is not necessary to mention that problems have existed concerning money and currency as risk in transition and developing economies (as occurred in the Russian crisis and Asian crisis).

We investigated in chapter seven the Daihatsu-FSO case in the 1980s in which the major issue was credit policy to Poland. This means that the critical situation with regard to monetary and financial factors like foreign exchange reserves and foreign debt was almost the same as in the FDI case in the 1980s. As indicated in the Daihatsu-FSO case, FDI is closely connected with the large amounts and long-term capital movement, and to foreign exchange reserves and foreign debt. Thus for both Japan and Poland it took many years' negotiation.

Another important message from the statistical investigation above is that, based upon the significant result of foreign exchange reserves with FDI, one can recognize the financial effects of FDI. This means that FDI inflow could make speculative capital movement (which is often called "currency crisis") less probable.

One of the most interesting pieces of research on currency crises was done by MITI in 1999 (MITI/1999). Usually a currency crisis is defined as an economic phenomenon in which, when a country suffers ·from a long-lasting current account deficit financed by foreign capital and cannot cover the deficit and the authority cannot keep up the exchange rate level clearly coming from decreasing foreign exchange reserves, then a rapid depreciation of the exchange rate happens. By defining currency crises as more than ten per cent depreciation of the exchange rate compared with the previous year, MITI started off examining currency crises by separating 1980s cases from 1990s cases (in order to avoid the heterogeneity of structure and interdependence in the global economy), focusing their main attention upon the currency crises in Asia.

Table 8.8 Correlation coefficient with foreign exchange reserves

	GDP growth rate (%)	Budget Balance (% of GDP)	Current account balance (US$ Billion)	Average wage rate (US$)	Industrial production growth rate (%)	Unemployment rate (%)	Inflation (%)	Foreign debt (US$ billion)
Poland	0.537	0.226	-0.665*	0.989*	0.409	-0.162	-0.391	-0.753*
Hungary	0.701*	-0.218	-0.606	0.854*	0.764*	0.629	-0.529	0.759*
Czech	0.616	0.335	-0.561	0.947*	0.745*	0.581	-0.541	0.906*

Source: Business Central Europe and author's calculation.

* Significant at the 0.05 level.

In this 1980s research, the significant variables for the research attempting to recognize significant variables with currency crisis by regression analysis could be summarized as follows:

(1) "Current account balance (per cent of GDP)", which indicates that the more current account surplus the less probability of currency crisis. We can say therefore that the increase of current account surplus, which also means an increase of foreign exchange reserves, significantly indicates less probability of a currency crisis.

(2) "Ratio of FDI inflow to foreign debt" which shows that the more the ratio financed by FDI to foreign debt the less probability of a currency crisis. Because FDI is usually involved in a long-term commitment of capital inflow, and also because it would make rapid large-scale capital outflow less probable, it could be insisted that the more foreign debt is financed by FDI the less probable a currency crisis is.

(3) "Overvalued exchange rate" which shows that the more overvalued

exchange rate, compared with the equilibrium market rate, would make a currency crisis more probable.

(4) "Budget balance (per cent of GDP)" is not significant enough. We would therefore indicate that budget deficit (per cent of GDP) might have no significance with the currency crises.

The significant variables recognized by the 1990s cases are:

(1) "Averaged short-term interest rate in advanced industrialized countries", which means that the higher interest rate of advanced industrialized countries the more probable is a currency crisis.

(2) "The greater share of short-term debt to foreign debt", which indicates that the more dependence upon short-term capital there is the more probable a currency crisis is.

(3) "Ratio of foreign exchange reserves to the (monthly) import amount", which shows that the more foreign exchange reserves there are the less probable a currency crisis is.

In summing up, indicating significant variables for currency crises in the 1980s and in 1990s, and in the Asian currency crises in 1997, the MITI report (1999) shows six variables to be significant: (1) current account balance; (2) foreign direct investment; (3) short-term debt; (4) foreign exchange reserves; (5) overvalued exchange rate; and (6) interest rates differences.

From the viewpoint of this chapter, the above emphasis upon FDI opens up many possibilities. The FDI inflow with technology transfer and capital movement would contribute not only to more scale and more efficient production but also make a currency crisis less probable. The reasons seem to be clear: (1) as mentioned in MITI (1999), FDI means the long-term commitment of capital inflow, and (2) the greater FDI inflow would show an evidence of trust in host countries' markets by FDI investors.

In other words, for preventing currency crises (rapid movement of short-term capital) and for growing foreign exchange reserves the inflow of FDI has been significant, and as far as foreign exchange reserves is concerned, variables related to economic growth indicate significant correlation.

Something else to be confirmed is that, as pointed out in MITI (1999), the situations in the 1980s and in 1990s were not the same and the characteristic feature in the 1990s was (MITI (1999), pp.148-49) the remarkable increase in the effects of international and monetary factors caused by the development of financial engineering.

However, we think that it might make the issue unclear if we consider the effects of the development of financial engineering too much. Arguments by Strange (1998) seem to be good examples to examine here.

Hereafter in this chapter there is a short consideration of speculative capital movements with an international relations approach, chiefly as preparation for the following chapters in which we investigate diagnosis and prescription on speculative capital movement into commodity futures markets in the third part of this book. (Needless to say, the main work and the preparatory work could be reversed if the topic concerned is approached from another viewpoint.)

In an international relations framework international relations like US-Japan, and France-Germany have been very important factors in understanding the instability of the international monetary system causing large scale capital movements (see, for example, Strange (1998) chapters three and four). When we approach the issues from within the international relations framework, the main focus is in which international economic relations would money supply be excess and in which would it be scarce. However asking questions about the nature of capital movement (FDI or portfolio investment or financial crime or aid) would not be the main issue, (therefore the issues themselves might be rather ambiguous).

What seems to be important is that we should recognize the situation of probable built-in instability concerning money supply and capital movement in the mechanism of the international political economy, and also that we should recognize the shortage of enough "will" and "skill" to adjust the instability. We expect that the greatest discrepancy of views has been among the measures of adjustment. There is more detailed consideration in the third part of this book and in this chapter we focus our attention upon a framework of international relations to approach capital movement.[3]

The targets of Strange's consideration (of 1998) might be interpreted as: (1) the instability of the domestic and international financial system accompanied by globalization; (2) the cause and effect of it; and (3) measures for adjusting it etc. After the very careful investigation with enormous literature, Strange reached a conclusion mentioning that neither international arrangements nor national policies by individual countries have ever been enough to control short-term speculative capital movement. By suggesting some ideas like writing off foreign debts, she reached a final point of emphasizing the need to create a new kind of political organization (whose detail is unfortunately not clear), and not to leave it to a market mechanism.

However, as Strange herself suggested, (as a good question raised by Santiso (1997)) it would be important to ask: "Whether the technology available to markets has not run ahead of the capacity of government or international organization to respond quickly enough" (Strange (1998), p.177). Thus: "Digital money would certainly make it much easier to evade the Tobin tax" (p.178),[4] and as Santiso (1997) has suggested, "there is a widening time-lag, ever since the Mexican crisis of 1994/5, between events in financial markets and the responses of governments, and that financial technology may explain this" (p.191).

It was the Bank for International Settlements (BIS) that Strange had in mind in terms of the creation of a "new kind of political organization". It was as she said: "When crises struck - as they certainly would - the hot-lines constantly open between regulators linked to the BIS were one way in which the speed of response to markets could be matched - or nearly so - by the speed of political decision making" (p.163).

However, we can quickly respond to her that analyses taking into consideration the adjustment speed of markets and the quantity of capital inflow and authority's regulation are not new, but fundamentally are similar to the "crisis problem" asserted by Mundell (1969). (See chapter ten in which we attempt to apply the crisis problem argument to the case of a corner market in the natural rubber market). In addition to the long history analysis, the idea that "the speed of response to markets could be matched or nearly so by the speed of political decision making" is nothing but establishing measures of markets when there is a crisis. It would be an idea classified as putting more weight upon the market mechanism, and the criterion to classify might be rather ambiguous.

Needless to say, Strange attached importance and emphasized through her writings, like Strange (1998), that development of financial technology would contribute to response speed and response size of capital movement. However, as indicated earlier, in the field of economics there have been improved analytical tools for many years (some of which will be demonstrated in the third part of this book). The characteristic features of quality (not quantity) in the development of financial technology can be recognized, and if there are areas of extreme difficulty, they arise from functions that have always been extremely difficult, such as the forecasting of stock prices and grain prices.

Conclusion

We have examined here the current FDI situations in Central Europe, and have recognized foreign exchange reserves to be a significant variable in statistical investigation, and with a correlation test we could understand that the growth factors are significantly correlated with foreign exchange reserves. Statistical investigations suggest, therefore, that both finance and growth have significance for FDI.

As far as determinants of FDI are concerned, as Dunning and Rojec (1994) identified, there are four major motives for FDI: (1) natural resource seeking; (2) market seeking; (3) efficiency seeking; and (4) strategic asset seeking. Based upon the general idea, by focusing our attention upon Central Europe, these are mostly dominated by market seeking.

The statistical investigations above indicating finance and growth to be significant might confirm market seeking as a dominant determinant because market expansion might be a dominant motive for attracting FDI inflow.

The FDI correlating with foreign exchange reserves could be recognized, through investigations into currency crises, as one of the effective factors in preventing currency crises.

Thus, we think that the FDI investigations suggest that, in Central Europe, growth oriented transition policies might be important from the viewpoints of attracting FDI and of preventing currency crises.

Concerning the effect of FDI in preventing a currency crisis, when we approach the issue of capital movements with international relations, this issue has never been new and the tools for analyzing it have been improved over many years. (Although an interdisciplinary approach would always be necessary) over-evaluation might not be a good way to reach reasonable solutions.

With such a point of view, we can focus our attention upon more specific issues in the following third part.

Notes

1   Both this and the next section are based in part on McMillan and Morita (2000).
2   The calculations in this section were based upon *the Business Central Europe Database*.
3   Needless to say, because FDI directly increases Foreign Exchange Reserves, we have some tests asking if FDI inflow explains Foreign Exchange Reserves. Results of the tests might mean that FDI would be one of the factors to increase Foreign Exchange Reserves.
4   A short comment on the "Tobin tax" to which Strange (1998) often referred, is needed here. The aim of it "would be to discourage those speculative transactions made possible by futures trading without discouraging productive foreign direct investment" (p.173). Referring to the Institute of Developing Economies, Topic Report, it suggested that the East Asian currency crisis pointed out a possibility of ill-function of markets by such factors as moral hazard, mob psychology behavior, self realizing expectation, etc., coming from asymmetry of information. It discussed also the regulation of capital transactions, that such ideas as the Chilean model and Tobin tax are regulating capital movement, particularly short-term capital transactions, against which such proposals as Malaysian exchange rate regulation are to secure freedom of macroeconomic policies

(monetary policies in particular) to put the emphasis upon economic recovery, not upon regulation of capital transactions (see http://www.ide.go.jp). That is to say, it would be important to clarify the priority of economic recovery, not limit the measures of macroeconomic policies, even when dealing with short-term capital movement.

PART III
INTERNATIONAL COMMODITY AGREEMENTS AND FUTURES MARKET

In the first part and second part in this book, we have examined commodity futures markets in Central Europe and characteristic features of risk connected with economic transition. We have focused our attention upon the necessity for a well equipped market and upon the importance of when and how government intervenes. In the third part, based upon the above investigations we consider the questions of what kind of function government or any other organization have, when and how.

In terms of the main topics of this book, our focus is on commodity exchanges and primary commodity markets. That is to say, we have selected here in this third part several issues (to be analyzed in the future) on capital movement and speculation concerning economic reforms and commodity exchanges in Central Europe. In this book therefore (although whether or not speculative behavior is in its nature destabilizing needs serious investigation, destabilizing cases could undoubtedly be observed), when we recognize speculation as "excess speculation" or "distorted speculation", we examine the nature of this and what measures can be effectively taken against it. We choose actual cases to study and, as good examples of effective measures, we investigate intergovernment agreement as shown in International Commodity Agreements and examine the effect of price limits on price movement.

In the chapter nine, we examine a phenomenon called "excess speculation", examine the nature of it and effective policies against it.

In the chapter ten, our attention is focused on a concrete case of a corner market, after we define "destabilizing speculation". By investigating the case concerned, we suggest here the possibility to recognize a corner or bang market at an early stage, with plausible signals to catch the behavior.

In the chapter eleven, we examine the issue that, when we observe significant volatility in price movement, effective intervention measures through governmental or intergovernmental schemes are needed. In order to do this, we analyze International Commodity Agreement schemes and their effects.

In the chapter twelve, we investigate the possibilities of placing International Commodity Agreement schemes in a sociological framework and examine the *raison d'être* of each scheme.

In the chapter thirteen, we try a similar exercise as in the chapter twelve in the framework of political economy. Also we try to interpret changes which have occurred in International Commodity Agreements schemes.

In the fourteenth and final chapter of this book, macroeconomic effects are considered, where the conditions of artificial stability created by, for example, International Commodity Agreements have the results of destabilizing effects in a macroeconomic sense.

Chapter 9

An Analysis of Excessive Speculation

Introduction

It might be necessary to ask a question about the effect of government intervention when speculative short-term capital movement, which is recognized as "abnormal", occurs.

In this chapter, we consider the possibility of a scientific approach in examining abnormality in speculative behaviors and of investigating an appropriate prescription against the abnormality. However, we have never had enough data and materials, both quantitatively and qualitatively, and never had enough accumulation of scientific analysis. In this chapter, therefore, we try to provide an effective theoretical framework to consider some aspects of such questions and try to interpret them appropriately.

Excessive Speculation

In approaching the excessive speculative behaviors, what we first try to examine is the extremely upward movement of prices of international commodities observed from the beginning of the 1970s (1972-74) when world-wide speculation started to receive attention. As mentioned in chapter eight with reference to Strange (1998), from viewpoints of international relations, the main problem has been the lack of ability to cope with the short-term capital movements caused by hedge funds, etc., which has been coming from money supply institutions and flexible money movement.

Particularly for the Central European transition economies which have experienced more than ten years of reforms, coping with the short-term capital movement toward commodities, stocks, bonds, etc., would have rather serious problems, but also the economies should be fully equipped with the market infrastructure for futures transactions. Having in mind the issues we examine in this chapter, we start by observing the situation at the beginning of 1970s.

Analysis by Walter Labys

Walter Labys (1974) observed the volatile movement of speculative capital at the beginning of 1970s and his diagnosis was as follows.

Labys started with the fact that the transaction volume in the futures market increased significantly. If, as Labys expected: "Most futures markets have roughly the same hedging needs from year to year"[1], the significantly increased volume of transaction could be recognized as coming from speculation. Concerning the degree of increase, if we could expect in the market transaction that hedging is in the net short position and speculation the net long position, it would be reasonable to assume that the volume of which speculative volume of net long position is above the hedging volume of net short position is "excessive speculation". In terms of the proximate index, it might be appropriate to think that a presumed ratio of physical transaction volume to futures market transaction volume could be a speculative index. The speculative index for the period in question was remarkably increased.

As prices of international commodities were also significantly increased after 1972 (until the middle of 1974), the price instability index showed remarkable growth. The price instability index indicates,

$$\frac{100}{\bar{p}} \sqrt{\frac{(p_t - \bar{p})^2}{n}}$$

Here $\bar{p}$ shows mean value of prices, p_t indicates observed value of prices, n means the number of observed value.

The relation between the speculative index and price instability index could be statistically significant. Why then do we observe the significant relation between the two indices?

According to Labys, it could be coming from monetary factors. This means that, when uncertainty of the monetary situation, like inflation and currency instability prevails, having international commodities could be an advantage in terms of risk dispersion and price expectation in international commodities. (It would be the same behavior as seen in a hedge fund when they expect a particular country's bond to be of comparative advantage.) Therefore, inflow of speculative capital by "shifting toward international commodities" could make their prices rise.

Mechanism of Excessive Speculation

From the analysis of Labys (1974) we understand that the Labys scientific contribution was about the process toward equilibrium for the individual economic agent. However, it is difficult to systematically recognize what kind of functions there were in the market and what processes there were in the market. In this section, we try to create a theoretical framework for approaching excessive speculation.

The following is an analysis of the phenomena and what Labys found.

The first analysis is shown in figure 9.1 (figure 9.2 is the excess demand curve).

As Labys assumed that the hedging need would be constant, if speculation meets the hedging need, it would not be probable that, all of a sudden, a huge amount of speculation at a particular period would take place. It would be more likely that the equilibrium of this period would exist at the neighborhood of the equilibrium of the previous period (shown as ε in figure 9.1). (Therefore, supply would become more inelastic when toward (q^{**}, p^{**}) from (q^*, p^*)).

However, speculative demand suddenly increased at a particular period (as in 1972), which indicated that the DD curve shifted to $D`D`$ curve. Unless such excessive speculative capital flows in, the price would increase to $\bar{p}$ from p^*. Actually, however, the price was raised much more toward p^{**} from p^*.

Moreover, it could be recognized that an implicit implication of the Labys' analysis might be the effect to spot market. As Labys mentioned, if there was a huge demand for raw materials and/or supply shortage of raw materials this might become one of the factors for the inflow of speculative demand, the big rise of prices in futures market would create supply at the futures market and would create demand at the spot market. This demand rushed into the spot market would undoubtedly cause a big price rise in the spot market.

As often assumed in this kind of issue,[2] we can here assume to exist multiple equilibria at the spot market,[3] which is shown at figure 9.3.

We would assume that the equilibrium E_1 holds when the excess demand curve is N_sN_s. When in this situation, a rushed demand in the spot market would shift the N_sN_s curve toward the $N_s`N_s`$ curve reaching the E_4 position. Then we could observe the close relationship between the rise of the speculative index and the price instability index.[4]

The above was the framework originally from Labys' observation.

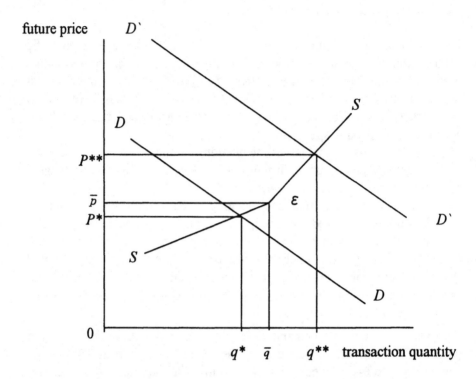

Figure 9.1 Futures market

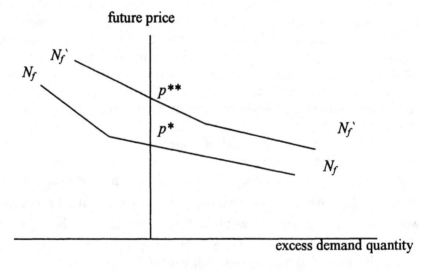

Figure 9.2 Excess demand in future by non-arbitrage

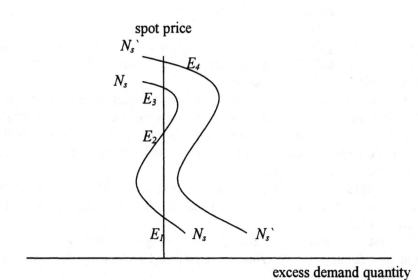

Figure 9.3 Excess supply in spot by non-arbitrage

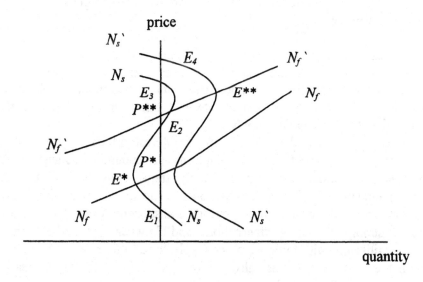

Figure 9.4 Arbitrage equilibrium

A Function of Arbitrage Transaction[5]

When we investigate the framework, what kind of adjustment mechanism should we consider? The basic necessary mechanism might be the "buffer mechanism to adjustment elasticity".

More concretely, it could be said that due to the adjustment (1) enough arbitrage trade would be done among markets and price volatility would become smaller to ensure the stable equilibrium; and (2) authority could make price volatility smaller through buffer stock operation; and also (3) a combination of (1) and (2) above.[6]

In this chapter, we try to examine the function of (1) above and try to find the applicability of coping with a speculative capital movement by the function (1) or (3).

We first try to make clear how interest arbitrage transaction could have a stabilizing function for the situation mentioned previously. We make the following assumptions:

(1) A spot market and a future market with a single delivery month (of nearby delivery).

(2) Arbitrage supply is fully elastic.

(3) Both interest cost and storage cost can be neglected.

(4) Therefore, interest rate differences would be also neglected.

Here we would assume that:

(5) Authority would not intervene in the market.

Interest arbitrage behavior usually means that they have the cover transaction in the futures market for spot market transaction, which indicates both transactions of spot market and futures market.[7] (Hereafter, just for convenience, we concentrate our attention upon spot market demand and futures market supply.)

In order to have the equilibrium of interest arbitrage, it would be necessary to meet the following conditions: (1) enough to be supplied by spot market excess supply of non-arbitrage transactions to satisfy the spot market demand of arbitrage transactions; (2) to be satisfied with futures market excess demand of non-arbitrage transactions to meet the futures market supply of arbitrage transactions; and (3) when spot market demand is in equilibrium with futures market supply for arbitrage transactions, spot market excess supply must also be in equilibrium with futures market excess demand for non-arbitrage transactions.

In other words, a condition for interest arbitrage to exist is that, for non-arbitrage transactions, the spot market excess supply curve would have an intersecting point with the futures market excess demand curve.[8]

Therefore, by making the above five assumptions, if the interest arbitrage mechanism works, the resulting situation would be expressed as in figure 9.4, which is given from figure 9.2 and figure 9.3. This would clearly indicate that the moving range of spot market prices is stabilized from $E_4 - E_1$ to $E^{**} - E^*$.[9]

If the above framework is approximately correct, it might not be clear enough as the price instability that Labys observed could be uncertain, which is a movement from E_1 to E_4 or a movement from E^* to E^{**}. If it is a movement from E_1 to E_4, by the arbitrage function the movement would be stabilized from E^* to E^{**}. However, it could not be assumed that the movement from E^* to E^{**} would be stabilized enough in an absolute sense. If the movement from E^* to E^{**} seems to be still unstable, additional measures (of government intervention) would be necessary.[10]

Analytical Tools

Own-rate of Interest

As was indicated, Labys examined the degree of the relationship of commodity prices with the general price level, exchange rate, and other various monetary assets. However, as far as the movement of commodity prices are concerned, they had to exchange them with a key currency (we will call it here US$). Thus, we have to examine first how an exchange of commodity with US$ is done.

When currency instability occurs and US$ are sold in exchange for DEM, JY, gold, etc., the monetary authority of each country has several measures to regulate short-term capital movement. When such measures have some effect, the US$ supply moves toward commodity demand such as for platinum, silver, copper, wheat, corn, soybean, etc., the demand for which are usually recognized as speculation toward commodities.

This kind of speculation would, as Labys indicated, occur through a behavior toward international commodities as a type of asset holding. Thus we understand that, in the meaning of providing profitability, the same kind of behavior occurs in DEM, JY, silver, wheat, etc.

When asset holders have a certain asset with comparatively larger value for a certain period and they expect the value to decrease, they would shift the asset toward other types of assets. (When such behavior occurs suddenly toward specific currency or assets in the short term, we usually call it a "currency crisis" or "monetary crisis".)

What is the value of assets then?

This question could be interpreted with J. M. Keynes[11] in mind as the following three factors for increasing value:

(1) Some assets produce a yield or output, measured in terms of themselves, by assisting some process of production or supplying services to a consumer.
(2) Most assets, except money, suffer some wastage or involve some cost through the mere passage of time (apart from any change in their relative value), irrespective of their being used to produce a yield; *i.e.* they involve a carrying cost measured in terms of themselves.
(3) The amount (measured in terms of itself) which they are willing to pay for the potential convenience or security given by this power of disposal (exclusive of yield or carrying cost attaching to the asset), we shall call it liquidity-premium.

As Keynes mentioned: "It follows that the total return expected from the ownership of an asset over a period is equal to its yield *minus* its carrying cost *plus* its liquidity-premium" (p.226).

Keynes called it the own-rate of interest measured by the commodity itself. It is just a value of asset measured based upon the commodity itself which would vary for a certain period.

However, even if the asset itself is measured as the growth rate of production for a certain period by the unit of its own, the values of various assets could not be compared. As a criterion for a common measure it would be necessary to select a specific asset. When money is taken as the standard of measurement, it could be possible to compare various assets' degree of intertemporal value volatility in terms of money. Keynes called this "the own-rate of interest of houses, wheat and money in terms of themselves".[12] (Hereinafter we call them the own-rate of interest of commodities.)

When the economy concerned is in equilibrium, the own-rate of interest of all commodities and all assets would be the same. There could be no shift in assets holding in an equilibrium situation.

Based upon the above framework, the footprint that Labys observed might be interpreted as the adjustment process toward a new equilibrium, with new relative prices.

Interest Arbitrage Transaction

The explanation mentioned in the previous section might not be enough, particularly in taking into consideration the volatile price movements of currencies and international commodities.

We should consider also the price movements of spot prices and futures prices, and here we could have an example of currency movement.

For convenience, we assume that futures transaction is contracted for a single delivery month and the exchange rate moves flexibly. We suppose here the currencies, US$ and JY. The spot exchange rate of US$ is r_0 for one JY, and three months interest rate in the US is i_a and in Japan i_j.

If we do not take into consideration the movement of the exchange rate for three months, for the investor who has asset D in terms of US$ it makes no difference whether the asset is in US$ or in JY because he would have the same asset value three months later, which is,

$$r_0 = \frac{1+i_j}{1+i_a}$$

because,

$$D(1+i_a) = \frac{1}{r_0} D(1+i_j)$$

If

$$r_0 > \frac{1+i_j}{1+i_a}$$

it might be better to have the asset in US$. On the contrary, if

$$r_0 < \frac{1+i_j}{1+i_a}$$

it would be better to have it in JY. In the former case the capital would move from Japan to the US, and the latter case from the US to Japan.

However, if the exchange rate is rather volatile, it would be risky to move the capital depending upon only r_0 and $(1+i_j)/(1+i_a)$.

When the capital is shifted from the US to Japan with the spot exchange rate r_0, as with keeping the interest rate unchanged but with a volatile exchange rate, the capital movement could suffer a loss. That is to say, this shifts the capital to Japan as,

$$r_0 < \frac{1+i_j}{1+i_a}$$

The exchange rate, however, changes to be r_t three months later and the inequality becomes,

$$D(1+i_a) > \frac{r_t}{r_0} D(1+i_j)$$

In order to avert the risk accompanied with the volatile exchange rate, the risk on the spot market demand could be covered by the futures market supply at the same period for the same volume in the foreign exchange markets.

Assuming the investors behave in this way, the capital movement would depend upon the interest rate difference and futures margin. This means therefore that three months' futures exchange rate is expressed as r_t, investors shift the capital comparing the values of $D(1+i_a)$ and,

$$\frac{r_t}{r_0} D(1+i_j)$$

When adjustment is finished, the situation would be called the equilibrium of interest arbitrage, which indicates,

$$D(1+i_a) = \frac{r_t}{r_0} D(1+i_j)$$

If it is,

$$D(1+i_a) < \frac{r_t}{r_0} D(1+i_j)$$

the capital is moving from the US to Japan, as holding JY might be preferable. The capital movement makes the spot market demand of JY increase and futures market supply increase, which would decrease a value of (r_t/r_0). The adjustment would be finished when reaching the equilibrium. When the inequality is the opposite way, the adjustment process would reach the equilibrium in the opposite way.[13]

The relations upon the capital movement could be approximated as follows. When p means futures premium and if it is that,

$$p = \frac{r_t - r_0}{r_0} = \frac{r_t}{r_0} - 1$$

at the equilibrium, the equality,

$$\frac{r_t}{r_0} = \frac{1 + i_a}{1 + i_j}$$

holds, and we have,

$$p = \frac{1 + i_a}{1 + i_j} - 1 = \frac{i_a - i_j}{1 + i_j}$$

By expressing the futures margin as a per cent we could have interest parity. When neglecting $p \times i_j$, there could be,

$$p = i_a - i_j$$

which shows that the interest parity could be approximated as the interest rate difference.[14]

The meaning of the above equality is as follows. Expressing the exchange rate as US$ for one JY, and as the futures premium means the higher rate of JY futures prices, as far as the capital movement by only the futures margin is concerned movement from US$ to JY would be more profitable. Meanwhile, when the interest rate in the US is higher than in Japan, as far as the capital movement by only the interest rate difference is concerned, movement from JY to US$ would be more profitable. Therefore, when futures premium (discount) equals the interest rate difference, no capital movement would occur.

A more general way to explain, it would be as follows.

When the futures premium is above the interest rate difference $(i_a - i_j - p < 0)$ and when the interest rate difference is above the futures discount $(i_j - i_a - d > 0)$, it would be more profitable to move the capital from US$ to JY and the capital moves from the US to Japan. The difference between the futures premium and the interest rates difference and the difference between the interest rates difference and the futures discount would be called the intrinsic premium. On the contrary, the difference between the interest rates difference and the futures premium $\left(i_a - i_j - p > 0\right)$ and the difference between the futures discount and the interest rates difference $\left(i_j - i_a - d < 0\right)$ would be called the intrinsic discount. When the existence of intrinsic discount can be observed, it could be more profitable to move the capital from JY to US$ and the capital movement would occur.

We could say, therefore, that the capital movement by interest rate arbitrage might be due to an intrinsic premium and intrinsic discount.

Application of Analytical Tools

The above mentioned interest rate arbitrage transaction seems to be applied to the transaction between the commodity and US$ by using the own-rate of interest measured by the commodity.

For convenience, we use the letter for JY to express the commodity. Under the situation in which a similar condition with interest arbitrage equilibrium holds, the following equality holds,

$$D(1+i_a) = \frac{r_t}{r_0} D(1+i_j)$$

That is to say, in such a situation, whether the asset holding is in US$ or in the commodity would be indifferent. When the equilibrium is disturbed for any reason that results in the following inequality,

$$D(1+i_a) < \frac{r_t}{r_0} D(1+i_j)$$

asset holders would shift the asset from US$ to the commodity. We observe the capital inflow into the commodity then. As the capital inflow is shown to be spot market demand and futures market supply in the commodity, it would make r_0 increase and r_t decrease. As a result, the decrease of (r_t/r_0) would finish the capital inflow and would return to the equilibrium.

On the contrary, if the inequality is,

$$D(1+i_a) > \frac{r_t}{r_0} D(1+i_j)$$

as asset holders wish to shift the assets from the commodity to US$, the capital would move toward US$ from the commodity. The capital moves to the spot demand of US$ and makes the spot market price of the commodity fall. The result of adjustment would be restored to the equilibrium by increasing the value of (r_t/r_0). The capital movement by arbitrage has a function of adjusting the difference between spot and futures in the exchange rate of US$ with the commodity.

As previously mentioned, the function of arbitrage transaction would make the market more stable but it would not ensure enough stability of price movement in an absolute sense. Even if the (r_t/r_0) is constant, r_0 and r_t might be heavily volatile; this suggests thus that the phenomena Labys observed might have effectively-functioning arbitrage transactions.

If that explains the situation, it would be necessary to have additional measures to ensure enough stability in the absolute level of prices. Such measures mean regulation to limit the movements for the absolute level of r_0 and/or r_t.

We can consider necessary measures.

Futures Market Intervention

With the above situation, we would assume that, by the inflow of speculative capital, excess demand could be observed in the market and both r_0 and r_t would start to rise. Then we also assume that the authorities start to intervene only in the spot market by a selling operation upon the level of r_0.

The futures price would be raised as far as excess demand exists through the function of the market. Therefore, with the spot market intervention by the authorities, when the (r_t/r_0) increases, the inequality,

$$D(1+i_a) < \frac{r_t}{r_0} D(1+i_j)$$

exists and capital movement by arbitrage would occur. As there could be more demand in the spot market and more supply in the futures market, the capital movement would work to decrease the level of (r_t/r_0). Due to the intervention of the authority upon the spot market, such an adjustment mechanism could not fully work. Rather it would be probable that, with a huge demand in spot market by capital inflow, it would be impossible to defend the ceiling price and because of the intervention the level (r_t/r_0)

could be raised by making the increasing rate of r_0 less than the increasing rate of r_t. Even if the authorities could defend the ceiling price by a selling operation, when the buffer stock is exhausted as the intervention has taken longer than is appropriate, it would be probable that spot market prices would rise fiercely due to the expectation of a supply shortage.

That story would show the necessity that, in order to fully implement the selling operation, the authorities have to prevent the shortage in a buffer stock.

What would occur if the authorities are intervening not in the spot market but the futures market by having the selling contract?

As the futures market price levels are regulated, just a small rise in the spot market price level would make the (r_t/r_0) decrease and the inequality of,

$$D(1+i_a) > \frac{r_t}{r_0} D(1+i_j)$$

would exist to move the capital outflow.[15] Demand for the commodity asset would be decreased. The capital outflow would produce the commodity supply and US\$ demand in the spot market and would make the spot market prices decrease; the (r_t/r_0) level would be increased to restore the equilibrium.

What is necessary would be for the authorities to implement the futures supply contract. Everything else is left to the function of market. Neither the level of buffer stock nor worries about a spot price rise are necessary with a buffer stock shortage. Also as it was when there were lots of international short-term capital, with a rather small rise of spot market prices it would be sufficient to shift enough arbitrage capital. When comparing with a case of spot market intervention, it might be almost the same in terms of spot market levels.[16]

It is easy to see that the futures market intervention is much more effective than spot market intervention. It could be claimed that spot market intervention would clash with the market mechanism, but futures market intervention would be compatible with the market mechanism.

Notes

1   Labys (1974) p.5.
2   For example, see Kaldor (1952).
3   This assumption is just for simplicity to show the situation drastically. If we assume an

inelastic demand and supply curve, there would be no crucial change.

4 Opposite causal relations between the increase of the speculative index and the increase of the price instability index is probable. See, for example, Telser and Higinbotham (1977).

5 As we make clear, we investigate here the interest arbitrage transaction.

6 Sohmen (1966) mentioned that arbitrage transaction had a role as a buffer to stabilize the foreign exchange rate random shocks which were produced by physical traders' inactive transactions. The functions of arbitrage transaction and of buffer stock operation have a quite similar nature.

7 See the next section.

8 See Sohmen (1966), chapter 4.

9 E^* and E^{**} are both stable equilibria.

10 Labys classified the transaction units as hedgers and speculators, and he did not explicitly mention arbitrage behaviors. Needless to say, however, it did not mean that there was no arbitrage.

11 Keynes (1936) chap. 17, pp.225-226.

12 If a very efficient futures market does exist, the price system would supply it.

13 In this case, when increasing the capital in Japan at the same time, it would make i_j decrease, and decrease the capital in the US, which would make i_a increase. That is the adjustment. Actually, as interest rate adjustment would be slower than foreign exchange rate, here we would assume that the adjustment is done by the foreign exchange rate.

14 If it is futures market discount and it is $(r_0 - r_t)/r_0 = d$, with the same calculation it would be $d = i_j - i_a$.

15 If originally the market had no capital inflow, the decrease of (r_t/r_0) would work to create capital inflow and would work to prevent excess demand expansion. It is not, however, necessary to mention this in this chapter. Also if the market received a speculative capital inflow, enough flexible arbitrage transaction would absorb the profitable opportunity.

16 The case of excess supply at the market could be analyzed in the way.

Chapter 10

A Diagnosis of Destabilizing Speculation

Introduction

On 4 and 5 July 2001, *Nihon Keizai Shimbun* announced that the listing of crude oil by The Tokyo Commodity Exchange would start with many serious problems. The original decision to list naturally began because "Japan's crude oil import reaches annually 250 million kilo liters, of which 90 per cent came from the Middle East. Asian countries including Japan are the biggest customers for Middle Eastern oil, the crude oil price is determined with reference to crude oil prices of US produced and European produced oil at the markets in New York and London etc. The dissatisfaction against the price determined mechanism in foreign countries has been a main initiative for the establishment of crude oil futures market" (*Nihon Keizai Shimbun*, 4 July 2001).

What were the problems? As announced in the above article, "The focus for permission is a way to secure confidence to the market. It is about the crisis management issue to assuredly correspond when price levels are heavily volatile and commodity trading companies etc. would become unsettled", and "The competence of the chairman of the board of directors has become stronger in more strict regulation of the volume of members' commitments to prevent excessive inflow of speculative capital and in quicker response to prevent more amount of damages when there might become a commodity trading company unsettled". At the same time, however, "it would have a problem of trade off between more regulation to prevent unsettled affairs and less possibilities for physical traders like oil refinery companies to join the market."

That is to say, the volume of a member's position in a crude oil futures market transaction at the Tokyo Commodity Exchange is limited to 16 thousand kilo liters for near future hedging, which means only 1/20 of 250 thousand ton tanker capacity. "It would make it difficult for general trading companies and oil wholesale companies who counted to buy crude oil amounting to ten tankers to join" (*Nihon Keizai Shimbun*, 5 July 2001). Also as the price movement limit per day is regulated to 900 yen per one kilo liter, this means that the price movement could be allowed to be 1.1 dollar per barrel in terms of the current exchange rate. It is not unusual for the crude oil price to move around two dollars in one day, and it might be easily imagined therefore that "they could not hedge when they need it" (*Nihon Keizai Shimbun*, 5 July 2001).

The Tokyo Commodity Exchange has put a priority on securing reliance through transaction regulation and this makes it quite possible to limit market participation.

The main problem to be considered is how to prevent "excessive speculative capital inflow" effectively. If we could have reasonably effective measures against "excessiveness", it might be unnecessary to have strict transaction regulation to prevent capital inflow.

We could look back to the 1970s, when this kind of issue was very hot, since then questions about futures trading and speculative phenomena have become rather commonplace. As mentioned in chapter nine, groundbreaking analyses were done by Labys (1974) and Telser and Higinbotham (1977), etc.

Needless to say, large-scale phenomena in commodity speculation has happened rather often as has (particularly recently) large-scale phenomena in financial speculation occurred often.

The idea about effective measures against some serious unstable problems in international commodities started with McKinnon (1967), in which McKinnon investigated the income stabilization policies of primary commodity producers. McKinnon's idea has widely focused experts' attention.

Such an idea is extremely interesting and needs to be examined thoroughly. However, though the idea of stabilizing producers' income has been quite meaningful, from a more technical viewpoint the necessary conditions for successful practical implement are still immature. The basic condition necessary to successfully investigate abnormal speculation, and the effectiveness of regulatory measures has been quite limited.

The purpose of this chapter is, in the context of the above situation, to investigate what abnormal speculative capital movements are and what effective measures can be used against them. In that sense, undoubtedly it is necessary to examine the functions of markets in New York, London, etc. We will consider cases in such markets later. However, using readily accessible data and with the purpose of clarifying the questions we are dealing with in this chapter, we will examine a Japanese case of abnormal speculation which happened in the market (appropriate market in international standard) and will consider possibilities for correcting the situation. It might be said that the case considered is rather old and the region covered by the abnormal speculation is relatively limited. However, because the approach used in this chapter has never been tried before, it is useful to investigate the question about the futures market in the light of this approach.

Abnormal Speculation

Classification and Regulation Measures

When the price level of an international commodity is observed to be heavily volatile, the nature of the volatility varies from one market to another.[1] However, the markets can be classified into two types, (A) and (B), where (A) is a competitive market but with price expectations, transaction actors' anticipation may be biased, thus heavy volatility in price movement is observed, and (B) the market is monopolized by a specific transaction actor who has a significant market share and by whom the market is manipulated, thus heavy volatility in price movement is observed. (Here in this chapter we will call the former "excessive speculation" and the latter "distorted speculation".)

Moreover, excessive speculation is classified into two types as follows: (A)-1 means that speculative behavior is synchronously observed among many commodities, and (A)-2 shows that speculation is limited to a particular commodity or some closely related commodities. Distorted speculation is also classified into two types as follows: (B)-1 points out the price manipulation mainly for corner and bang[2] cases and (B)-2 shows the price manipulation mainly for arbitrages. It seems therefore that the abnormal speculations can be classified into the above four types (as is shown at table 10.1).

Table 10.1   Abnormal speculations

(A) Excessive speculation	(A)-1 to many commodities
	(A)-2 to particular commodities
(B) Distorted speculation	(B)-1 for corner and bang
	(B)-2 for arbitrage

The four types of speculative behavior each have specific characteristics and occur with different phenomena. The counter measures employed by exchange would undoubtedly be different for the different characteristics. We can first indicate the differences in the characteristics and phenomena, and then investigate the measures for appropriate regulation.

(A) type speculative behavior is done to get profit from price difference of intertemporal exchange between monetary assets and commodities. In the case of (A) type speculation, thus, speculative capital would be moved towards spot and nearby delivery months.

(B) type speculative behavior is as follows. The (B)-1 type speculative behavior for corners is behavior in which the speculator has a long position with forecasting the limit of supply capacity in the market concerned and has a request to take an actual transaction after having a big share of the market and after a big rise in the price level. To accomplish this, sellers have to have settlement of the outstanding accounts and have to pay money guarantees. For sellers, as they have a corner market beyond the supply capacity, it is difficult to clear the position by physical transaction and it might be unavoidable to take a huge amount of loss to clear financially the position because of the higher price level. After all, the exchange will intervene between the sellers and the buyers to clear the positions with the available level of loss for the sellers to reach a compulsory settlement. From the beginning, speculative behavior for a corner has the aim of profiting through compulsory settlement without the intention of receiving the physical commodity. Therefore, in case of (B)-1 type speculation, it would be more likely to succeed with a less elastic supply. Also speculative capital would inflow into spot and the nearby delivery months as when taking a long position.

The (B)-2 type speculation for arbitrage is usually with the following behavior. (Here in this chapter, for convenience, we will consider a re-sale case.) For example, if there are six trading months from the start month to the current month, usually the speculator would have a bigger long position in the forward months, because there would be larger trading volume in forward months and it would be possible for speculative capital to flow in without any recognition. Furthermore, the aim of (B)-2 type speculation is to disturb the normal price system. This means that, when a futures market works well, the price level will become higher in the forward months. By utilizing this function, first the speculator takes a big position at the start of the trading month, and, in the next trading month, as the whole volume in the life of the contract becomes less, the concerned speculator's share at the market becomes more significant reaching the position of a power to control the market. In such cases, usually the price rise makes followers join the market which makes for more of a price rise. The situation would be advantageous for the speculators concerned here because by re-sale the speculator could take a profit from the buying position. At the same time, by the long position which the speculator has in the nearby months he could take a profit through re-sale behavior, because when the price rises at the market one month in advance, the price difference between the two consecutive months becomes more than the carrying cost, and in terms of the downward movement of trading a month in advance, would be small enough (which would be correct if the speculator concerned takes a significant share of the trading volume of the trading month), because price levels are mainly adjusted by the trading month levels concerned. This adjustment process would make the trading contract in the long position of the bull speculator profitable. As is clarified above, in the (B)-2 type speculation, by assuming enough financial capacity, the greater trading volume and the more elastic demand (which means more efficiency), the more probable is the success such speculative behavior. The speculative capital would inflow into rather deferred futures.

In the case of the (A)-1 type, as mentioned above, many commodities would be targets for this type of speculation, and in the case of the (A)-2 type, particular commodities would be targets when supply and/or demand for the particular commodities are distorted by such factors as political instability and bad harvests. Generally speaking, therefore, commodities for the (A) of type speculation would be gold, platinum, silver, copper, tin, soybean, corn, natural rubber, etc. In the case of (B) type speculation, the target commodities in (B)-1 and (B)-2 are different. Basically, it would depend upon supply possibilities.[3] That is to say, it might be said that, as far as taking profit is concerned, the appropriate target commodities for corners would be agricultural products like soybean, and for arbitrage, natural rubber and nonferrous metals.

What then are reasonable measures by the exchange against abnormal speculation (both implicit and explicit)? In the case of excessive speculation, the excessiveness would be caused by capital inflow as "a temporary abode of purchasing power".[4] Some measures, therefore, should be taken against the inflow of speculative capital. In the case of distorted speculation, when the market is distorted by a particular participant's significant share of the trading volume, it might be reasonable to regulate the speculative capital inflow of the particular participants and to promote the outflow of them to weaken their shares.

In that sense, the effective measure against the distorted speculation would be regulation of trading volume by the particular participants. (However, in the case we are concerned with in this chapter, the exchange did not have such a measure.) Also, even if it is not possible to regulate the trading volume, it might be possible for the exchange (1) to regulate against particular participants who have more trading volume than a certain volume (noticed beforehand) and (2) to take money guarantees beyond the original margin against particular participants who have significant trading volume for the additional trading volume or the newly traded volume; these are called "additional margin" and "advance margin".

The effective measure against excessive speculation and against distorted speculation which come to the front after the "latent period" might be "incidental margin" (needless to say, the above regulation would be effective against distorted speculation). The characteristics of regulation by incidental margin would be recognized as being (1) a rather arbitrary exchange and (2) applicable to whole trading participants.

To complement the explanation above, we can mention the functions of margins. Margins can have two functions. One is the function of a "mortgage", and the other is the function of a "entry barrier". Needless to say, they are closely related and it would be difficult to separate them exactly, however we could say that, when the margin drops to a rather low level, the former margin would work, and when it becomes rather higher the latter would work. From the beginning, as it could be traded for participants with a low level margin, the capital for hedging and for speculation could flow in. It would be the *raison d'être* of a futures market. In that sense the "mortgage" function could be said to be an "entry promotion" function.

In classifying the margins, we can see that the original margin and maintenance margin call are mainly with the mortgage function, and that incidental margin, additional margin and advance margin are mainly with the entry barrier function.

Theoretical Framework

We present first in this section a theoretical framework for considering speculative behavior in an abnormal sense.[5]

The conditions for a commodity futures market to accomplish risk aversion or supply information are, generally speaking: (1) to be able to neglect transaction cost; and (2) to be dominant by physical factors.[6] In other words, it could be said that: (1) there is a large amount of trading volume because of an active market; and (2) an appropriate level between speculation and hedging.[7] Therefore the basic conditions are (1) the optimal combination of safety and stability in transactions at the exchange - that is, without excess volatility - and of a large trading volume, and (2) the attainment of optimality in speculation.

In addition to the above, condition (1) reflects confidence by participants in exchange management. That is to say, participants carry out transactions with confidence in the quality and quantity of commodities provided by the exchange. Actually it is necessary for the exchange to meet the physical demand of participants by supplying necessary commodities at any time with the necessary quality and to reserve an appropriate stock by assuming a maximum limit of liquidity for the commodity concerned.[8] It might be said that the transaction is similarly to be done in the commodity reserve currency. Needless to say, the quantity corresponding to the optimum condition would request the appropriate transaction volume.

Condition (2) seems to be a situation held in the equilibrium of perfectly competitive speculation.[9] From a viewpoint of relations between speculation and hedging, the following relation of:

Net long position of speculation = Net short position of hedging[10]

could be held (or something in the neighborhood of it), in whose relations price is structurally raised by the carrying charge as a result of deferred futures.

The above relations could be expressed graphically as follows.

Figure 10.1 shows condition (1). On the horizontal axis a reserve stock A_1 is plotted. On the vertical axis is a level achieved by multiplying A_1 by the reverse of a reserve rate. The reserve rate could be interpreted as a rate of margin. On the vertical axis, the maximum limit of transaction volume (which is assumed by the exchange) would be measured traded at the exchange concerned. Needless to say, $A_1 < A_2$ would be held.

We can examine figure 10.2 the axes common to the figure 10.1 with regard to the condition (2). On the horizontal axis net short hedging needs is plotted, which is assumed to be constant year by year according to Labys' assumption (1974).[11] Thus as far as the above assumed relation of,

Net long position of speculation = Net short position of hedging

is concerned, the inflow quantity B_2 holding $B_1 = B_2$ is plotted on the vertical axis.

Based upon the above assumptions, $B_1 > A_1$ and $B_2 < A_2$ would be held, because A_2 means inflowed speculative capital is desirable for the exchange with the aim of maximizing trading volume and B_2 indicates the inflowed capital compatible with a yearly constant quantity of hedging. As in figure 10.2 the equilibrium in complete competitive speculation is assumed, decreased volume of short hedging equals to decreased volume of long

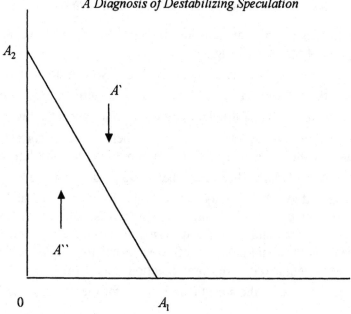

Figure 10.1 The condition (1)

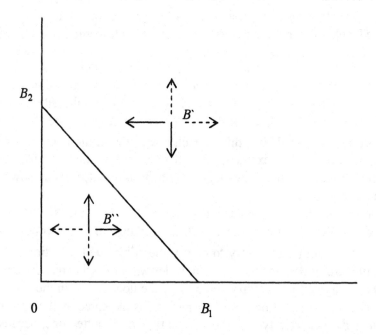

Figure 10.2 The condition (2)

speculation and the quantity of short hedging on the horizontal axis means that B_1 is a point of zero short hedging.

All the points on the A_1A_2 line of figure 10.1 satisfy condition (1) and all the points on the B_1B_2 line of figure 10.2 satisfy condition (2). As far as whether the absolute value of the slope of the A_1A_2 line equals the reverse of the rate of margin and the rate of margin is below one is correct, the absolute value of the slope of the A_1A_2 line is more than the absolute value of the slope of the B_1B_2 line. Therefore, when $B_1 > A_1$ and $B_2 < A_2$ are held, the two lines have, without fail, a unique cross point. In figures 10.3 and 10.4 this is expressed as point E. At point E the optimum situation both for the exchange and for speculators is realized. Based upon figures 10.3 and 10.4, it can be seen that the abnormality of inflowed speculative capital is shown as the area to the right and in an upward direction from A_2EB_1.

First we need to clarify the adjustment process for the exchange and for speculators.

The exchange will work to regulate the situation when it deviates from the A_1A_2 line.

When the situation is recognized to be the right side of the A_1A_2 line, A' point of figure 10.1 for example, the market has more liquidity than a reasonable level compared with reserve quantity which would show enough trading volume but would have some problems from the viewpoints of safety and stability. The exchange would thus try to reduce the capital inflow. The adjustment would be done as illustrated by the downward arrow direction from the A' point. On the contrary, when the situation is indicated as to the left of the A_1A_2 line, the A'' point of figure 10.1 for example, the market would be "thin" which means that transaction cost per actor might be high. The exchange would therefore attempt to grow the transaction volume and the adjustment would be illustrated as an upward arrow from the A'' point.

Speculators would show adjustment behavior when the situation is recognized to deviate from the B_1B_2 line. Figure 10.2 illustrates the adjustment. It would be necessary to clarify the adjustment direction if (1) it is in an upward or downward direction, or leftward or rightward direction and if (2) it is shown by the straight line or by the dotted line. In the several abnormal cases of speculation, an excessive type is indicated by the upward dotted line and a distorted type is shown as a rightward dotted line, because it could be simplified that in excessive speculation speculators would not be attached to physical transactions and that in distorted speculation for corners[12] they would always take into consideration physical transactions.

Therefore, in the case of convergence in the excessive type behavior, the adjustment done is shown by the downward straight line, and in the case of convergence in distorted type behavior, the adjustment is pointed out in the leftward straight line. In either case, in order to have the adjustment shown as a straight line, it is necessary for markets to be competitive. In the case of adjustment shown in a straight line, it could quickly reach the E point (see the mentioned below when it is a case of left and downward from the $B_1 B_2$ line).

What about the adjustment behavior indicated by the dotted line?

We first consider the case of excessive speculation which is illustrated in figure 10.3. In figure 10.3 the area (I) - (IV) is shown separated by two lines. When speculation is in area (I), it might excessive. Then the situation would become area (II). In area (II), it would be decided whether the adjustment direction should be upward or downward depending upon relations between regulation by the exchange, shown as a straight line and movement by speculators, shown as a dotted line. When speculators' ability for liquidity control is more powerful than the exchange authority's ability for liquidity control, speculation would have an excessive nature. On the contrary, the areas illustrated as (III) and (IV) are recognized as the cases of too little speculation. Namely, it would be a case in which too little attractiveness for speculation would make too little demand to meet the short hedging, and it might not be enough for risk aversion. Area (III) indicates the situation moving in that direction and area (IV) depends upon the movement direction shown as the straight line representing the effort to increase trading volume by the exchange and the dotted line indicating avoidance of the market concerned (due to too stable a price level and transaction costs which are too high, etc.).

We investigate next the case of the distorted speculation which is shown as figure 10.4. In the same way as figure 10.3, areas (I) - (IV) are expressed by the two straight lines. Areas (III) and (IV) might be in the too little speculation case, which are the same as in figure 10.3. However, in figure 10.3 it would be approached from the viewpoints of liquidity and in figure 10.4 it would be with behavior of physical sales. In areas (I) and (II), it would depend on convergence toward the E point and disturbance of relations between the exchange's control shown by the straight line and speculators' movement toward market share expansion indicated by the dotted line. If speculators' ability to control liquidity is more than the exchange's ability to control liquidity, the market situation would reach a point (near A` point) on the vertical line $A_1 A_1$` and be heavily disturbing. The point reached indicates successful corners, which would have a politically resolved final result (and not by the market mechanism).

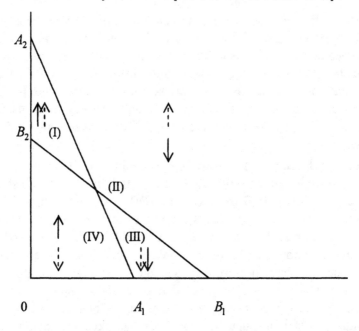

Figure 10.3   Case including the excessive speculation

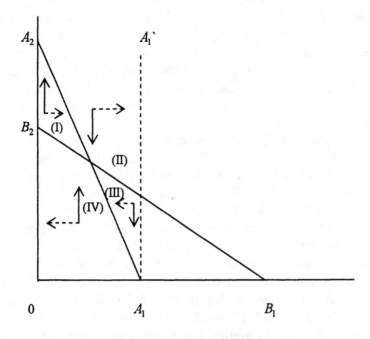

Figure 10.4   Case including the distorted speculation

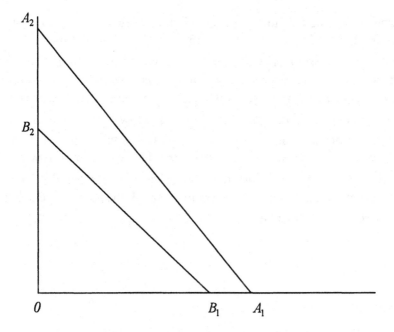

Figure 10.5 Long-term pathological case

Needless to say, abnormal situations are not only limited to the case illustrated by the A_1A_1 line. If the speculator has much more financial ability than the exchange and repeats re-sale and buy-back, the market would heavily fluctuate.

By the way, the above abnormal speculation should be seen as a "short-term" pathological phenomenon. If we mention the E equilibrium point, it would be unique, but it would be unstable.

In a commodity futures market, it could be seen as a "long-term" pathological phenomenon rather than "short-term" (that is, like corners) not even "permanent", which is presented in the figure 10.5.[13] In that case, although the ratio between short hedging and long speculation might be reasonable, the market would be too inactive for exchange management. It would be the case without equilibrium E. If this situation were permanently maintained as "normal", the necessity for commodity futures markets would be weak and there would be no *raison d'être* for commodity futures markets.

In order for the market equilibrium shown in the figure 10.5 to exist: (1) the necessity for short hedging would be increased, which makes the B_1B_2 line shift towards the right and in an upward direction; and (2) the exchange would be able to decrease the liquidity level of the market, which shows the leftward and downward shift of the A_1A_2 line. (1) above and /or (2) might be necessary. (1) is the qualified condition for commodity futures transactions in which prices are not too stable but rather fluctuate. The reason why the B_1B_2 line exists as in figure 10.5 would keep the price level stable (sometimes abnormally stable). (2) shows the point A_1 moving leftward. It indicates that, as the market is weak and the reserve stock of the exchange is decreased, when $B_1 > A_1$ there could be equilibrium. However, if the *raison d'être* of commodity futures market will be secured because of the movement of the (2) and as $0A_1$ would be small, the speculative behavior for corners is very attractive.

Case Study

Background

The case considered here is the abnormal speculative behavior which occurred from May to July 1968 in the Natural Rubber Market of Japan. As mentioned earlier, it could be said that the case is rather old, but it cannot be denied that this case had fairly interesting phenomena as will be explained below.

The Natural Rubber futures markets were established in 1952 in Japan. The direct motivation for this came from the abolition of price regulation. As a result of this, (1) there was a resolution of general trading companies closely connected with *zaibatsu* and (2) the *garapon* system was adopted and a rapid increase in importers with low financial ability was observed. However, the risk caused by the price fluctuation in international natural rubber trade was too great for the importers and a futures market was necessary to avoid the risk. After that there were a number of transitions in the market and there were several differences with the markets in New York, London, Singapore etc. which surely made the Japanese market unique. At the same time, however, domestic market prices moved by reflecting demand and supply in the international natural rubber market.

Focusing our attention upon price movement in 1968, data is presented in figures 10.6 and 10.7. Looking at several years before, 1960 to 1967 were 8 years of "low level prices" and also the six years from 1962 to 1967 showed "extremely stable movement which was extraordinary in the natural rubber history".[14] From February 1968 the prices started to rise.

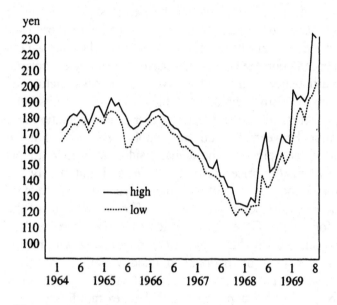

Figure 10.6 Domestic market price (R.S.S. 3, current month)

Source: Commodity exchange concerned.
* Price is per kilogram.

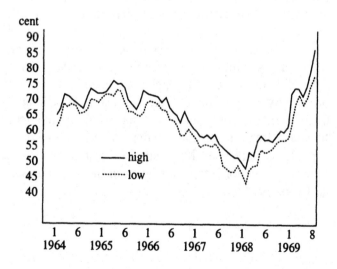

Figure 10.7 Singapore market price (R.S.S. 1, nearby)

Source: Commodity exchange concerned.
* Price is per pound.

Needless to say, price decreases were caused by excess supply and price increases came from excess demand. The basic factor of the extraordinary long-term stable (with downward trend) prices of the natural rubber excess supply market was based upon the continual release of a strategic stockpile of natural rubber (particularly by the US). As well as this basic factor was an additional one coming from synthetic rubber as a close substitute. Generally speaking, factors related to natural rubber price fluctuation are: (1) regional separation between demand and supply which would make effects independent of each other on the demand side and supply side as market disturbing factors; (2) price elasticity of demand and supply are both extremely small; and (3) as natural rubber has been a strategic commodity strategic stockpile policies have been effective in terms of the price level. They (or some of them) are observed to be more or less common for international commodities, factor (3) in particular with regard to the US was crucial for some international commodity markets. Anyway, the price stability during the period we are concerned with here was mainly caused by each country's release policy and led to extraordinary price stability.

This price stability finished on 2 February 1968 and prices started to move upwards. This upward price movement can be separated into two periods by the principal factors. The first one was from February 1968 to February 1969, when the upward price movement was due to the increase in demand because of currency fluctuation and the decrease in supply from the main producing countries. In this period the US strategic stockpile release policy for natural rubber was kept the same as the previous years, thus factors of extraordinary stability of natural rubber prices was still in effect. However, the US did not increase the stockpile release to correspond with the upward price movement. The US press release describing its policy to increase the stockpile quantity on 20 February 1968 undoubtedly contributed to the "upward" trend. In addition to the US policy, demand by socialist countries, political unrest in Malaysia and a border dispute between China and the Soviet Union, etc. contributed to the heavy upward price movement after February 1969.

The Case

1. The market trend
Based upon the background described earlier, the first half of 1968 seemed to be a turning point towards upward movement after the long period of stability and downward trends. Thus for this period the natural rubber futures market had poor demand for risk aversion and with low level stock

quantities. Also one of the fundamental factors causing upward movement during this period was shift in demand toward commodities because of currency fluctuation. In other words, (although the result was not so serious) there were symptoms of excessive speculation phenomena in the international economy.

Looking back upon this case as a person concerned, it was considered to have started with the information that a stock quantity in warehouses designated by the exchange fell significantly in the middle of May 1968 (for convenience hereinafter we refer explicitly to the year 1968). This case seems to have shown, from the phenomena, distorted (in the first half) and excessive (in the second half) speculation. The upward price movement continued for the whole month of June and even into July. The exchange actually started to regulate against corners by margin control from 1 July. The outcome of the case came about as follows. That is to say, on July 19 the speculator concerned with the corners left because of the position, even when there was an additional short position by some brokers. That made the prices in the August and September delivery months at the lowest level and the price in the July delivery month fell heavily. The speculator concerned needed around 200 million yen to be paid to cover the unrealized loss for July 19 trade and the incidental margin. Finally the speculator fell into difficulties to pay and requested that the exchange resolve the situation through negotiation. With the requests not only by the speculator concerned, but also by other trading members, the exchange effected the compulsory resolution in the July, August and September delivery months.

We can see several factors supporting the case retrospectively.

Figure 10.8 shows the movement of the contractor's price in futures transactions. It clearly indicates a rapid increase from the middle of May. Furthermore, although (because many figures are needed) it is omitted here, the figure showing all delivery months for the whole year of 1968 indicates that, from January to the middle of May, the price structure among delivery months generally moved systematically with a certain difference (of contango). It can be recognized from the figures that the market was in a situation of having no disturbing factors. From the middle of May, however, the situation drastically changed. The fluctuating situation continued in June (whole month) and in July led to the price situation in the current month becoming extremely abnormal. It is interesting to mention that at the end of 1968 currency unrest did become heavy and a workers' strike in US harbors happened. The international natural rubber market was diagnosed as in the early stage of excessive speculation, and the abnormality of July in this case was fairly different compared to several months later. What is clear from the figures is that the continuity between the current month and other delivery months was much less in July than at the end of 1968.

Figure 10.9 shows the ratio between the quantity of natural rubber import in Japan and the trading volume share to the import quantity.   It shows the

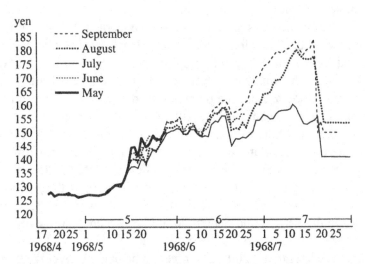

Figure 10.8 Futures market prices, April 1968-July 1968

Source: Commodity exchange concerned.

remarkable increase of trading volume from May to July.

Details of the movement are as follows.

Table 10.2 shows the price instability index. The aim of this table is to specify a particular time when we observe a rapid increase in the differential coefficient. The result clearly says that it was the middle of May, particularly from 15-20 May, when the index rapidly increased. If we estimate the normality from past data and have a strong doubt about abnormality when we observe significant deviation, it would be reasonable to conclude that the specific time that the abnormality was introduced was from 15-20 May.

Table 10.3 indicates a change of trading volume in each delivery month. The way to read the table is illustrated by the example of the July 1968 delivery month as shown in the note to table 10.3. The trading period in the Japanese natural rubber market covers six months (which is the same as in August 2001) and the trading for the July current month started in February. Therefore, February is the beginning month and July the current month, which includes the March to June delivery months. The total trading volume for these six months is the whole trading volume of the life of delivery in the July delivery month. This table therefore shows that the whole trading volume is allocated between each delivery month. The nearer to the beginning month, the bigger the uncertainty and, as there is much more time for re-sale and buy-back, the more trading volume. Therefore, the beginning month would have the biggest share and the share would then decrease the current month which would have the smallest share. For reference, the table 10.4 shows the mean value from the January delivery month of 1975 to the December delivery month of 1977 in the Tokyo Rubber Exchange (at that time) and Kobe Rubber Exchange (at that time).

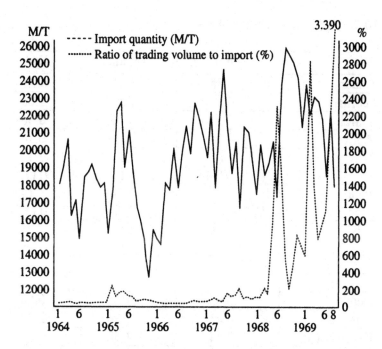

Figure 10.9 Import quantity and a ratio of trading volume to import quantity

Source: Commodity exchange concerned.
* M/T is metric ton.

It might be usual to judge normality in terms of ordinal allocation of the share number between each delivery month. If we use a criterion of normality by past data, in this case it is the previous several months' numbers starting from May 1968 (in this chapter we observed numbers from June delivery month of 1967 - which shows the beginning month of it was January 1967). The result is indicated in the table 10.3. With this table

we should say that a strong doubt on abnormality can be put on the May
delivery month but not on June delivery month. If we recognize that the
May delivery month might be abnormal, we would mention that the
September delivery month might also be said to be abnormal. However,
there could be no abnormality sign at all in the September delivery month
of 1967. To make sure (although there is not enough data and it would be
difficult to analyze exactly) assuming the percentage share of each delivery
month would take a normal distribution for June 1967-April 1968, for
September 1967, January 1968,[15] May 1968, June 1968 and July 1968 we

Table 10.2   Price instability index*

	Beginning	Middle	End
1968 January	0.38	0.74	0.77
February	0.88	0.72	1.00
March	0.59	1.17	0.36
April	0.58	0.11	0.16
May	0.44 (0.11) (0.47)	5.35 (0.99) (2.23)	2.13 (1.09) (1.16)
June	1.32 (1.57) (0.90)	2.16 (2.36) (1.76)	3.14 (0.53) (1.79)
July	1.34 (1.18) (0.34)	7.04 (1.03) (8.67)	
August **			
September**			
October	0.65	0.61	0.84
November	0.43	1.90	2.28
December	0.44	1.52	0.44

Source: Commodity Exchange data.

*   Price Instability Index means variation coefficient by 100. Price is for the current
delivery month (end of month includes that of next delivery month).
** In August and in September, price was fixed at the certain level because of this case.

investigate the probability which each delivery month could have. This is
shown in table 10.5. Needless to say, although it would be difficult to judge
scientifically from the numbers in table 10.5, it might be plausible to
estimate that June and July were abnormal and other delivery months were
normal. Anyway, as far as the change of trading volume for each trading
month is concerned, it is most probable to conclude that June was
abnormal.

Table 10.3 Percentage movement of each delivery month volume of trade (%)

	New delivery month	Fifth delivery month	Fourth delivery month	Third delivery month	Second delivery month	Current delivery month
1967						
June	24	13	12	11	20	20
July	33	14	6	9	24	14
August	27	11	15	18	15	14
September	17	11	37	8	15	12
October	18	38	8	15	13	8
November	32	16	18	20	7	7
December	33	25	20	7	11	4
1968						
January	34	26	12	13	10	5
February	29	17	16	11	10	17
March	24	20	10	14	18	14
April	25	20	14	10	20	11
May	14	15	13	24	11	23
June	8	8	15	9	34	26
July	4	5	4	27	40	20
August	5	3	12	28	52	0
September	4	19	25	52	0	0
October	28	28	34	6	2	2
November	42	37	11	2	4	4
December	56	20	4	8	7	5

Source: Commodity exchange data.

* A way of looking of this table is as follows (for example July 1998 transaction). (See table 10.6 regarding the meaning of 'lot'.)

February volume of trade (1968) (new delivery month)	981 lots,	4 %
March volume of trade (1968) (fifth delivery month)	1,328 lots,	5 %
April volume of trade (1968) (fourth delivery month)	1,013 lots,	4 %
May volume of trade (1968) (third delivery month)	7,184 lots,	27 %
June volume of trade (1968) (second delivery month)	10,361 lots,	40 %
July volume of trade (1968) (current delivery month)	5,143 lots,	20 %
Whole volume of trade (of July 1968) (life of the contract)	26,010 lots,	100 %

Table 10.4   Average percent, January 1975-December 1977 (%)

	New delivery month	Fifth delivery month	Fourth delivery month	Third delivery month	Second delivery month	Current delivery month
Tokyo Rubber Exchange	48	25	12	7	4	4
Kobe Rubber Exchange	46	26	13	7	4	4

Source: Commodity exchange data.

Table 10.5   Probability of each delivery month's share (%)

	New delivery month	Fifth delivery month	Fourth delivery month	Third delivery month	Second delivery month	Current delivery month
1967						
September	3.7	15.0	0.2	15.3	50.0	42.0
1968						
May	1.1	30.2	40.1	1.1	21.0	0.6
June	0.03	5.8	50.0	22.1	0.007	0.08
July	0.002	3.4	8.2	0.006	0.00003	3.0
Reference: January 1968	11.0	18.0	35.0	40.0	16.0	11.0

Source: Commodity exchange data.

The purpose of table 10.6 is to find the change in the market share of the speculators concerned and to find the difference between the total net position and the net position by the speculators. The former is to get the information about the market structure in the period concerned and the latter is to get information on the trading volume of the followers. What is clear from the table is that the time when market share and its growth rate increased significantly was the middle of June (latest 15 June). If the net position is accepted, the speculator concerned included lots of followers' net positions, and these net positions would be decreased in a share sense but would not be significantly decreased in an absolute sense (until the middle of July). It is useful for reference to judge the effects upon a scale of periodical margin.

Table 10.7 shows the growth rate compared with the previous month in import and stock in Japan. This table shows a rapid increase in imports and stock in July and in August 1968. It also shows that the import decisions for natural rubber related to this case might have been made at around the middle of June because it would take (at this time) 2-4 weeks for domestic supply after spot purchase in the Singapore market. Also, although we cannot specify the exact time, we can recognize the arbitrage transaction from the other domestic exchange.[16]

As was mentioned earlier, a key factor for the possibility of increasing the reserve stock would be to have a successful corner market. Needless to say, in the natural rubber case it would be possible to take and import the natural rubber from the Singapore market to make more reserve stock. Were there any indications during this abnormal speculation of international effects through imports? As far as this case is concerned, we cannot see any strong indications of it (see figures 10.6 and 10.7).

Based upon the above information, we can examine possibilities of finding the existence of abnormality at an early stage and the nature of it in the speculation market.

From the price movement, as clearly shown in figure 10.8 and table 10.2, the strongly upward price movement started in the middle of May. Needless to say, exactly speaking, even if it were reasonably expected that the price movement would deviate from past trends and the market might be recognized as abnormal, the price movement does not present enough evidence to say whether the price move was due to normal market workings (meaning due to physical demand and supply), excessive speculation, or market control.

Figure 10.9, indicating the volume of trade, tells us that the rapid increase started in May. Needless to say, however, this index points out the rapid increase of the demand side quantity related with the price movement. Even if it were a helpful sign, it is nothing more than that.

From the change of trading volume in each delivery month, from table 10.3 and table 10.5, it is plausible to judge May as normal and June as abnormal. To be sure, the change of trading volume in each delivery month (except successful speculation for arbitrage) would be effective data for finding abnormal speculation. The weak point would be: (1) full information would be available only after the whole trading volume of the life of the contract is available; (2) if the first delivery month and the fifth delivery month have rather a big amount of volume, it might be difficult to recognize abnormal action (which must have happened at the second delivery month and current delivery month); and (3) even if we could judge a doubtful delivery month with abnormality, it might not be easy to judge which month is the one the abnormality was introduced; (4) also even if we

Table 10.6   Shares of the speculator concerned

(%, lots) **

Month/Day	(B/A) × 100 (%)	A - B (lots)	Month/Day	(B/A) × 100 (%)	A - B (lots)
May / 1	7	403	July/6	47	2,039
15	9	463	8	56	1,856
June / 1	5	1,018	9	53	1,998
5	9	1,000	10	50	2,055
10	10	1,089	11	48	2,144
15	22	1,388	12	61	1,885
20	35	2,167	13	62	1,847
25	41	1,905	15	70	1,577
July / 1	38	2,115	16	75	1,332
2	40	2,119	17	77	1,214
3	46	1,985	18	77	1,272
4	44	2,056	19	77	1,252
5	49	1,925	20	77	1,287

Source: Commodity exchange data.

* A: Total net position.   B: Net position of speculator concerned.
** 1 lot is 3 tons.

could clearly recognize abnormality, it might not be easy to judge which type it is, excessive or distorted (we could not judge from the data concerned because in (A)-1 type, (A)-2 type, and (B)-1 type speculation, speculative capital would move into the spot or nearby delivery month). With reference to table 10.3 and table 10.5, what we could say is that the period in which the abnormality could be recognized should be the second delivery month of the June market and if we could recognize the abnormality at the June stage, it would be "not too late" but "not early".

When we observe the market share of the speculator concerned, it was ten per cent on 10 June, and quickly increased to be 22 per cent on 15 June. If we judge abnormality by extreme discontinuity from past trends, we could recognize the time of this to be after 10 June and at latest 15 June. However, in this way also we would not have enough of a theoretical base to combine the market share with the market control in the light of market performance. However, in the period concerned, the market did not regulate

Table 10.7   Growth rate of import and stock (% of previous month)

Year/ month	Import	Stock	Year/ month	Import	Stock	Year/ month	Import	Stock
1967			1968			1969		
1			1	- 10	2	1	12	1
2	15	- 3	2	18	- 12	2	- 8	2
3	- 20	- 2	3	- 9	- 5	3	5	1
4	21	22	4	4	- 12	4	- 1	1
5	15	13	5	7	- 10	5	- 5	1
6	- 14	- 8	6	-16	- 16	6	-16	- 10
7	- 12	- 3	7	33	16	7	21	- 8
8	11	- 1	8	13	28	8	-19	- 3
9	- 20	-10	9	- 2	18	9	44	20
10	30	1	10	- 2	- 4	10	14	13
11	- 6	- 1	11	- 3	- 1	11	- 2	18
12	- 3	- 11	12	- 12	17	12	- 15	0

Source: Commodity exchange data.

in terms of position limit and it was not possible for the exchange to remove abnormality from the market share. It could be easily imagined that, if the exchange had regulated position limit, such market share in this case had never been gained. Therefore, if there had been position limit regulation, it would have been difficult to recognize actual market share of particular participants or a particular group early and the focus of the problem might be attributed more to conspiracy than relations between market share and market power. Needless to say, from the viewpoint of economics, to regulate market control it would undoubtedly be the regulation of position limit that would be one of the most important measures (as mentioned at the beginning of this chapter with regard to the issue of listing crude oil in the Tokyo Commodity Exchange when the issue of the volume of a member's position limit became the main point). By the way, probably the most important information that data on the market share of the speculator concerned provided is that related to the dominant factor of rapid and heavy upward movement from the middle of May, which may or may not be market share. Although we do not have enough scientific criteria, we could not judge market power with a single number share. Also (omitted in this chapter) the price data for each delivery month for the whole of 1968 would reject a possibility that the concerned speculator's commitments volume was effectively concentrated. The price level of each delivery month was raised similarly. In that case the market should be understood as competitive until the middle of June. We should conclude therefore that, based upon the information about the market share of the speculator concerned, until the time when the speculator's market share reached a significant level the price upward movement would be rather similar to that which happens in excessive speculation. Needless to say, it would be another issue to ask whether the speculator concerned had the intention of corners, and the criteria do not exist to judge whether the upward price movement from the middle of May came from excessive speculation or from a normal price mechanism.

Anyway, as mentioned above, to try and judge abnormality might become a serious obstacle and the analysis mentioned above might not be enough. Therefore, to find abnormality in this kind of speculation might be said to be fairly difficult. As Hieronymus (1971) indicated, "Seemingly erroneous courses of prices often, if not usually, turn out to be quite correct when we gain the advantage of hind sight" (p.321). Actually in this case, regulations by the exchange seemed to be neither "early enough" nor "reasonably correct".

2. Regulations by the exchange

The exchange concerned took measures against the abnormal speculation when and on what? An official document announced as follows.

On 20 June, the exchange talked over the abnormal speculation upon the decision on a course of action to take incidental margins and countermeasures against the increase of trading volume (although they did not have any actual measures).

Then on 28 June, they decided to collect ten thousand yen incidental margin from the 1 July position.

In addition, on 8 July, from the 10 July position they decided on the additional collection of 20 thousand yen incidental margin (which meant 30 thousand yen incidental margin in all).

On 15 July, they decided that, from 22 July to 26 July on the July trading (26 July was the closing day for current month delivery), it was necessary for sellers to deliver commodity and for buyers to pay the total amount, and in the August trading they decided to collect 30 thousand yen incidental margin from the 19 July position.

On 19 July, as the fourth measure, they decided that additional incidental margin became 60 thousand yen from the 20 July position on the July delivery month (the total amount of incidental margin equaled 130 thousand yen), in the August delivery month became the additional incidental margin became 50 thousand yen (total 80 thousand yen), and in the September delivery month they collected 40 thousand yen incidental margin.

As mentioned earlier, at the second session of 19 July trading the speculator concerned did not participate and this started the heavy price decrease in the July delivery month transactions reaching a final negotiation of compulsory resolution in this corner market case. Needless to say, this came from the inability of the speculator to make the necessary payment (amounting to 200 million yen).

Viewpoints of the Case

We consider in this section that the case described above can be rearranged within the framework mentioned previously, and we try to provide a reasonable viewpoint on the case.

The case started, as mentioned above, when a reserve stock in the exchange fell to a very low level. Previously there had been a long period of price stability (the conditions first experienced by natural rubber). The extraordinary price stability coming from the strategic stockpile policy of each country (the US in particular) made the situation as illustrated in figure 10.5, and, as counteraction to it, the left and downward shift from the A_1A_2 line happened. The situation made (B)-1 type speculation more attractive.

In fact, it took about four weeks for the (B)-1 type speculator to gain significant market share. The upward price movement during the period should be interpreted as a feature of excessive speculation. Thus the situation happened then and it can be understood that first it started from area (I) and crossed the A_1A_2 line, and finally the action shown as a rightward dotted line became rather significant in the area indicated in figure 10.4. In July, the exchange rapidly increased the margin and, because of imports from the producing country's market, the reserve stock of the exchange increased. This meant that the right and upward shift with a decrease in the absolute value of the slope of the A_1A_2 line occurred, and that the action shown as a downward line in area (II) of figure 10.4 was started or expanded. Judged from the characteristics of the commodity concerned and taking into consideration the financial ability of the speculator concerned, for the (B)-1 speculation to succeed it undoubtedly took too long. Because of this, the line shift was reached. In that sense, this case of speculation should be interpreted as being outside the fundamental rules. As mentioned earlier, natural rubber might not be good for (B)-1 type speculation, which finally caused the big difference between A_2 and B_2 and reached a resolution by negotiation among all the members because of the speculator's inability to pay. This indicates that the action reached the point on the horizontal axis both because of regulation by the exchange and because of movement of the A_1A_2 line. The results occurred because of speculation outside fundamental rules and because of excessive adjustment (due to late timing).

We can investigate the case concerned with a more exact analysis of the nature of adjustment in a case with distorted speculation (shown in figure 10.4).

We examine the nature of resolution to the following simultaneous differential equation.

Equation (1) indicates adjustment by the exchange, and equation (2) shows movement of speculative capital by the speculator.

As figure 10.4 indicates, the speculator shows deviation from the B_1B_2 line, which means that S becomes bigger and that β is a positive constant. (If the dotted line is leftward in the area (I) and (II), and rightward in the area (III) and (IV), β is a negative constant.) When we redefine L and S to be

$$\frac{dL}{dt} = \dot{L} = \alpha(F - S - \xi L) \tag{1}$$

$$\frac{dS}{dt} = \dot{S} = \beta(L + S - M) \tag{2}$$

Where:

   L : maximum limit of liquidity judged as safe by the exchange
   S : quantity of capital inflow by net purchase speculation
   F : quantity of reserve stock by the exchange (constant)
   M : total quantity of liquidity warranted on the B_1B_2 line (constant)
   ξ : margin rate (constant, $0 < \xi < 1$)
   α : financial ability of the exchange (constant, $\alpha > 0$)
   β : financial ability of the speculator (constant, $\beta > 0, \beta < 0$)

deviation from the equlibrium, the characteristic equation is,

$$\lambda^2 + (\alpha\xi - \beta)\lambda + \alpha\beta(1 - \xi) = 0$$

as $(1 - \xi)$ is positive, in order for the real part of the characteristic root to be negative (which means that it would be converged toward the E point of figure 10.4), this is only when,

$$\frac{\alpha}{\beta} > \frac{1}{\xi}$$

If β is negative, the characteristic equation is,

$$\lambda^2 + (\alpha\xi + \beta)\lambda + \alpha\beta(\xi - 1) = 0$$

and as the discriminant is,

$$(\alpha\xi - \beta)^2 + 4\alpha\beta > 0$$

it would be understood to be converged to the E point. That is to say, in such an adjustment mechanism, if the market is competitive, it would finally be restored to the best situation for the exchange and the optimal situation for speculation.

We have further consideration of the case of positive β. As is shown above in figure 10.4, it would be the case that $\alpha\xi$ is larger than β when it could be appropriately defended against a heavily disturbed market. This clearly indicates that, when abnormal speculation is introduced, it is necessary for the financial ability of the exchange to be several times greater than the financial ability of the speculator in order to be reasonably adjusted. That "several times" means the inverse of the rate of margin. For example, if the rate of margin is ten per cent, during the period concerned the exchange has to have ten times more ability to decrease the capital from the market than the speculator(s)' ability to have capital inflow. If the ability is just ten times, the situation would not be kept stable in convergence or in disturbance. If the ability is a little less than ten times, abnormal speculation would occur and the market function would be heavily hurt.

It goes without saying that the "multiple" could be decreased by making the rate of margin increase. Making an additional collection of margins contributes this function, which means that the $\alpha\xi$ indicates a regulation ability of the exchange.

It seems to us that, once a symptom of abnormality of speculation is observed, the necessary conditions (though this depends upon subjective judgement) to successfully adjust might be fairly difficult. In addition to the above, when speculation is of the (B)-1 type, even if the exchange has much more ability (as is held of $\alpha\xi > \beta$) for liquidity management, if it is difficult for the exchange to flexibly increase the reserve stock, successful adjustment toward convergence would be impossible. This shows the market to be reached on the A_1A_1`line of figure 10.4. This means that market functions of the exchange would be stopped in reaching "a cessation of the rules of the game".[17]

The above is an interpretation of the case concerned arranged within a theoretical framework. The fundamental viewpoints to argue the case for abnormal speculation (distorted speculation for corners in particular) and to successfully and flexibly adjust for it are the following:

(1) A strict use of position limit - the prescription for "crisis problem" from Mundell (1969) mentions the application of the principle of effective market. It is about the inverse of control variables. In the case concerned here the implication would certainly not be neglected. However, when the target is speculation, first of all, the adjustment mechanism shown in figure 10.4 should be the direction indicated by the straight line converged monotonously on the E point. This indicates the importance of the market being competitive.

(2) Early and strong liquidity management - once abnormality is recognized in the market, it is necessary to take strong measures early. That must be much more able (more the inverse of rate of margin) than the speculators.

(3) Establishment of criteria to take measures for liquidity management - a concern for the measures described in (2) above is that they would have problems in the long-run. In order to supplement them, as a fundamental viewpoint it is necessary to pay attention to the timing for taking strong measure(s) early. It would be necessary therefore to establish criteria for rather abstract concepts, with reference to the A_1A_2 line and the B_1B_2 line.

Conclusion

We have examined the case described above focusing our attention upon the above three viewpoints.

With regard to (1), in the period concerned the market had no regulation of position limit. However, they could have adjusted with additional margins and advance margins. We should not ignore some problems in actual implementation, but basically we would indicate that regulations which should have been taken were not actually taken.

With regard to (2), it would be difficult to evaluate the liquidity management policies as being early and strong enough, because (a) it took more than four weeks to settle the disturbed situation after the market share of the speculator concerned reached 22 per cent and he was not to a good strategic speculator in terms of financial ability and price manipulation strategy because it took four weeks to gain a significant market share and natural rubber was selected as a speculation for corners, and (b) it was not enough effectively to significantly decrease the followers' position.

Probably the viewpoint (3) would provide the root of the above judgments. In our objective view, the main reason for disturbance came from the exchange's mistaken recognition with regard to the timing of crossing from area (I) in figure 10.3 to area (II) - in the beginning it was in figure 10.3 and later it seemed to be in figure 10.4. Namely, for the natural rubber market which had been extremely thin since its establishment, the rapid increase of trading volume since the middle of May became "the merciful rain in the drought".[18] If the speculative capital inflow was the "merciful rain" for the exchange, it could be that the situation in question occurred in area (I). As a logical possibility it would be logical to interpret the whole case concerned as having occurred in area (I). However, if it did, it could never be understood why the exchange took the measures. Also if it was, the market would be too disturbed. We should recognize therefore that there was a transition from area (I) to area (II). Based upon viewpoints (1) and (2), we could easily expect that the exchange wrongly recognized over rather a long time the situation in area (II) to be in area (I). Early and strong measure(s) should have been taken as soon as possible after the situation transited from area (I) to area (II). Also at the stage when they could recognize the market monopolization, they should have implemented a margin management policy with "entry barrier"[19] functions (that is, to prevent the internal expansion) for the particular participant.

The main problem is to establish the time when the case transited from area (I) to area (II). Examining the case concerned would suggest that the time was probably during May and at latest 15 June (if it was 15 June, the area would be in figure 10.4).

Concerning establishing the time (that is, confirming viewpoint (3)), it is desirable that, based upon the framework presented in this chapter (although it is necessary to be more exact and more real), more quantitative and more practical criteria was needed for early stage recognition. It might be thought that, in light of well arranged futures markets, the above is one of the most important investigations.

The commodity futures markets in Central Europe are still in a very early stage of development, and it would be necessary for them to have active arrangements for development and to establish appropriate measures particularly against abnormal speculation.

Notes

1 Judging abnormality in speculation has been very difficult. The purpose of this chapter is to examine any helpful tests to find it at a significantly early stage. The description of the case concerned was based upon the time when this corner case occurred. The Japanese natural rubber markets in which this case happened were the Tokyo Rubber Exchange and Kobe Rubber Exchange. Since the event in this case took place, the Tokyo Rubber Exchange was unified with the Tokyo Textile Exchange and the Tokyo Gold Exchange with the Tokyo Commodity Exchange in November 1984. Also after that Kobe Rubber Exchange was unified with Osaka Textile Exchange to be Osaka Mercantile Exchange in October 1997.

2 Hereinafter for the purposes of this chapter, we would say this case is an example of a corner. The opposite of a corner case could be described as a bang case. In either case they do not intend to make physical transaction, but to corner or bang, finally reaching a compulsory resolution through negotiation.

3 The supply possibility depends not only upon physical and biological environment, but also upon financial ability.

4 L. G. Telser and H. N. Higinbotham (1977), pp. 969-970.

5 The theoretical framework in this chapter is basically dependent upon the "crisis problem" by R. A. Mundell, which is adjusted and expanded to be applicable to the issue concerned. Needless to say, figures presented in this chapter originally came from Mundell. See R. A. Mundell (1969).

6 See M. J. Farrell (1966).

7 This statement might be rather ambiguous for practical purposes. That is to say, (1) there is not a clear definition in practical use of speculation and hedging and (2) it is not clear yet what the "appropriate level between speculation and hedging" is. Unfortunately, we have to start our argument with such ambiguous concepts.

8 By rate of reservation, we mean the amount of value.

9 This concept originally comes from J. E. Meade (1949/50).

10 Hereafter saying long speculation and short hedging means in a net sense.

11 According to Labys (1974), "Most futures markets have roughly the same hedging needs from year to year ... " (p.5). This assumption seems to be real and to be convenient of simplification.

12 We would say for convenience this case is one of distorted speculations.

13 The opposite position of figure 10.5 would not actually be possible (as shown in figure 10.A) concerning A_1A_2 and B_1B_2. Because, on the B_1B_2 line, as long speculation and short hedging exist in appropriate ratios, it would not be risky for the exchange to lose trust.

14 Mase (1978), p. 24. The description of the natural rubber market in this chapter is based upon Mase (1978) and Tokyo Rubber Exchange (1975).

15 The figure of January of 1968 is included as it is the closest figure in table 10.3 to the
    figure in table 10.4 for reference.

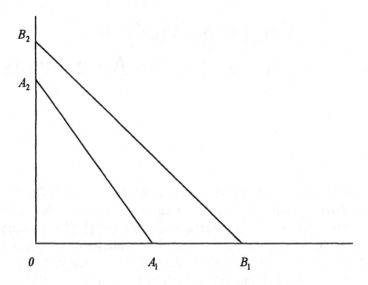

Figure 10.A   Unreal case

16 *Monthly Bulletin* (July 1968) of the other domestic exchange announced that it was
    often reported the physical transportation was as expected.
17 Mundell (1969), p.347.
18 From the report on this case of the exchange concerned.
19 That is to say, in the case concerned, from any viewpoint of (1)-(3), the regulation
    measures were not correct. Anyway, it would be reasonable to adjust to such a case
    concerned here by establishing better functioning markets not by governmental or
    inter-governmental intervention.

Chapter 11

An Economic Analysis of
International Commodity Agreements

Introduction

As shown in the previous chapters, when prices are in volatile fluctuation with speculative capital movement, measures to make the market mechanism work well are sought. According to Strange (1998), it would be rather difficult for an individual country or for an international cooperation agreement to have effective regulations. We will not investigate here in this chapter whether Strange's argument is plausible. However, it undoubtedly seems to be hard to adjust to the market response with international agreement.

In order to investigate such issues from various viewpoints, we will examine the issues of international commodity agreements and commodity futures markets in this chapter, chapter twelve and chapter thirteen. In this chapter we consider the issues and what mechanisms are researched when commodity prices are heavily fluctuating and what functions are accomplished by such mechanisms.

What we would mention first is that it would be difficult to effectively adjust (stabilize) spot market price fluctuation without depending upon quantity regulation. The author put this opinion forward first in Morita (1978), and has recognized that this argument is correct.

In this introduction, we describe the current situation of international commodity agreements.

Nihon Keizai Shimbun (27 May 1989) reported the Primary Commodity Common Fund Agreement, which came into force 19 June 1989, ten years after reaching the basic agreement at United Nations Conference on Trade and Development (UNCTAD) in May 1979. The fund concerned was to strengthen the nine international commodity agreements from the financial side. It was a 750 million US$ fund in which Japan would contribute around nine per cent (more than 60 million US$), the biggest contributor among the 103 member countries. However, *Nihon Keizai Shimbun* also reported that the US did not join.

June 1989 was a significant month as there were (partial) free elections in Poland, which were a turning point in the collapse of the socialist regime and towards the end of the Cold War. Although this primary commodity common fund agreement came into force, we had faced a crisis of international commodity agreements (*Nihon Keizai Shimbun*, 4 November 1993 - it is a matter of opinion whether or not it was a crisis). This was the situation of international relations in the 1990s. A report on the same day in *Nihon Keizai Shimbun* said that the end of the Cold War and the crisis of international commodity agreements was closely connected. That is to say, the conclusion of the International Coffee Agreement in 1963 came from the confrontation between the US and USSR (due to the Cuban Missile Crisis), the aim of which was to prevent the movement toward communism in Central and South American countries. Also the International Cocoa Agreement in 1973 was led by the USSR to expand its influence into African countries. Since the end of the Cold War, therefore, the US has never been enthusiastic about the conclusion and management of international commodity agreements. Actually the US withdrew from the International Coffee Agreement in September 1993 and has lost interest in the International Natural Rubber Agreement. If the US thinks that the financial contribution to international commodity agreements (with the aim of strategic aid) was "a waste of money" (*Nihon Keizai Shimbun*, 4 November 1993), it was quite reasonable that it did not join the primary commodity common fund agreement started in 1989.

(Apart from the strategic aim of preventing communism, etc.) it is also reasonable that international commodity agreement has never been compatible with the market mechanism. It is the same way of thinking as the Havana Charter treating the primary commodity trade as the exceptional case and planning the stabilization of primary commodity prices through regulation of the market.

It might be a rather difficult issue whether or not the financial contribution to international commodity agreements is a waste of money and what the reasons are. It is because the issue is about opportunity cost, which means that another way of using the money (the financial contribution) could get more economic welfare than in the case of international commodity agreements. Therefore the issue is closely connected with the size of financial contribution.

The environment in the 1980s and 1990s was fairly hard for international commodity agreements, of which there were nine in the 1980s and 1990s. They are the International Wheat Agreement (changed to be International Grain Agreement in 1995), International Sugar Agreement, International Natural Rubber Agreement, International Tin Agreement, International

Cocoa Agreement, International Coffee Agreement, International Jute Agreement, International Tropical Timber Agreement and International Olive Agreement. The International Tin Agreement ceased to exist in 1990 mainly because in October 1985 the International Tin Organization purchased tin stock at an extraordinarily high price, resulting in bankruptcy by exhausting the buffer stock fund (*Nihon Keizai Shimbun*, 31 October 1995). The "economic clause" aiming to stabilize price levels by buffer stock operation, export regulation, etc. was abolished in almost all international commodity agreements in the 1980s (if not abolished, then the functions were suspended), most agreements have actually become a way of organizing research and development and for collecting information. The International Jute Agreement, International Tropical Timber Agreement and International Olive Agreement have been without economic clauses from the beginning.

As mentioned above, the reason why the International Tin Agreement, which was said to be the "world's strongest cartel with an economic clause of buffer stock and export regulation" (*Nihon Keizai Shimbun*, 31 October 1995) ceased to exist was after all due to exhausting the buffer stock fund and this was because of purchasing stock with an extraordinarily high price. In other words (from the viewpoint of market level) it came from the establishment of an unreasonable price range.

The reason why the International Natural Rubber Agreement, which was said to be one of "the few commodity agreements with a workable economic clause" (*Nihon Keizai Shimbun*, 29 October 1986) was abolished basically the same. Directly it was mainly caused by a price fall because of strong selling behavior resulting from the Asian currency crisis. However a more correct interpretation is that several years ago, Thailand and Malaysia were very dissatisfied with the price range level and buffer stock operation, and the countries intended to have a cartel forward from a producers' association to support the price level. Actually at the stage of negotiation for the 1995 agreement (and started in the work February 1997), there were lots of problems (mainly at the level of price range) and we had varying information on the withdrawal of the main producing countries, Thailand and Malaysia, and on the exhaustion of the buffer stock fund and the floor price level negotiation. The situation with regard to the International Tin Agreement was about the same. The main producing countries like Thailand and Malaysia aimed to have a price stabilized at a high level through the monopolizing behavior of a producing countries association, not through an international commodity agreement which was not effective enough.

As far as the International Natural Rubber Agreement is concerned,

Japan's proposal, submitted for modification, seemed to be interesting. It included: (1) modification of markets for calculating the criteria of index price; (2) shortening the payment period for fund contribution of market intervention from 60 days; and (3) possibility for futures market intervention not only for spot market intervention, the purpose of which was to have practical management of buffer stock operation (*Nihon Keizai Shimbun*, 10 October 1992). In the 1995 agreement, one of the characteristics was to allow buffer stock managers to have futures market contracts. (The modification approving futures market contracts was extremely interesting as there were intentions common with the investigations in this book. Unfortunately, however, it must be said that the International Natural Rubber Agreement concerned here did not fundamentally have features of utilizing the market mechanism. As was mentioned, it must be said that the main aim of agreement negotiation was to support the floor price through the cartel behavior of a producing countries association.)

In the 1980s and 1990s, the tin and natural rubber agreements were abolished by exhaustion of the buffer stock operation fund, and the economic clause were deleted from the grain, sugar, cocoa, coffee, jute, tropical timber and olive agreements, or these agreements did not have an economic clause from the start. The main purpose of the agreements is to enable research and development and to collect information. The International Sugar Agreement indicates a purpose to provide a framework for negotiating a new agreement, with an economic clause, in the future.

However, in the sense of an international commodity market, countries producing tin and natural rubber whose international commodity agreements abolished their functions for price stabilization would have a new opportunity to establish a producers' cartel (although it might be difficult to succeed as OPEC could), which should be paid attention.

As has been mentioned briefly, in the circumstances, there could be several arguments concerning international commodity agreements. The standard argument is to ask if price stabilization is feasible and to ask if (when the price stabilization is achieved) economic welfare could be increased with the attempt. Also it is a standard discussion to investigate concrete measures when an international commodity agreement is actually managed.

In this chapter, in view of the above circumstances and as a basis for the following chapters, we try to analyze the schemes of management with as simple tools as possible and with as continuous a spectrum as possible. In order to do this, we focus our attention on the International Wheat Agreement (as we are able to study the multilateral contract scheme, currently it has been changed to the International Grain Agreement - hereinafter we would call it International Wheat Agreement). We will investigate the following questions here in this chapter: (1) we pay attention to a particularly appropriate period of a particular international commodity agreement for our purpose (even if it is rather old); and (2) try to establish a criterion to be employed for the particular scheme for stabilization.[1,2]

In this chapter, we first have an overview on the types of agreement, mention analytical tools to be employed, and investigate how the types are organized using the analytical tools. Then we have a brief look at the short history of the International Wheat Agreement, and finally try to interpret the short history of it, within the framework studied in the first section.

Theory

Schemes of International Commodity Agreements

Needless to say, the international commodity agreement is an international arrangement to achieve price and income stability on primary commodities, which has various schemes. The schemes are usually classified as the following three types; (1) multilateral contracts, (2) buffer stocks, and (3) export regulation.[3]

These three schemes can be summarized as follows.

For each scheme, the board of directors first establishes the ceiling price and the floor price. When a difference between market price and price range happened, each scheme starts to work. The scheme in which the difference disappears by buffer stock operation is called the buffer stock scheme, and the scheme in which the difference is eliminated by export quantity (or production quantity) regulation is called the export regulation scheme.[4] In the multilateral contract scheme, they first decide a portion of guaranteed quantity of the whole transaction quantity[5] and concerning the quantity the price difference could be absorbed by either party, the importers or exporters. When a market price is above the ceiling price, the difference would be adjusted and absorbed by the export countries. On the contrary when a market price is below the floor price, the adjustment difference would be absorbed by the import countries. The former could be interpreted as an excise tax imposed on export countries and the latter could be thought as an excise tax imposed on import countries. Needless to say, the portion from the guaranteed quantity could be traded at the market without regulation.

Analytical Tools

There are two analytical tools used in this chapter as follows.

One is coming from Becker (1971)[6] whose idea is that an economy with a price range could be arranged as the economy imposed a discontinuous excise tax.[7]

This means that, when a transaction is done within the price range, it has zero excise tax, however a transaction outside the price range would lead to an imposed excise tax as a penalty. Thus, if no member violates the regulation, the price is stable. In this case, as the motivation to violate the ceiling price regulation is on the sales side and to violate the floor price regulation is on the purchase side, the penalty should be imposed on sellers in the former case and on buyers in the latter case to be effective.

Figures 11.1 and 11.2 show the ceiling price case. Assuming the ceiling price is set up to be p_c . Figure 11.1 indicates the case in which the excise tax rate is t and producers would increase the quantity even by paying the tax. Then E is the equilibrium at which supply meets demand. However, in comparison with the competitive equilibrium E , the quantity would be decreased from q^* to q , the price for producers would fall from p^* to p_s and the price for consumers would rise from p^* to p_d . The area shown $q \times (p_d - p_s)$ would be paid to the regulation authority as excise tax, which is the excise tax imposed on producers.[8] Figure 11.2 shows the case in which producers would not violate the regulation as the penalty becomes greater. In that case, at the price p_c excess demand $(q_d - q_s)$ exists, which should be adjusted through some measures. It is clear from the two figures that if $t \leq t^*$, this is indicated in figure 11.1, and if $t > t^*$, this is shown in figure 11.2.

On the contrary, figures 11.3 and 11.4 illustrate the case of a floor price. Assuming the floor price is set up, the level is p_f . Figure 11.3 shows the case of $t \leq t^*$ in which the excise tax rate is t and consumers would increase the consumption quantity even by paying the tax. Then the demand meets the supply at the equilibrium E . Compared with the competitive equilibrium E , however, the quantity would fall from q^* to q , the price for producers would decrease from p^* to p_s , and the price for consumers would rise from p^* to p_d . The area indicated as $q \times (p_d - p_s)$ would be paid to the regulation authority as excise tax imposed on consumers.[9] Figure 11.4 points out a case of $t > t^*$, in which the rate of excise tax is raised and consumers would not violate the regulation as the penalty becomes greater.

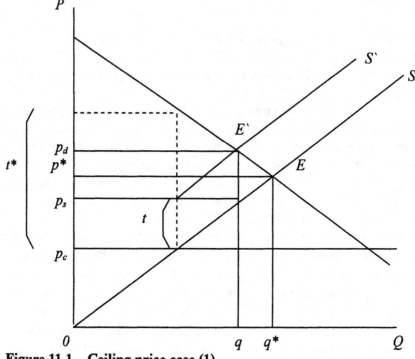

Figure 11.1   Ceiling price case (1)

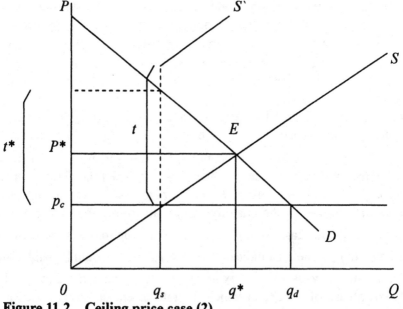

Figure 11.2   Ceiling price case (2)

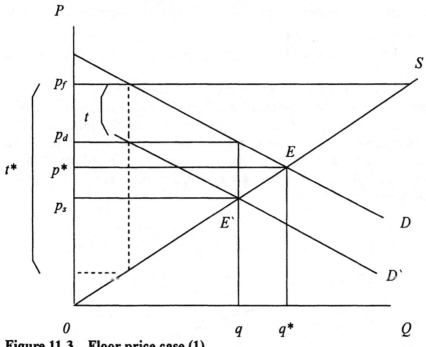

Figure 11.3   Floor price case (1)

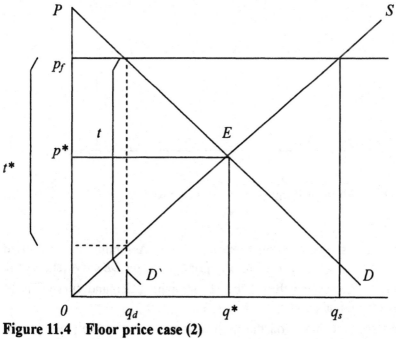

Figure 11.4   Floor price case (2)

Therefore, at the price level p_f there would be excess supply which should be adjusted through some measures.

   Another analytical tool useful for this chapter is the all or nothing demand curve.[10]

   As is well known, a demand curve is usually shown as a "continuous locus" expressing the combination of goods purchased to maximize a consumer's utility corresponding to the change of relative price ratio. The all or nothing demand curve is not like the usual demand curve, and it would be expressed as a case in which consumers are forced to buy "all" or "nothing". In the most extreme case of this, consumers have to transfer all their surplus[11] to producers.

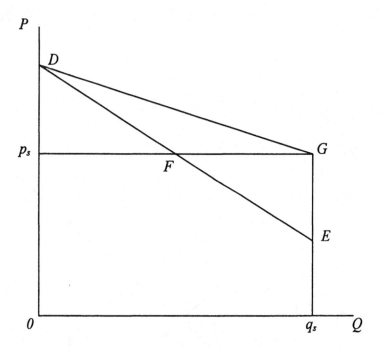

Figure 11.5   All or nothing demand curve case

   Figure 11.5 shows the most extreme case. Assuming the proposed quantity from the seller is q_s, and the price is p_s, the DE curve shows the usual demand curve and the DG the all or nothing demand curve. The F would be the middle point of the line $p_s G$.

   If a consumer behaves on the usual demand curve at the price p_s, the demand quantity would be $p_s F$ which means the consumer surplus equals the area of the triangle Dp_sF. In this case, however, when a consumer faces the extreme situation of an all or nothing demand curve, the consumer has to select either all the quantity q_s or nothing (the G or the origin in figure 11.5). When the origin is selected which means nothing is bought, it shows a zero consumer surplus. Also in the extreme case shown as figure 11.5, even when the consumer selects G, the consumer surplus would be also zero.[12] In figure 11.5, the area above the usual demand curve (portion of consumer surplus which is shown in the area of the triangle Dp_sF) equals the area below the price level (portion transferred to producer which is shown in the area of the triangle GFE). The DG line shows the most extreme case of an all or nothing demand curve and usually an all or nothing demand curve would exist between DE line and DG line.

Needless to say, the reason why consumers have this kind of demand curve is because of significant monopolization by producers.

A Theory of International Commodity Agreement

Based upon the analytical tools examined above, in this section we will present a theoretical framework by which three schemes of international commodity agreement could be arranged as continuously as possible. Taking into consideration the following applied work, we will study a case of protecting the floor price.

We can consider first here what the conditions would be for a multilateral contract scheme to be employed.

As examined in the previous section, this scheme would best utilize a market mechanism, which means that employing market workings has less inconvenient. The inconvenience assumed in this chapter is a phenomenon of price instability. Setting up a price range indicates planning to stabilize price levels, as price instability seems to have some inconvenience.[13]

For example, assume the price movements shown in figures 11.6 and 11.7 are observed in wheat and cocoa. We plot time on the horizontal axis and price level on the vertical axis in which p_c is the price range ceiling and p_f the price range floor. Needless to say, the two figures have a common scale. According to the observation assumed in the figures, the wheat market price would be at most w above the ceiling price and at most w below the floor price. Also the cocoa market price would be at most c above the ceiling price and at most c below the floor price. The question we will investigate is how the price could be stabilized as quickly as possible. First we can approach the question with a multilateral contract scheme.

When a multilateral contract scheme is employed this indicates that

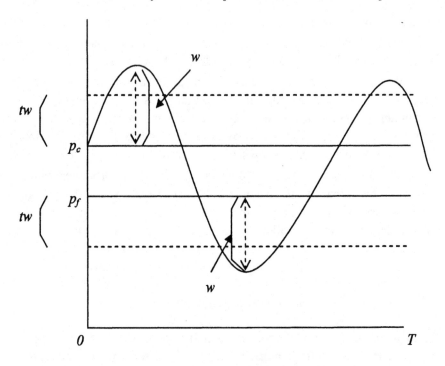

Figure 11.6   Price movement of wheat (supposition)

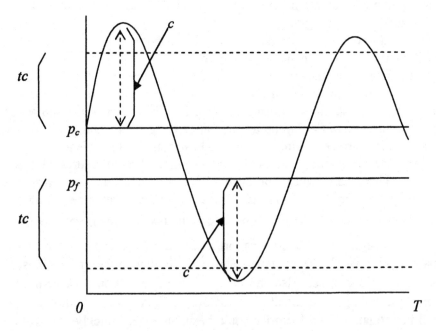

Figure 11.7   Price movement of cocoa (supposition)

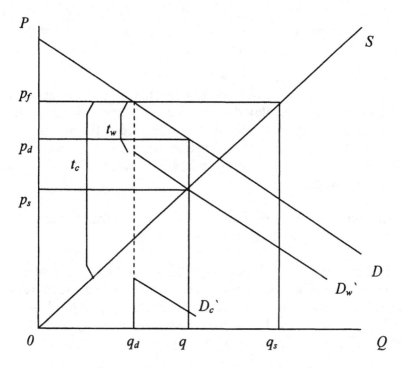

Figure 11.8   Case for the multilateral contract scheme

when there could be a difference between the market price and price range and the market mechanism can be utilized if the penalty is paid. The purpose of imposing a penalty is to have price stability. The more there is a deviation tendency of market price from the price range, the more it is necessary to impose a greater penalty. The multilateral contract scheme therefore shows that the penalty might be less if necessary. As the penalty indicates the market price instability, the case in which a multilateral contract scheme could be employed tells us when market instability is relatively less.

Applying this way of thinking to the assumed case of wheat and cocoa, it would be necessary for the rate of excise tax for wheat and cocoa to be near the rate of w for wheat (t_w for example) and of c for cocoa (t_c for example). As the wheat price is relatively more stable, the penalty is less, but as the cocoa price is relatively less stable, the penalty is greater. For example, we would assume both the wheat market and cocoa market being as in figure 11.8, where there is excess supply of $(q_s - q_d)$ at the floor price p_f. Then in the wheat market, consumers would pay tax amounting to

$q \times (p_d - p_s) = q \times t_w$ to have transactions of q quantity. In the cocoa market, however, consumers would not violate the regulation because of the higher rate of excise tax t_c and they have transactions of q_d quantity at p_f price. The excess supply of $(q_s - q_d)$ could not be adjusted.

Therefore, with such a framework, we could have a result saying that the wheat market could employ the multilateral contract scheme but that the cocoa market could not employ it. The difference of the results is coming from the difference of rates of excise tax,[14] which is caused by the difference of stability of market prices. We could, therefore, have the following criterion:

> Criterion (I): The condition to employ a multilateral contract is the relative stability of the market price concerned.

In other words, the criterion for a multilateral contract scheme to be employed (as opposed to a buffer stock scheme or an export regulation scheme) is the relative stability of the market price. Needless to say, stability here means the low rate of excise tax which says that the market price would not heavily deviate from the price range.

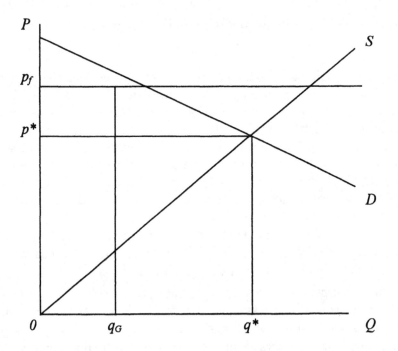

Figure 11.9 Excise tax amount

In order to make clear the relationship with the following analyses, we can discuss further the relationship between the mechanism of a multilateral contract scheme and the discontinuous excise tax rate.

The mechanism of a multilateral contract scheme, it is intuitively illustrated in figure 11.9. It shows that the floor price is p_f, the guaranteed quantity is q_G, the equilibrium price of the market is p^* and the equilibrium quantity of the market is q^*. Then, concerning the guaranteed quantity q_G, though the market price is equilibrated to be p^*, importing countries have an obligation to import the quantity at the floor price p_f, which means that the importing countries impose the excise tax amounting to the area $q_G \times (p_f - p^*)$.

However, figure 11.9 seems not to tell the correct story. According to Tyszynski (1949), "... the volume of the wheat trade may be lower than in a free market, ...".[15] That is to say, because of the excise tax, the trade quantity might be lower than q^*. We would call the quantity q, which is $q < q^*$. The price level which importing countries would pay might be higher than p^* and lower than p_f, which we call p_d. It indicates the price levels as $p^* < p_d < p_f$. The practical value of the tax to be actually paid means that the amount of excise tax is divided by quantity of trade. Therefore, the amount of excise tax $q_G \times (p_f - p^*)$[16] is thought to be,

$$q \times \frac{q_G \times (p_f - p^*)}{q}$$

The criterion of employing a multilateral contract scheme is heavily dependent upon the rate of excise tax t which is,

$$t = \frac{q_G \times (p_f - p^*)}{q}$$

(We will use the t equation later.)

The next question is how the excess supply $(q_s - q_d)$ will be adjusted. Roughly speaking, the measures to adjust the $(q_s - q_d)$ are either (1) with market[17] or (2) without market.[18] When it is (1), it is necessary to have some mechanism of absorbing $(q_s - q_d)$. When it is (2), it is necessary for producers to hold the stock of $(q_s - q_d)$ to eliminate the supply quantity. It is adjusted by demand in (1) and by supply in (2). Neither measure uses the function of prices.

As we are using the terms in this chapter, (1) includes the buffer stock scheme and (2) includes the export regulation scheme.

Then what are the criteria for using (1) and (2)?

Finding the answer to this question is a little more complex than having a criterion to use a multilateral contract scheme. First it has to confirm the following. For the export regulation scheme is it necessary to distinguish between positive export regulation and passive export regulation? Here in this chapter we investigate the passive case. It would be easier to imagine that an example of positive export regulation is OPEC (Organization of Petroleum Exporting Countries) and an example of passive export regulation is CIPEC (Consejo Intergubernamental de Paises Exportadores de Cobre - Intergovernmental Council of Copper Exporting Countries). This means that the OPEC case has no need of an international institution for stabilization. It could be approximately correct to say that there is a unique correspondence of quantity and price similar to a simple monopoly market, and it is not necessary to establish a price range by international cooperation. In the CIPEC case, however, even if they wanted to conclude an international commodity agreement with a price stabilization fund and to plan to stabilize prices through buffer stock operation, they could not accomplish it.

As the aim of this chapter is to examine how an international commodity agreement could be effective through intergovenmental cooperation, excluded commodities are not a target of the analysis here in this chapter. The export regulation scheme considered here is a passive export regulation scheme. The excess supply $(q_s - q_d)$ would be adjusted by a buffer stock operation if possible, and if impossible then the adjustment would be accomplished by export regulation.

What is a criterion for employing a buffer stock scheme? This could be presented in several ways, but we will present it here the following two ways.

The first is that it could be up to the limit when a transaction of quantity q_s is possible with the floor price p_f. In other words from a theoretical perspective, it would be when an all or nothing demand curve could exist, which is shown in figure 11.10. In order to adjust the excess supply $(q_s - q_d)$ which the market faces, the authority would join as a buyer. The situation for the demand side, including the authority, would be the same as consumers when they are offered a certain quantity with the price p_f. The buyers including the authority face (all or nothing type) demand curve shown as Dd. As was seen earlier, this type of demand curve could be assumed until when $p_fF = Fd'(p_fF + Fd' = 0q_h)$ could exist. The curve Dd'' shown in figure 11.10 could not exist. Therefore, if a supply quantity with the price p_f is more than q_h, the demand curve would disappear.

According to such a framework, the criterion to employ a buffer stock scheme is that excess supply $(q_s - q_d)$ would not be more than the quantity q_d which is a quantity of free market transaction. Therefore, we could say:

> Criterion (II): It would be possible to employ the buffer stock scheme whose burden is imposed more to consuming countries only when the market is significantly monopolized and the excess supply quantity is not more than the demand quantity presented at the floor price.

As is clear from criterion (II), taking into consideration the all or nothing demand curve means taking into consideration consumers' surplus. Therefore, the criterion would assume consuming countries would pay the major part of the buffer stock management cost.

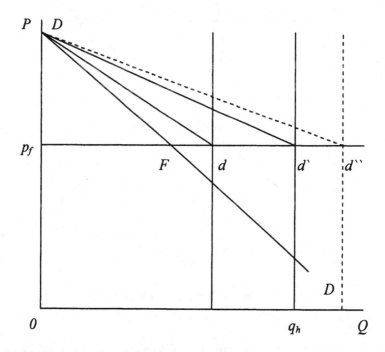

Figure 11.10   Case for the buffer stock scheme (1)

It is necessary thus to examine another criterion in which producing countries cover more of the share of the buffer stock fund.

To consider this case it would be necessary to deduct the cost of the buffer fund from the producing countries' profit, even if it is successful in protecting the floor price. Dividing the cost of the buffer fund by transaction quantity gives a unit cost which should be deducted from a unit profit. Therefore, for producing countries the unit profit would mean not the floor price but deducting the floor price from the unit cost for buffer stock operation (which is the actual floor price). As examined, with the all or nothing demand curve, the triangular area above the usual demand curve should be transferred from consuming countries to producing countries which is a benefit for producing countries.

Figure 11.11 illustrates the above situation as follows.

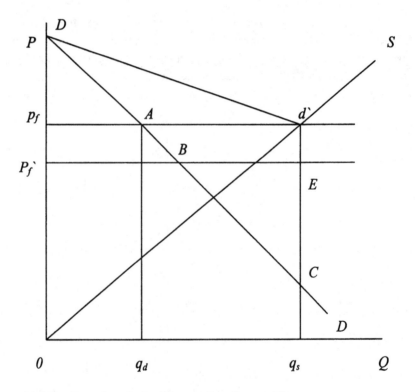

Figure 11.11   Case for the buffer stock scheme (2)

The floor price p_f would actually fall to $p_f{}^\grave{}$ due to a necessary unit cost $\left(p_f - p_f{}^\grave{}\right)$. Therefore, the necessary cost imposed on producing countries is shown to be $q_s \times (p_f - p_f')$ - the area of a rectangle $p_f p_f' Ed'$. The benefit for producing countries is indicated as the area of triangle ACd' by a transaction of quantity q_s with the floor price p_f.

Therefore, it could be argued that the buffer stock scheme sharing the major burden of producing countries would be employed when the area $ACd' \geq$ the area $p_f p_f' Ed'$, and would be abandoned when the area ACd' < the area $p_f p_f' Ed'$ (then the export regulation scheme would be employed). If the floor price p_f and the supply quantity q_s are already established, it depends upon the potential price level of p_f' whether or not the above mentioned condition is satisfied. Therefore, we could say the following criterion applies:

> Criterion (III): The buffer stock scheme sharing the major burden of producing countries would be employed only when a unit cost for stock is relatively small.

The reason why the buffer stock operation is not widely available is mainly due to criterion (III).[19]

Application

International Commodity Agreement Events

In the previous section, we examined some criteria for employing international commodity agreement price stabilization schemes. In this section, we will study the case of the International Wheat Agreement until the beginning of the 1960s. (The reason why we choose the International Wheat Agreement at this time is that it had a multilateral contract scheme, which is interesting for our research.)

First we follow the historical events of the International Wheat Agreement.

1. International Wheat Agreement in 1947-48

A remarkable feature of this period was the excess demand just after the Second World War. Both market price increase and stock decrease of export countries were easily recognized (see figures 11.12 and 11.13).

Such an environment in the international wheat market, however, did not cause adjustment behavior in export countries. It was only the US (until 1954) where a high level international price caused a domestic price rise that resulted in the increase of the cultivating area. In Argentina, the government utilized the wheat export earnings in an industrialization policy and did not utilize the domestic wheat environment. In Canada and Australia, the governments pooled the wheat export earnings and controlled the domestic price. The background of the Canadian and Australian government policy to separate the domestic market from the international market was based upon the "surplus complex" which was coming from the hard experience against the excess supply policy before the Second World War and was coming from deep-rooted excess supply anxiety.

Faced with an international wheat market in which present excess demand and anxiety about future excess supply co-existed, the first conference to make an International Wheat Agreement after the Second World War was held in London from 18 March to 23 April 1947. For this conference, the preparatory committee of the International Wheat board of directors submitted two drafts of the agreement. The first draft included export and production regulation, which was abandoned mainly by Argentine opposition. The second draft included the multilateral contract scheme which characterized the International Wheat Agreement. However, at that time this draft was abandoned because of UK opposition, main complaint of which was the very high ceiling price level.

Then, from 28 January to 6 March 1948, the second International Wheat conference after the Second World War was held in Washington DC, which came to a successful conclusion because they reached an agreement for establishing the International Wheat Agreement. The main reason for this was that, although the price range of the draft was US$ 2.00-1.50,[20] the average monthly price was US$ 3.28 (at the highest level in November and December 1947) and even the lowest level was US$ 2.75 (in February 1948). (However, because the US was in the opposite position, the draft was abandoned again. This was caused by the US persistence in claiming that the agreement hindered free trade.)

The agreement established through a series of negotiations for the International Wheat Agreement was a fundamental policy which was necessary: (1) to utilize free trade as much as possible; (2) to approve free domestic policy of each member country by excluding quantity regulation, as some agreements before the Second World War had; (3) to avoid measures to impose a big financial burden on each member country through the stock as existed just after the Second World War. In taking into consideration the above situations, introducing a multilateral contract scheme was appropriate.[21]

2. International Wheat Agreement in 1949

The international Wheat conference was held in Washington DC, from 26 January to 23 March 1949, and the first International Wheat Agreement since the Second World War was established.

This was the period when the excess demand after the Second World War became eliminated and a sign of excess supply was recognized (see figures 11.12 and 11.13). Thus market price was in a downward tendency and fell below US$ 2.00.

Also figure 11.12 clearly shows that, although quantities of domestic stock in Canada, Australia and Argentina were unchanged or a little decreased, only the US had increased the quantity of wheat stock. The above difference seemed to be caused by the difference in domestic agricultural policy. As far as the stock quantity was concerned, the US policy realized the excess supply anxiety.

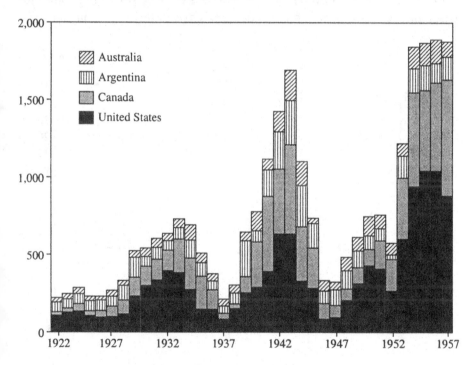

Figure 11.12   Wheat carryovers of four major exporters, July 1923-July 1957 (million bushels)

Source: Farnsworth (1958) p.5.

The International Wheat Agreement was not, however, concluded smoothly. Argentina refused to join as they said the ceiling price (US$ 1.80) was too low, and the USSR (which was an export country then) also refused to join as the guaranteed quantity was too small.

To be sure, as is clear in figure 11.13, market price was above the ceiling price. This was the characteristic of the 1949 International Wheat Agreement. According to Chiba (1966): (1) Farnsworth thought that it was a puzzle why export countries agreed to establish an International Wheat Agreement with such a low price range; (2) there was more than US$ 0.7 billion to be transferred from export countries to import countries during the 1949 Agreement (1949-53).[22] However, it should be indicated that in actual management of the agreement export countries had several regulations, which were, for example, as follows.[23]

(1) There was the differential problem[24] which was still ambiguous and wheat prices traded were left to negotiation between sellers and buyers.

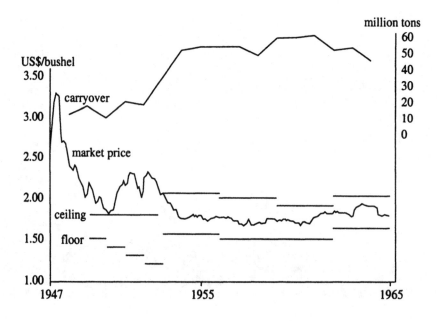

Figure 11.13   Movement of price and exporters carryovers

Source: Chiba (1966) p.35.
* Market price is Manitoba Northern 1 (delivered at the warehouse in Fort William/Port Arthur).

(2) There was no definite rule upon the cost of stock management. Therefore, in 1951, Canada unilaterally declared without any discussion with the import countries that about six cents stock cost should be added to the export price, and as the US and Australia immediately followed suit, actually around a six cents price rise was realized, which meant a three-four per cent price rise based on the price range.

(3) As a result of exchange rate adjustment by each country in September 1949, the price range fixed by the International Wheat Agreement had the same effect actually as a 35-40 per cent increase.[25]

(4) Export countries satisfied the guaranteed quantity restricted by the ceiling price with low grade quality wheat, and high grade quality wheat was left to free market transaction because there was no restriction in the agreement.[26]

3. International Wheat Agreement in 1953
International Wheat conferences were held twice; (i) from 17 April to 10 May 1952, and (ii) from 2 February to 13 April 1953.

Figures 11.12 and 11.13 points out that just at the period concerned the built-in chronic excess supply mechanism finished. Probable reasons for this were: (1) increase of area for cultivation, and/or (2) increase of average quantity of harvest. Table 11.1 showed that, although almost no change in the area of cultivation was observed as the world figures for 1948-52 and 1952-57 indicated (from 249 million acres to 250 million acres - a 0.4 per cent increase), average quantity of harvest showed a remarkable increase (from 15.5 bushels per acre to 15.7 bushels per acre - a 13.6 per cent increase). Undoubtedly this was due to the increase of the average harvest quantity. Furthermore this increase seemed to be the effective result of a remarkable technology innovation.[27] As Farnsworth (1958) indicated, the progress was undoubtedly strengthened by government policy.[28] The biggest contribution to the innovation came from the US.[29]

Then how did the US try to adjust the excess supply? As mentioned earlier, the International Wheat Agreement employed a multilateral contract scheme and respected each country's independence of domestic policy. Based upon this independence, the US started the wheat special trade (which meant the transaction by low prices was not restricted by the price range of International Wheat Agreement and also, in particular, transactions in local currency (not in transferable currency) under the terms of the Mutual Security Act (the so-called MSA Amendment 550) of 8 August 1953. This was followed by Amendment 402 of 1954 and by PL 480 of 1954 (the share of developing countries in the world wheat trade was around 40 per cent during 1954-65 - before then it was about 20 per cent -

most of which was coming from imports under special trade).

By the way, at the International Wheat Conference the main issue was how much the price range was raised. It was quite reasonable when we look at the level of price range in the 1949 agreement and of market price shown in figure 11.13. However, when taking into consideration the rapid increase of stock and rapid decrease of market price, the proposal of the export countries seems to be rather high. The US proposal was US$ 2.50-US$ 1.90 and the proposal by Canada and Australia was US$ 2.25-US$ 1.75 (the proposal by import countries was US$ 1.95-US$ 1.55 and finally the price range was determined as US$ 2.05-US$ 1.55, excepting the stock cost). Besides, because after the price range was determined and the new agreement was established the market price did go down, it was suspected that export countries had engaged in price supporting cooperative behavior.[30]

These were the events in this period. There was, however, serious counteraction. The UK refused the price of more than US$ 2.00 accompanied with a decrease in the guaranteed quantity from 15.8 million tons to 10.7 million tons (a 32 per cent decease).

Therefore, these events were understood as: (1) the beginning of US special trade; (2) a radical decrease in guaranteed quantity accompanied with UK non-participation; and (3) the existence of non-member countries like the USSR made the *raison d'être* of the International Wheat Agreement more meaningless.

Table 11.1   Wheat supplies, acreage, and yield per acre in the non-Soviet "world", specified period 1922-57

	Production (million bushels)	Wheat acreage (in millions)	Yield (bushels per acre)
1922-28	3,132	219	14.3
28-34	3,431	242	14.2
34-38	3,188	252	12.7
38-40	3,848	251	15.3
1945-48	3,455	237	14.6
48-52	3,856	249	15.5
52-57	4,408	250	17.6

Source: Farnsworth (1958) p.6.

4. International Wheat Agreement in 1956

In the above environment, there were three conferences to renew the agreement: from 26 October to 16 November 1955, from 20 February to 28 March 1956, and from 16 April to 25 April 1956.

The international wheat market was along the lines of the 1953 agreement, which had no significant change in major member countries. This meant that the main remaining issues of the 1953 agreement were taken over, and the International Wheat Agreement was described as being in a crisis of collapse. It was said that, if Germany and Japan had decreased the guaranteed quantity (whose total was 2.5 million tons), the International Wheat Agreement could never have existed.[31] The guaranteed quantity was greatly decreased from 10.7 million tons in the 1953 agreement to 8.24 million tons, which was 23 per cent less (48 per cent less than the quantity of the 1949 agreement). The price range came to be US$ 2.00-US$ 1.50, which indicated five cents up both from the ceiling and floor level.

This would have the following two consequences.

First, for import countries, the sales obligation of export countries because of the agreement restriction became less meaningful because of the significant quantity of wheat stock in export countries, supply from non-member countries like the USSR, supply from US special trade and domestic production and domestic stock. Second, it could be interpreted that the export countries' attitude in negotiation with import countries was that even if it were possible to accept the decrease in guaranteed quantity, it was not be possible to accept a decrease of price range.

More explanation is necessary for the above two points. As noted earlier, the US tried to adjust the excess supply quantity by PL 480, and also caused the UK not to participate because of proposing an unrealistically high price range. Moreover the special trade quantity increased year by year. It could be said that the International Wheat Agreement was in a crisis of collapse due to the major export member country, the US. In other words, it was suggested that the US was urgently adjusting the excess supply and the multilateral contract scheme in the International Wheat Agreement and it could not satisfy the US needs. Canada seemed to wish to ensure a reasonable level of price[32] for producers. From the start, wheat production in Canada was more uncertain than in the US because of the geographical and meteorological condition, and Canada was more stability oriented than the US (for the same reason that Canada was quite positive toward a bilateral long-term trade agreement). In that sense, it could be said that there were reasons for Canada to strongly request reasonable prices which were characteristic features for primary commodity issues. We could insist, therefore, that the combination of a US request to eliminate excess supply and a positive Canadian request to establish a stable price range contributed to the 1956 agreement and the events that followed.[33]

We could also say that it would be extremely difficult for the International Wheat Agreement with a guaranteed quantity formula to work appropriately both to satisfy the intention of export countries to eliminate excess supply and to give an incentive to import countries (most of which lost the incentive to participate) through a multilateral contract scheme.

5. International Wheat Agreement in 1959

In order for the International Wheat Agreement to exist, it was necessary for it to deal well with: (1) the US, which might cause a crisis for the agreement through domestic policy and special trade; (2) the UK, which contributed to the rapid decrease in guaranteed quantity by refusing to participate; and (3) the USSR, which worked as a non-member export country. It was possible therefore for the International Wheat Agreement to overcome the crisis of collapse if it could apply a limit to the US policy and could make both the UK and USSR participate. In other words, it was possible for the International Wheat Agreement to continue to exist by (1) eliminating excess supply, and (2) stabilizing the price range.

The measure to overcome the crisis was the change to the obligation ratio formula. As a result of the International Wheat Conferences held from 28 October to 6 November 1958 and from 26 January to 10 March 1959, the obligation ratio formula was employed in place of the guaranteed quantity formula. Canada mainly contributed to employing the new formula.

What was the obligation ratio formula? The characteristics in the context of the aim of this chapter are as follows.

(1) Each import country would buy a greater quantity of wheat than the percentage predetermined for each country in the table attached to the agreement of the whole quantity of commercial purchase of wheat in each harvest year. Namely, as the total quantity of demand (which became clear afterwards) changed, the obligation quantity for purchase could change. As was clearly written, the demand quantity of the import country was limited to commercial transaction and the US special trade was not included (examples of obligation ratio were 70 per cent of Germany, 50 per cent of Japan, 80 per cent of UK, 75 per cent of the Netherlands, 80 per cent of Switzerland etc., whose average was 71 per cent).

(2) Each export country would sell enough wheat to satisfy the commercial purchase of the import country, within the price range, in the harvest year concerned in cooperation with each other. That is to say, it would be necessary for all export countries to satisfy the needs of import

countries.

Also

(3) Both the sales obligation of export countries and the purchase obligation of import countries would be applied when the market price was within the price range. Until reaching the quantity of the predetermined percentage, even if a non-member country like the USSR had a price discrimination policy (an export dumping policy), import countries would not be able to buy from the non-member country. This was undoubtedly a trade restriction policy against outsider countries.

Besides, however,

(4) It was confirmed that the import country needed to purchase the import quantity even above the obligation ratio with a price within the price range when it was imported from a member export country.[34] This might make the (1) above meaningless. The essential point of it was that, when a member country imported from member export countries, it was necessary to buy within the price range which had no connection with market price. Also because the USSR participated in the 1962 agreement, there was no non-member export country. It automatically meant that if the import country was a member, the country had to import at a price within the price range, and if that country was not a member, that country could not import wheat at all.[35]

The UK participated in the International Wheat Agreement on the condition of abolishing purchase obligation imposed by the guaranteed quantity formula.

Therefore, of the above three aims, which were (1) dealing with US special trade, (2) UK participation, and (3) USSR participation, both (2) and (3) were accomplished, but as far as (1) was concerned they could do nothing. Furthermore, special trade, which remained ambiguous was left free for each country, and (as table 11.2 shows) the trade was treated as trade "within" the agreement. However, it was clearly recognized as trade "outside" the agreement, which meant that the International Wheat Agreement could not participate in it.

What were the effects of it? (There follows a brief view only of the procedure without explaining the mechanism, because the mechanism of the 1962 agreement was the same as the 1959 agreement.)

As table 11.2 indicates, a percentage of the quantity of wheat traded through the agreement (the sum of commercial trade and special trade) as a share of the world wheat trade was almost restored to the 1949 agreement level. However, to identify the *raison d'être* of the International Wheat Agreement, it would be necessary to identify the share of the commercial trade quantity from member export countries to member import countries in terms of the world wheat trade quantity. As far as the share was concerned, the figure in the 1959 agreement was almost unchanged, compared with those of the 1953 agreement and the 1956 agreement. By employing the obligation ratio formula the commercial trade quantity increased (60 per cent increase from 1958-59 to 1959-60), and also the special trade quantity clearly acknowledged in the 1959 agreement increased significantly (96 per cent increase for the same periods). Most of the special trade (97-100 per cent of it) was exported from the US. The special trade seemed to detract from the basic *raison d'être* of the International Wheat Agreement. The more effective the price supporting function of the International Wheat Agreement, the more beneficial for special trade in trading with a low price.

This would indicate that the US attached great importance to special trade and to the elimination of excess supply. It would also imply that the chronic mechanism of producing excess supply could not be adjusted by the formula change.

Table 11.2   Performance of the International Wheat Agreement

	1949-50	1950-51	1951-52	1952-53	1953-54	1954-55	1955-56	1956-57
(1)World wheat production (million tons)	72.5	73.5	69.1	91.0	86.3	73.5	77.9	76.1
(2)World wheat trade (million tons)	21.9	24.8	27.1	25.4	23.4	26.4	29.2	36.1
(3)Guaranteed quantity (million tons)	14.3	15.3	15.6	15.8	10.6	10.7	10.7	8.0
(4)Commercial trade quantity between member countries (million tons)	15.5	20.9	22.9	19.8	13.7	14.3	15.3	13.0
(5)Special trade quantity within agreement (million tons)	-	-	-	-	-	1.8	2.6	5.0
(6)Recorded trade quantity by agreement (million tons)	11.8	14.5	15.6	15.6	6.1	7.9	6.9	5.8
(7) [(4)/(2)] · 100	71	84	85	78	59	54	52	36
(8) [{(4)+(5)}/(2)]·100	71	84	85	78	59	61	52	50

Source: Chiba (1966), Hemmi (1975-76).

What were the effects upon the price level and upon the carrying stock level? Major moves happened when (1) harvest quantity increased in 1958-59[36] and (2) harvest quantity decreased in 1961-62. In (1) we could recognize a big rise in stocks and stable, or a rise in, price levels. In (2), we could recognize a big fall in stocks and stable, or a rise in, price levels. The most dominant factor to explain the big change in stocks might be the harvest quantity (see table 11.2). Then what would be the most dominant factor to explain the extremely stable condition of prices? The revision to the obligation ratio formula seemed to be indicated as one of the explanations for it.

Table 11.2   Performance of the International Wheat Agreement (continued)

	1957-58	1958-59	1959-60	1960-61	1961-62	1962-63	1963-64	1964-65
(1)World wheat production (million tons)	73.3	90.8	83.2	90.7	80.4	93.8	97.2	106.3
(2)World wheat trade (million tons)	32.3	35.3	36.7	42.7	43.8	42.3	56.6	52.8
(3)Guaranteed quantity (million tons)	8.0	8.0	-	-	-	-	-	-
(4)Commercial trade quantity between member countries (million tons)	10.3	9.5	15.2	14.4	16.8	14.5	18.1	16.4
(5)Special trade quantity within agreement (million tons)	4.6	5.2	10.2	13.7	16.2	19.3	17.0	21.3
(6)Recorded trade quantity by agreement (million tons)	5.3	5.2	-	-	-	-	-	-
(7) $[(4)/(2)] \cdot 100$	32	27	41	34	38	34	32	31
(8) $[\{(4)+(5)\}/(2)] \cdot 100$	46	42	69	66	75	80	62	71

Source: Chiba (1966), Hemmi (1975-76).

Interpretation of the International Wheat Agreement

How could the events written about earlier be organized by applying the framework described in this chapter?

First we can summarize the events of the International Wheat Agreement outlined earlier. Faced with excess demand and future anxiety about excess supply, they did as follows.

(1) Taking into consideration respect for free trade, respect for each country's independent domestic policy and a shortage of financial ability in each country, the International Wheat Agreement employed a multilateral contract scheme.

(2) The domestic price policy of each country was a major factor in promoting the remarkable technological innovation, increase in average harvest and increase in domestic stock level in export countries. It was particularly remarkable in the US. A chronic excess supply mechanism was built in.

(3) As a result, the International Wheat Agreement was confronted with (a) US special trade to adjust the domestic excess supply, (b) low export prices by non-member export country, the USSR, (c) artificial price regulation by export countries, (d) a major import country's (UK) nonparticipation and request to decrease the guaranteed quantity of importing countries. The conditions for a guaranteed quantity formula to work effectively were lost.

(4) For Canada, which had significant domestic agriculture, the smooth function of the International Wheat Agreement coincided with the aim of domestic policy.

(5) Export countries (including the US) attempted (a) to support the price range and (b) to eliminate transaction routes, except the International Wheat Agreement. It was the obligation ratio formula which realized the UK and the USSR participation realized.

(6) As a result, it was necessary for import countries to import wheat at a price within the price range if they participated in the International Wheat Agreement. If they did not participate, they could not import wheat from any country.

(7) Therefore, as far as the wheat transaction within the International Wheat Agreement was concerned, export countries could attempt to shift the supply curve by stock operation.

(8) However, special trade (most of which was of the US) increased both in an absolute sense and in a percentage sense.

The carrying stock level in export countries was so high that a huge amount of special trade was necessary.

It is not necessary to repeat criteria (I) - (III).

The purpose of the applied work in this chapter is to investigate whether the criteria explained previously could be applied to interpret the events of the International Wheat Agreement.

First, we can clarify the reason why in the following analysis we need to examine the framework of protecting the floor price level.

As shown in figure 11.13, Manitoba Northern 1 (delivered to the warehouse in Fort William/Port Arthur, as hereinafter) was moving within the price range after 1953. However, despite this fact, we could not recognize that all the hundreds of different kinds of wheat were in the level of competitive equilibrium. If in fact the competitive equilibrium prices of all the kinds of wheat were within the price range, it would be difficult to explain the reasons why the export countries needed to decrease so much guaranteed quantity that the International Wheat Agreement was in a crisis of collapse, and why the formula revision from guaranteed formula to obligation ratio formula was necessary. It is better to interpret that since the second half of 1953 the International Wheat Agreement worked with the mechanism to protect the floor price. This was mainly due to the following reasons. The floor price set up by the International Wheat Agreement was based upon the highest grade of Manitoba Northern 1 and many other kinds of wheat were lower grade than Manitoba Northern 1. Because the differentials among the many kinds of wheat were not specified, it remained ambiguous that a certain specific kind of wheat was how much lower than Manitoba Northern 1. Therefore, the actual price range depended upon negotiation between sellers and buyers. Taking into consideration the structure of the international wheat market and chronic excess supply environment, it is reasonable to think that the mechanism to protect the floor price actually worked.

A tool available for this would be the equation shown below,

$$t = \frac{q_G \times (p_f - p^*)}{q}$$

According to criterion (I), the effect of a multilateral contract scheme depends upon the value of t. If t is too small, the effect on stability would be too small. If t is too large, the danger of the scheme to collapsing would be large. The value of t depends upon p_f, q_G, q and p^* (the greater t, the greater p_f, the greater q_G, the less q, the less p^*).

The direct effects are as follows. The special trade of (a) in (3) meant the decrease of q and the fall of p^*. The USSR supply of (b) in (3) also indicated the decrease of q and the fall of p^*. Also the price regulation of (c) in (3) attempted a p_f increase. Each of them worked to raise the value of t (which indicated an excise tax rate imposed on import countries). When there was such action to raise the value of t, it was natural for importing countries to reduce the value of t. If it was unavoidable of "p_f increase",

"$(p_f - p^*)$ increase because of p^* decrease" and "q decrease", in order to reduce the value of t, "q_G decrease" would be necessary. Decreasing q_G would be interpreted as adjustment behavior in import countries to reduce the value of t. This is (d) in (3). As is shown by the situation here, the International Wheat Agreement was in crisis almost to collapse in 1956, the direct reason for which was the decrease in the guaranteed quantity of importing countries.

Canada, which was keen to have stability from a domestic viewpoint, tried to keep the International Wheat Agreement in existence as a point of contact between import and export countries. Canada's reason was that it wanted the International Wheat Agreement to function effectively. As it was to keep the value of t at a reasonable level, in other words, Canada was tolerant of the import countries' request to decrease q_G, and to increase q and p^* in order to check the US special trade, and enforce a reasonable level of p_f.

We seem to have a framework of explaining the short history of the International Wheat Agreement with the movement of the value of t.

Canada also insisted on the obligation ratio formula. Canada wanted to change the management formula because it recognized that the value of t had become unreasonable because of actions by the US, USSR and UK, the function of a guaranteed quantity formula was lost, and it was indispensable to completely lose the functions of the International Wheat Agreement. We could interpret that the background of Canada's action was (4) and it attempted (5) with the purpose of (6) and (7).

We will continue to follow the situation.

The international wheat market became a "multiple" market with price discrimination after 1953 in which commercial trade from the agreement because of UK nonparticipation and special trade by the US after 1954 were included. It can be interpreted as a shift from the DD curve to the $D'D'$ curve shown in figure 11.14. The demand produced by the shift resulted in another international wheat market with price discrimination. That seemed to be a counteraction against the chronic excess supply mechanism by (2) above. Needless to say, it caused the decrease of q and of p^*.

The obligation ratio formula can be interpreted as aiming to put the brakes on against those movements. The targets of the brakes were (6) and (7), which are shown in figure 11.14 to have been approaching a $D'D'$ curve toward a DD curve and to have more ability to operate as a SS curve. Although it became more difficult to approach a DD curve by approving US special trade, it could be said that, as far as the market within the agreement was concerned, a right and upward shift from a $D'D'$ curve to a $D''D''$ curve resulted and the operation ability of the SS curve became much stronger. Therefore, this contributed toward supporting p_f and increasing q, which meant supporting the price range of (5) and increasing the trade quantity (except the special trade).

By the way, because (6) was produced by the obligation ratio formula this meant that q_G lost meaning. If it was necessary to import wheat within the price range in commercial trade, either absolute quantity or relative share made no sense in the guaranteed quantity. The function of q_G, which worked to adjust the value of t through import countries' behavior, was lost. It showed that the function of q_G in the multilateral contract scheme, which carried out a price stabilization function and a transfer function between import countries and export countries, almost completely disappeared. In that sense, as far as the viewpoint of criterion (I) is concerned, the obligation ratio formula did not have an important function in the multilateral contract scheme.

If the situation were as described above, the following two issues would come out. First, because the loss of the function of the guaranteed quantity formula did not occur suddenly, we should ask what the mechanism of the International Wheat Agreement actually was in the period when the malfunction of the guaranteed quantity formula became clear (in the second half of the 1956 agreement, for example). Second we should ask what the function of the obligation ratio formula was.

Concerning the first question, as described earlier, the shift from the DD curve to the $D'D'$ curve and the significant decrease of q and p^* happened. Based upon the facts, looking at table 11.2 and figure 11.13 makes us suspect that q_G might be in the position shown in figure 11.14. This is possible if the adjustment speed of q_G by importing countries is significantly slower than the adjustment speed of the shift toward the $D'D'$ curve. The import quantity of import countries, whether q_G or q_f, basically depends upon the market structure concerned. The approximate figures to correspond to the above assumption are that, as q meant commercial trade within the agreement and q_G indicated the guaranteed quantity, q equals 9.5 million tons and q_G eight million tons. The question was about the quantity of q_f and, as far as the second half of the 1953 agreement and the 1956 agreement are concerned, the approximate figure seemed to be the quantity recorded by the agreement, which was q_f as 5.2 million tons.[37]

If the situation was similar to that shown in figure 11.14, it suggests a possibility of an all or nothing demand curve. Criterion (II) mentioned above could possibly exist. As criterion (II) suggested, if (1) producing countries exercised market control (to monopolize), and (2) excess supply quantity was not more than the demand quantity presented at the floor price, the quantity q_G would be traded at the p_f price. If we speculate that the obligation quantity from export countries to import countries at this period was limited to q_G of eight million tons, as the q_f quantity was 5.2 million tons, condition (2) would be satisfied. Therefore, if import countries accomplished the purchase obligation of eight million tons guaranteed quantity at the p_f price, condition (1) seems to be also satisfied. On the contrary, if import countries purchased only 5.2 million tons at the p_f price, condition (1) seems not be satisfied.

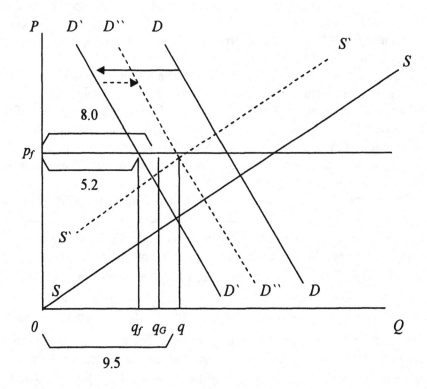

Figure 11.14   International wheat market

As far as the period of the second half of the 1953 agreement and the 1956 agreement were concerned, the import countries did not evaluate the *raison d'être* of the International Wheat Agreement because of export countries' wheat stock of more than 50 million tons, the price level, which was moving downward, and the existence of non-member export countries. It seemed to be plausible that the crisis would lead to collapse for import countries. In such a situation, it might be plausible that at the presented price of p_f, import countries would have purchased a quantity q_f, not a quantity q_G, which was reported as the recorded quantity within the agreement. If import countries purchased at the p_f price not q_f, or 5.2 million tons, but q_G, or eight million tons, it might not have been necessary for export countries to attempt to change the obligation ratio formula.

Import countries would be suspected of trading with the usual demand curve, in which q_f equaled to 5.2 million tons, not of trading with the all or nothing demand curve in which q_G equaled eight million tons.

If the above interpretation explains a lot of the facts, export countries did attempt transactions where import countries would share more of the burden through a buffer stock scheme, but the import countries refused this. It reasonably means that the market monopolization power of export countries was not so big as that applied in criterion (II). Also it shows that the price stabilization function and transfer function between import and export countries was completely lost.

What about the second question? As pointed out previously, the employment of the obligation ratio formula prompted the shift from the $D'D'$ curve to the $D''D''$ curve as shown in figure 11.14 and led the operation ability towards the SS curve (for example expressed as the shift from the SS curve to the $S'S'$ curve as in figure 11.14). The result was clearly observed with the price movement which was remarkably stable, even when faced with a good harvest in 1958-59 (stock increase) and a bad harvest in 1961-62 (stock decrease). Concerning this price stability, this is usually analyzed as a "voluntary stock holding policy".[38] This means that it comes about because of the voluntary operation of SS curve supporting price levels.[39] However, as examined with criterion (III), even when the case was shared by more producing countries, it was necessary that employing the buffer stock scheme would not cause such a high unit cost for stock holding. Therefore, when we have an interpretation based upon criterion (III), the so-called "voluntary stock holding policy" under the events of the International Wheat Agreement, it should be recognized as the "involuntary" result coming from the high carrying cost which made employing the buffer stock scheme impossible.

The destabilized mechanism of the international wheat market, which was built in and fixed through the 1953 agreement and the 1956 agreement, made excess supply more serious. Around 1959, the chronic excess supply which could satisfy neither criterion (I) and (II), nor criterion (III) seems to have been produced.

That is to say, as far as the functional aspect was concerned, when the obligation ratio formula was employed, the function of the multilateral contract scheme became weak and it could be understood, rather, that the function of the export regulation scheme in this chapter's sense was the major function of the multilateral contract scheme. In other words, it would be the case in which, through quantity regulation, there could have been a function to adjust prices.

Notes

1   It is possible to use multiple schemes jointly. In this chapter, we will assume that it is possible to point out the dominant scheme which will focus our attention on it. Concerning the International Coffee Agreement, see, for example, Akiyama and Varangis (1990), and concerning the International Tin Agreement, see, for example, Anderson and Gilbert (1988).

2   To make sure, regarding the following schemes and events etc., we would not have any value judgment to say "good" or "bad". Such a value judgment would depend upon "particular purpose" from the viewpoints of "particular individual or particular group" who have no relation with the author of this book.

3   It could be considered that the price compensation agreements insisted on by J. E. Meade (1964) was a possibly superior alternative to the multilateral contract. See H. G. Johnson (1967), p. 145. See also a critical investigation against Meade's idea by R. I. McKinnon (1967).

4   In broadly understanding the schemes of international commodity agreements, it could be said in general that for protecting the floor price the export restriction scheme is assigned and for protecting the ceiling price the buffer stock scheme is assigned. This seemed to be advantageous as they needed only commodities, not currencies, for counteracting measures.

5   As is clearly shown in this chapter, there were two cases in the multilateral contract scheme one of which was case predetermined as absolute quantity and of which was predetermined as a certain share in the whole trade quantity. The former used the guaranteed quantity formula and the latter the obligation ratio formula.

6   G. S. Becker (1971), pp. 106-108.

7   The scheme in which discontinuous excise tax is imposed across a border would be usually considered as a customs quota. We have had such a framework in economics for many years. For example, J.R. Hicks (1946) exactly analyzed the price range which indicated that an economy with fixed price could be analyzed as the important topic under a more general theoretical framework.

8   If we examine the case more practically from the viewpoint of this chapter, it could be recognized that the authority subsidizes the amount of tax to consumers and producers.

9   As in note 8.

10   On this idea, see, for example, M. Friedman (1967), p.15.

11   When partial equilibrium analysis is applied here and in the following investigation, we would assume that, if an income effect exists, it would be small enough.

12 In this case, strictly speaking it would not be indifferent between the origin and G. If it is the origin, the amount shown as the area of $q_s \times p_s$ is held and there is the opportunity to have positive consumers' surplus by using the purchasing power for other commodities. In the case of G, it was predetermined that the purchasing power shown as the area of $q_s \times p_s$ had zero consumers' surplus.

13 We will not investigate the question here.

14 It is necessary, more precisely, to add the following conditions. First, the excise tax rate, which consumers wish to transact even if it is imposed, has to be as follows. That is to say, in figure 11.A, the excise tax rate is $(p_d - p_s) = t$ when consumers could raise the consumers' surplus from the area of triangle $Pp_f q_f$ to the area of triangle $Pp_d q_d$ with market transactions by paying the penalty. The benefit is shown as the area of trapezoid $p_f p_d q_d q_f$. The cost when consumers pay is indicated as the area of rectangle $p_d p_s q_s q_d$. Therefore, when they wish to transact at the market, even paying the penalty, it means that the area of the trapezoid exceeds the area of the rectangle. The excise tax rate then would be,

$$t < \frac{(q_f + q_d)(p_f - p_d)}{2q_d}$$

Second, the higher rate of tax does not mean a larger amount of tax. In order to enforce that, the following additional condition is necessary. In case of figure 11.B, the tax amount when tax rate $BC = t$ is indicated as the area of rectangle $BCHG$ and when tax rate $AE = t'$ it is shown as the area of rectangle $AEJF$. Therefore, the condition says that, when $t' > t$, the area of rectangle $AEJF$ exceeds the area of rectangle $BCHG$.

15 Tyszynski (1949), p.33. It would be likely that this makes producers' stock increase. This kind of stock increase might produce serious problems, but we will not cover this here.

16 Actual market price would be lower than $p*$, but for convenience it is indicated as $p*$.

17 The market means here not the function but the institution and the place.

18 As in note 17.

19 The measure to deal with it might be the Integrated Program for Commodities.

20 Hereinafter the price is shown as US$ or US cents per bushel. US$ 2.00 - US$ 1.50 means for example that the ceiling price is US$ 2.00 and the floor price is US$ 1.50.

21 We will not examine here in this book whether that was appropriate from the viewpoint of criterion (I).

22 Chiba (1966), p. 34 and p. 36.

23 Chiba (1966), section 5.

24 The differential problem meant that, as a basis of Manitoba Northern 1 price, some hundred kinds of wheat prices were reasonably set up with a reasonable differential according to the quality differentials. As mentioned, in international wheat trade in this period there was no clear rule upon the differential. It was January 1965 when the clear concept to decide differentials (it was called "historical differential") was introduced. Therefore in the period concerned the price of Manitoba Northern 1 was actually the base upon which the actually traded wheat price was negotiated between sellers and buyers.

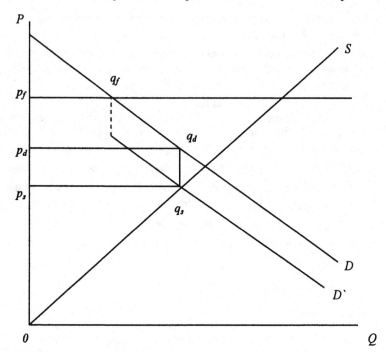

Figure 11.A   Excise tax rate

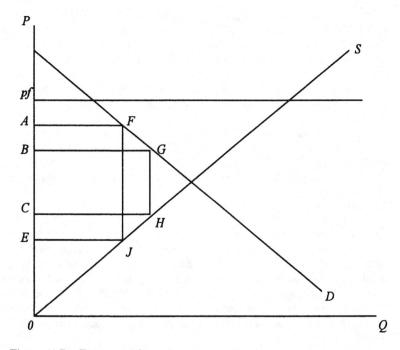

Figure 11.B   Tax rate and tax amount

25   This figure was said to come from H. C. Farnsworth (see Chiba (1966), p.36). Also it was said that in UK then there was criticism of the price rise caused by a monopoly market controlled by export countries (see Hemmi (1963), p.166).

26   According to Hemmi (1975/76,p.32), in *Commodity Trade and Economic Development* (United Nations, 1954) it was pointed out that such commodities as wheat with quality differentials and accompanying price differentials caused extreme difficulty in concluding the international agreement. Several restrictions mentioned here might indicate the importance of this.

27   It was called the "technical explosion" (Chiba (1966), p.42).

28   Farnsworth (1958), p.13. Needless to say, it might be very difficult to prove a causal relation insisting that government price policy accelerated technological progress, however, it seemed to be rather plausible to assume that if there had no government price policy, such accelerated technological progress would have never occurred.

29   According to Farnsworth (1958), from one third to half of the increase in production was shared by the US. See also *Ibid.,* p.6, chart II.

30   Chiba (1966), p. 40. Monthly average price in 1952 and in 1953 is shown in table 11.A (as US$ per bushel).

31   Chiba (1966), p. 44 and p. 46.

32   It was during the negotiations for the 1962 agreement that Canada's intention became clear. They pointed out that, when most developing countries requested a lower price because of their shortage of foreign exchange reserves and their need for food import, even developed countries had the right to request a reasonable price for primary commodity which they produce (Chiba (1966), p. 63). The reasonable price would not be exactly defined but the probable basic concept of it might be the mark-up rate in full cost pricing.

Table 11.A   Average monthly price of wheat

month \ year	1952	1953
1	2.29	2.25
2	2.30	2.22
3	2.20	2.24
4	2.12	2.19
5	2.13	2.14
6	2.04	2.08
7	2.00	2.04
8	2.25	2.05
9	2.27	2.03
10	2.28	1.99
11	2.33	1.95
12	2.28	1.94

Source: Chiba (1966), p. 34.

33   As far as the structure of the international wheat market at this time is concerned, McCalla (1966) presented a meaningful analysis. According to McCalla, the then structure of the international wheat market was duopoly by the US and Canada, in which Canada was leader and the US follower. It was the choice of the US government, however, because (1) the US government refrained from external appearances, and (2)

the US government put priority upon domestic agricultural policy and special trade. McCalla called the US government's behavior that of a "silent partner" to Canada. The McCalla analysis has undoubtedly interesting viewpoints indicating that players' behavior depended upon political considerations, although the theoretical model might not be enough clear.

34   It was the 1962 agreement when it was definitely confirmed (Chiba (1966), p.68).

35   Concerning the protection of ceiling price, when the market price exceeded the ceiling price, import countries had the right to purchase a certain quantity of wheat from export countries with the ceiling price. The certain quantity at that time meant the average purchase quantity of the last five years of import countries from export countries commercially (not in special trade) minus the purchase quantity of the year concerned. The term "export country" was defined as a country with Maximum Price Declaration by the International Wheat Board of Directors and any import country could trade with the export countries by the quantity by right. In that sense, as far as the obligation to protect the ceiling price for export countries was concerned, they had explicit rules. On the contrary, regarding the protection of a floor price, the rules were rather vague which said that when market price was below the floor price, the International Wheat Board of Directors advised measures to accomplish the right and obligation. With the above rules, the dominant view seemed to be that the obligations for export countries were disproportionately hard compared with import countries. Taking into consideration the situation of the international wheat market at this time, harder explicit rules of obligation might not have made any sense. As already noted, the structure of the international wheat market was already established to support the price level by export countries through supply control (even if the rules of obligation were hard enough, if there was no possibility to actually be put into effect, it could not be said that they were disproportionately hard).

36   Therefore, the effects would be included in views on the 1959 agreement.

37   It is difficult to estimate the figure of q_f from the recorded transaction quantity regarding the 1949 agreement and the first half of the 1953 agreement. Because, as regards the 1949 agreement, it was thought that the recorded transaction quantity seemed to be lower than the guaranteed quantity due to: (1) market price exceeding the ceiling price; and (2) lots of quantity was estimated without being recorded in the 1949 agreement. Also in the first half of the 1953 agreement, it should be interpreted that the report of recorded quantity by the agreement was almost meaningless as market prices of almost all kinds of wheat were within the price range and the International Wheat Agreement did not work at all. In the first half of the 1953 agreement, thus, the recorded quantity by the agreement seemed to be lower than the guaranteed quantity. However, for the reasons mentioned here, regarding the second half of the 1953 agreement and the 1956 agreement, the situation was completely different.

38   Chiba (1966), p.61.

39   Strictly speaking, export countries more or less regulated the *SS* curve almost all the time. The obligation ratio formula made this more powerful.

Chapter 12

A Sociological Study of
the Futures Market

Introduction

The author has analyzed in this book such issues as economic transitions from a centrally planned to a market oriented system and covered capital movements, particularly related with commodity futures markets, from several different viewpoints.

In this chapter, we will try to put such analyses in a sociological framework. As mentioned earlier, it has been recognized that it is difficult to write appropriate prescriptions, although there have been many prescriptions upon the primary commodity problems. The problems of international commodity agreement we have investigated here in this book have been typical ones.

Many arguments conducted in the past were imperfect because they could not fully explain the *raison d'être* of international commodity agreements, though from the viewpoint of economics, international commodity agreements are (or must be) considered failures. Also the way of thinking of introducing market mechanisms (like futures markets) to absorb the volatility of primary commodity prices is not generally accepted.

The purpose of this chapter is to examine which social level should we focus upon when investigating the above questions.

In the first section of chapter eleven, we studied the economic criteria which indicated a specific criterion that lead to particular schemes for several international commodity agreements. In this chapter, the same considerations will be attempted from the perspective of economic sociology.

We shall proceed as follows. In the first section, we will sketch how the problem starts. In the second section, we shall look at four devices to alleviate uncertainty. We will then, in the third section, give an overview of four functional exigencies of a social system mainly put forward by Parsons. In the fourth section, we will describe four patterns of transactions pointed out by Polanyi and further examined by Smelser. Finally, in the fifth section, we will attempt to arrange the above four according to their relationships with one another and to indicate the link with the schemes of international commodity agreements.

Intention of McKinnon's Proposal

In this book, as described in the first chapter particularly, McKinnon (1967) put forward the following proposal.[1]

We will assume here that there could be a well established futures market in the optimum situation.[2] If the authorities could successfully stabilize futures market prices in the distant future, it would mean that futures markets could play very important roles for economic society: (1) in supplying devices to alleviate risks, and (2) in supplying information about prices in the future. At the same time, it could also provide a social benefit indicating that the futures market system could be the alternative to the "inferior" method, i.e., international commodity agreement, by which primary commodity prices are unsuccessfully regulated by intergovernmental councils and resources are allocated in a distorted way. From the viewpoint of individual transaction actors, with the futures market devices they could utilize futures market transactions in the distant future, and they could utilize their own production factors more efficiently by having information on prices provided by a futures market.

According to the example originally described by McKinnon this would be as follows.

We will suppose here that it becomes possible for traders to carry out wheat transaction for two years in advance. Then a wheat producer decides at September 2001 to sell the estimated crop, 100 bushel, with a long-term average price of two US$ per bushel (the same as hereinafter) in September 2003. However, in 2002, they have a very good harvest of wheat and lots of stock is carried until 2003. As stocks are increased, the spot price of wheat is decreased to 1.2 US$ and also the futures market price of wheat is decreased to 1.2 US$. Then what could we expect the wheat producers' behavior to be when they plant for the September 2003 harvest? According to McKinnon's reasonable way of thinking, the wheat producer decides to have the planting upon the expected price of 1.2 US$ at the 2003 harvest. He actually plants 50 bushels of wheat, far less than the 100 bushels of estimated crop with an expected price of 2 US$. As a result, he settles the short position of 50 bushels sales contract at September 2003; at the same time he decides to plant oats on half of his farming land and have a sales contract for the estimated crop in oats at the futures market of September 2003.

Based upon the above way of thinking, McKinnon's intention seems to be that the wheat producer could flexibly adjust both his planting decision and hedging behavior to compensate for the unexpected harvest and unexpected price decrease. On the contrary, however, in international commodity agreements, they usually intervene directly through the spot market and might try compulsory production regulation. Spot market intervention is, therefore, undoubtedly an inefficient policy from a viewpoint of economic rationality.

In that sense, according to McKinnon's assertion, a policy in which the authority might not have intervened in the spot market, might have encouraged futures market transaction in the far distant future and successfully supplied information on long-term average prices instead. (Therefore, although the 1995 International Natural Rubber Agreement allowed the Buffer Stock Manager to purchase future contracts up to a maximum of two months ahead and this might be similar in meaning to utilizing futures contracts, it seemed to be basically totally different from McKinnon's idea).

Against McKinnon's assertion, Poole (1970) put forward a counter argument. We will not mention here Poole's counter argument,[3] but from this chapter's viewpoint it is useful to know that McKinnon clarified his theory through his dispute with Poole.

McKinnon's main points in (1967) seemed to be the following two. (1) Only when money is a stable numeraire is McKinnon's argument correct. This means (as Poole pointed out) that, if forecasting costs is fairly uncertain, hedging might be probable, on the contrary, to destabilize incomes and to prevent resource allocation efficiency. Also it would mean that hedging in distant futures might not be attractive. (2) A more important argument from the viewpoint of this chapter is that through Poole's critical discussion McKinnon's intention could become clearer. McKinnon's intention is actually a criticism against the authorities' improper intervention and is to propose an alternative which would be relatively more efficient. This means that, when an authority stabilizes primary commodity prices, McKinnon's idea is to propose a more efficient method than spot market intervention.

In this chapter, we can examine the appropriate position of the intention of the second point from the viewpoint of economic sociology.

Four Methods to Mitigate Uncertainty

As is well known and as mentioned in the first and second chapters of this book, Hicks (1946) suggested four possible causes of disequilibrium.[4] Disequilibrium according to Hicks means discrepancy between expected and realized prices. The discrepancy comes from inaccurate foresight (which means the existence of uncertainty) and causes wrong investment, waste and inefficient production.

Hicks mentioned that the first cause of disequilibrium (which was said to be the least important) occurred when different people's price expectations were inconsistent. However, if all buyers and sellers expect the same price, the total quantity all buyers plan to buy might not be equal to the total quantity all sellers plan to sell. This means disequilibrium coming from discrepancy between plans of buyers and sellers. This is the second cause of disequilibrium (which is said to be perhaps the most interesting cause of all four). Moreover, even if both price expectations and plans are consistent, people might not predict their own wants correctly, or might make wrong estimates of the results of technical production processes. If such a situation arises, they are unwilling or unable to buy or sell those quantities they had planned to buy or sell. This is the third cause of disequilibrium due to unforeseen changes in tastes, unforeseen results of technical processes, imperfect foresight of harvest fluctuations and unforeseen political upheavals, etc. Also, moreover, even if no disequilibium in any of the above three senses exists, the most perfect adjustment of resources to wants might not be achieved, because when risk and uncertainty exist, people generally act not on the price that they expect as most probable, but as if that price had been slightly shifted in an unfavorable direction.[5] This is the fourth cause of disequilibrium (also called Imperfect Equilibrium).

The discrepancies between expected and realized prices need to be eliminated to improve the efficiency of economic systems. As Hicks correctly indicated, however, the third and fourth causes of disequilibrium are inevitably found in every economic system.

The first two causes of disequilibrium appear differently and in different ways in any economic system. "In a completely centralized system they would be removed",[6] but according to Hicks, "a completely centralized system is a mere figment of the imagination".[7] Several sources of inefficiency could be contained by handing over the power. In the case of a private enterprise system, "expectations and plans can be (at least partially) co-ordinated".[8] Therefore, we could find the device to (at least partially) eliminate the first and the second causes of disequilibrium, which is, according to Hicks, the device of forward trading.

If neither the third nor the fourth cause of disequilibrium exists, expectations and plans could be coordinated by forward trading, and an efficient economic system could be achieved by removing the waste. However, actually, mainly due to the third cause of disequilibrium, expectations and plans cannot be coordinated. It might be real to mention that forward trading works to mitigate the risk coming from the difference between real and expected (usually described as a market for hedging). In other words, we could say that the futures market is the device to arrange the intertemporal market and to adapt to circumstances by market exchange, and to adjust the disequilibrium at the spot market. That is to say:

(1) Futures market is the device to mitigate uncertainty.

As Hicks explicitly mentioned, the term forward trading includes not only trade in forward markets, but also all the trade made in advance and all long-term contracts. Such frameworks, however, are inconvenient because they are not exact enough from the viewpoint of this chapter which focuses our attention upon the characteristics of transaction costs and recognizing devices to mitigate uncertainty. In dealings in futures markets, it is necessary to pay deposit money and there are transaction costs. In this long-term contracts, however, (supposing the fixed price and fixed quantity case as the typical example[9]) it is not necessary to pay some costs as in the case of futures market transactions. It also means that to have a long-term contract needs more limited conditions. It could be recognized that this indicates another type of transaction costs meaning anyone, any goods and services, could not have such contracts. That is to say:

(2) Long-term contract is the device to mitigate uncertainty.

A long-term contract is a transaction in which buyers and sellers decide transaction period, transaction volume, transaction price, etc. between themselves. It needs successful management to share the value system and to manage tension so as not to hinder confidence in holding contracts. It indicates the necessity for reciprocity between buyers and sellers and it might happen that (1) negotiations come to a standstill, (2) contracts repeat over and over again, and (3) contracts are threatened by market price fluctuation.[10] In order to avoid such cases as mentioned above, devices to evade friction and to cooperate between buyers and sellers are required. A device such as vertical integration is an example for integrating buyers and sellers. By vertically integrating, various resources can be redistributed more easily inside the organization and a much smoother flow of information can contribute to a less uncertain situation. Needless to say, such limited conditions are necessary to conclude any integrated transaction. We can say that:

(3) Vertical integration is the device to mitigate uncertainty.

We could examine government intervention to alleviate uncertainty, such as the international commodity agreement. The international agreement is a device among member countries with the goal-attainment of price stabilization for primary commodities and of export earnings stabilization for primary commodity exporting countries. In order to achieve this, member countries establish a fund and manage the device and the goal. A clear difference from other devices is the political will to mobilize resources to reach the social goal of stabilization. Anyway, we could point out the fourth device:

(4) International commodity agreement is the device to mitigate uncertainty.

As mentioned above, there could be some devices to mitigate uncertainty.[11, 12] Then are there any relationships between them? One of the main purposes of this chapter is to find any adequate position for the devices from the viewpoint of their dominant function in sociological approach.

Four Functional Exigencies

Uncertainty is one of the most important topics for sociological analysis, because one of the purposes for sociology is to explain reasons why human behavior makes a (stable) society, with deviation behavior not occurring frequently.

In throwing light on social phenomena, a new framework of sociology, which departed from nineteenth century methodology in explaining with single or a very few dominant factors,[13] has been based upon setting up a minimum postulate indicating that "everything is interdependent upon everything" or "every function has its feedback".[14]

According to Talcott Parsons, who developed this "new sociological synthesis",[15] the procedures in which the "theory of social system" comes from relations of interdependence can be summarized as: (1) establishing a structure in which there are relatively constant relations of systemic parts within analytical perspectives, and (2) confirming a functional mechanism to explain reasons why the structure could have relative constancy. It is mentioned that both of them are a type of "structural-functional analysis".[16]

We focus our attention in this chapter upon the function of giving relative constancy to the structure. Parsons' way of organizing the topic has already become common property in the theory of sociology. In this chapter, we will describe the main points in line with the viewpoints of this book.[17]

Parsons' framework is usually called the AGIL scheme. It means that, in order for a social system to keep relative constancy without collapsing, four functional exigencies are necessary. The system in that sense has four dimensions revealing the weight of superiority and inferiority for specific situations. With regard to why there are four functional exigencies, this chapter accords with Bales, which built a foundation for the AGIL scheme by a small group experiment upon the interaction process.[18] The experiment was to investigate how a small group carried out a task. It usually takes the following process: (1) recognize an orientation of task, and then (2) move toward resolving the task directly, (3) it is necessary to unite the members to resolve heated arguments, and finally (4) be satisfied with resolving both in duty and in emotion (or manage tension). This is expressed through moving dominance among the four functional exigencies during the course of events. We assume that the four functional exigencies necessarily exist for equilibrium and continuation of the system, irrespective of the level in which the system is located.[19] We usually call (1) Adaptation (A), (2) Goal Attainment (G), (3) Integration (I), and (4) Latent pattern-maintenance and tension-management (L), and they are abbreviated to AGIL. The correspondence could be expressed at a macroscopic level, that a sub-system for A function is economy, for G function politics, for I function social integration, and for L function culture, respectively. Each sub-system also has its own AGIL function (for example, they are expressed as A_A, A_G, A_I, A_L), and each sub-system has its own AGIL function (for example expressed as A_{Aa}, A_{Ag}, A_{Ai}, A_{Al}). This means that, "what may be treated as a unit for purposes of one level of analysis may be treated as a system for purposes of another".[20]

At this stage of the chapter we can focus our attention upon the more specific level, which is, needless to say, A function for Adaptation. That is to say, as the function of A, "the goal of the economy as a whole is the production of wealth or utility for the society or its sub-systems". And "Fulfilment of this goal maximizes adaptation for the social system".[21]

As was examined previously, an economy that is a unit function for a social system could be a system for a lower analytical level and, needless to say, it would have the four functional exigencies, A_A, A_G, A_I, A_L, respectively.

There could be a sub-system of A_A for Adaptation. This has a function of adapting to the current request of economic production. In other words, it could be expressed as a function to mitigate an external disturbance to maximize wealth and utility (under some restrictions).

A_{Ag} is, according to Parsons and Smelser (1956): "The most salient mechanism" and "a certain *guarantee of the liquidity of securities* which permits continuous adaptation to the production needs of the society" (italic in original).[22] Also: "In a highly differentiated capitalization system such liquidity is healthy, for it sensitizes investors to production needs and opportunities and allows for quick adaptation to changes in these".[23] In other words, with coming uncertainty and profit opportunity in sight, A_{Ag} could be interpreted as a mechanism which could be quickly adjustable for uncertainty in consideration of profit maximization (A_A which Parsons and Smelser (1956) diagrammatized by analogy with the enterprise organization is shown in figure 12.1). A_{Ag} takes the function of regulating the production of wealth by producers (because, as is mentioned later, A_G has the function of regulating production and distribution).[24] A_{Al} has the function of making a framework of capital movement. Institutional arrangements, like stock exchange and commodity exchange are included to be in the A_{Al} function. A_{Ai} has the function of taking "a balance between short-term investment and long-term investment".[25] This means the function of hindering distorting intertemporal resource allocation, and "for correctives to excessive speculation", and also the concrete examples are "a government transfer tax on all transactions, the requirement of a cash percentage for the purchase of securities, etc."[26]

Guarantee of liquidity	Production of productive capacity
a	g
l	i
Credit and investment mechanisms (flow of credit and capital)	Guarantee of enterprise

Source: Parsons and Smelser (1956), p. 200.

Figure 12.1 A_A investment-capitalization sub-system

Therefore, when the economy is confronted with uncertainty and that

Commitment to long-term productivity	Commitment to productivity
a	g
l	i
Economic values(economic rationality)	Commitment to planned allocation of resources

Source: Parsons and Smelser (1956), p. 204.

Figure 12.2 A_L economic commitments

functional differentiation is dominant, a function of the futures market could have priority. We can say that:

(1) A_A includes a function of the futures market as a particular case.

A_L is a sub-system for the economic commitments shown in figure 12.2, involving "the classification - in system-problems terms - of the motivational commitments underlying the whole economic process".[27] Therefore, when this function is prevailing, the economic agents would behave in such a way as to cooperate each other.

A_{La} is a sub-system for the commitment to long-term productivity and has the function of being adaptive "relative to certain special exigencies such as changes in long-term demand, in market structure, in pool of resources, etc".[28] A_{Lg} is the commitment to productivity and indicates allocation productive factors and technology of the goal attainment. A_{Li} is the commitment "to supply the motivation and skills necessary for planning, which regulates commitments merely to capitalize and commitments to change the form of the factors of production".[29] A_{Ll} is "the most general statement of positive valuation of economic activity as a form of activity".[30]

When the economy faces uncertainty and this functional differentiation prevails, the method of long-term contract is given a priority. Therefore, we could say as follows:

(2) A_L includes a function of long-term contract as a particular case.

A_I is a sub-system of the enterpreneurial one, as shown in figure 12.3. This means that A_{Ig} represents "the actual process of innovation, or the offer of new combinations of factors of production, which is the goal of the entrepreneurial function", and A_{Ii} is "the complex of entrepreneurial decisions based upon the opportunities and incentives for innovation. These decisions are integrative in that they control the introduction of new combinations, limit the demand for inventions, resources, etc., limit the demand for risk capital, and change the market demand for re-allocating the uses of the factors of production".[31] Therefore, this sub-system has the function of judging opportunities for introducing new schemes of combining production factors (which undoubtedly means vertical integration) by mixing the use of production factors with demands. A_{II} is a sub-sector that, through the institutionalized mobility, flexibility and substitutability of the factors of production, "includes those particular

Financing of innovation		New combination of factors of production
	a	*g*
	l	*i*
Mobility, flexibility and substitutability of factors of production (flow of resources)		Opportunity of innovation

Source: Parsons and Smelser (1956), p. 203.

Figure 12.3 A_I enterpreneurial sub-system

Procurement of facilities		Production, distribution and sales
	a	*g*
	l	*i*
Technical production(flow of production line)		Production co-ordination

Source: Parsons and Smelser (1956), p. 199.

Figure 12.4 A_G production sub-system

elements of economic rationality which are the values requisites for the pursuit of long-term economic adjustments".[32] A_{Ia} represents "the actual process of innovation, or the offer of new combinations of factors of production, which is the goal of the entrepreneurial function".[33]

When the economy faces uncertainty and this functional differentiation is dominant, the method of vertical integration is given priority. We could say therefore:

(3) A_I includes a function of vertical integration as a particular case.

A_G is a sub-system of aggregate production units in an economy as shown in figure 12.4. Here A_{Gg} involves "manipulation of the production goals themselves, which is usually accomplished by means of policy decisions".[34] This means that A_{Gg} has the function of deciding a policy based upon a goal and of regulating the production goal, and if we observe a function to make a goal of production regulation for maintaining price levels, it is a function of A_{Gi}. A_{Ga} is a sub-system for the procurement of facilities which is the mode of adaptation to certain situational exigencies. "The most common of these exigencies is the need for generalized facilities, in the form of liquid assets, to implement a change in the production process or to meet crises such as debt or mortgage foreclosure".[35] A_{Gi} has the function of production co-ordination. It indicates neither regulating production quantity nor maintaining production line, it indicates the function of "trouble-shooting activities of the executive".[36] In other words, when price levels suddenly decrease, the regulating organization has the function of absorbing the fluctuation shock through supply adjustment (which undoubtedly means stock adjustment as it does produce the stock). A_{Gi} therefore represents the function of maintaining the production line and of ensuring "smooth operation of the production sub-system as a whole".[37] Also in other words, this function shows the work of smoothing the production process as a function of a factory manager as well as concluding a contract of long-term transaction with the demand side, and ensuring a sales network for the production process.

When the economy is confronted with uncertainty and functional differentiation prevails, the method of international commodity agreement is given priority. Therefore, we can say as follows:

(4) A_G includes a function of international commodity agreement as a particular case.

Four Transaction Types

When focusing our attention upon Karl Polanyi, we recognize his way of thinking, usually called economic anthropology, mentioning that the

Polanyi's purposes were to recover the integration of motives for economic agents in everyday life behavior as producers, and to embed the economic system into the social system. In order for them to be accomplished, the main intellectual obligation was to develop a wider frame of reference in which the market is recognized as a portion.[38] As Tominaga (1999) correctly mentioned, a necessity "to investigate economic behavior not as a closed system but as a system closely related with the entire systems" is expressed by Karl Polanyi as "the embedded economy".[39]

The attention of this chapter is not focused upon the evaluation of the above way of thinking from the viewpoints of economics and sociology but upon the types of economies classified by the dominant integration form[40] extracted from Polanyi's wider viewpoints. (We will not explicitly here raise the question of whether such classification might be impossible without focusing our attention upon the substantial meaning[41] of "economic"). Here the term integration means the institutionalization of movements of economic factors, which indicates therefore that the integration form means the movement patterns of goods, factors and services. The main movement patterns proposed by Polanyi are: (1) exchange, (2) reciprocity, and (3) redistribution. Needless to say, those three types are not exclusive to each other, but come into existence in some combination in different historical dimensions and in different sectors of the economy.[42] To illustrate this, exchange indicates movement of goods, factors and services between any two points within the system concerned, reciprocity means symmetrical movement patterns (in a sense of equilibrium), and redistribution shows the movement inward to the centre and (due to any legitimacy) outward from the center.

Corresponding to the integration forms, we can observe each characteristic: (1) forms of trade, (2) uses of money, (3) market elements, and (4) types of social structure.[43]

We will focus our attention here upon the forms of trade. According to Dalton, the term "trade" used by Polanyi usually indicates foreign trade or external trade.[44] Therefore, hereinafter we will mention it "foreign trade".

The above mentioned foreign trade could be classified into three main types, which are: (1) market trade, (2) gift trade, and (3) administered trade. In the framework of Polanyi, each type has its own integration form, meaning market trade corresponds to exchange, gift trade is reciprocity, and administered trade is redistribution.

Market trade is a form in which, under the market mechanism, trade agents each have their own voluntary transaction with prices as a signal. Gift trade is a form in which trade agents are combined in reciprocal relations. The characteristic of gift trade form is that it needs much less time for transaction compared with market trade. In other words, it produces a saving in transaction costs because in this system trade agents share a value system. In administered trade, transactions are implemented through intervention by authority. They are done by more or less formal treaty. Administration covers a wide range of transactions including transaction rate, storing and keeping, payment system, etc.

Neil Smelser (1959) tried to integrate Polanyi's argument of economic anthropology described above into economic sociology.[45]

Smelser's investigation is composed of: (1) ways of thinking about scarecity, (2) relations between redistribution and administered trade, and (3) bringing this together with the AGIL scheme. Here in this chapter, we focus our attention upon the (2) and (3)[46] above.

As mentioned earlier, redistribution is a form of integration, whose corresponding form of trade is administration trade. According to Smelser, however, redistribution and administered trade are concepts which should be separated (as occurred in the cases of the port of Whydah and the kingdom of Dhomey).[47]

However, the Smelser's argument might not be completely correct. Because, in line with Polanyi's classification of the movement pattern of goods and services, when the movement inward to and outward from the center can be recognized, such patterns would be classified as redistribution. Smelser's classification argues that administered trade is a resource mobilization that governments use to attain a goal when a certain public situation (like a war) exists, and redistribution is a resource mobilization in which government first collects wealth and then mobilizes it once again toward socially justified groups. In other words, while Polanyi focused his attention upon the *scheme* of a moving pattern, Smelser focused attention upon the *function* of a moving pattern.

Apart from this difference, Smelser's viewpoints have the following interesting development.

Through investigation into relations between administered trade and redistribution, the fourth form of integration would be added, which is called mobilization by Smelser. As Smelser correctly stated, types classified by forms of integration should be described not as various economies but as various types of exchange, because what is directly investigated there is movement of goods, factors and services. In this chapter, we also call them types of exchange (classified by forms of integration).

Those types of exchange are embedded in the social structure. In that case, a way to recognize the characteristic social structure is to examine the correspondence between the social structure and potential instability of types of exchange. In other words, as it could be interpreted that the (positive) function of types of exchange could contribute stability to the social structure concerned, observing factors on which stable types of exchange depend could lead us to characteristics of the social structure. In connection with the above argument, we could indicate that the structure and function focusing upon economy could mitigate uncertainty and could call for stability.[48] Therefore, investigating the predominant type of exchange could also estimate the method of mitigating uncertainty for the social system. In other words, we could try to find the *raison d'être* of the particular method of mitigating uncertainty from the above framework.

Correspondence between potential instability by Smelser and types of exchange could be argued as follows.[49]

We do not think we should go into the details of market trade. Adjustment of costs coming from instability is left to the market mechanism.

In a reciprocative system, transaction is done on the principle that "the exchanging partners are segment units ... which base the exchange of goods and services on an implied reciprocal equivalence at appropriate times and places".[50] If this type of transaction collapsed, it would come from not (in the short-term) demand and supply relations but more social factors. It is mainly due to such a dimensional factor as a shift of sharing part of the value system between exchange partners. Thus, change would be gradual and this system could produce cost saving effects as a result of the stability.[51]

In a redistribution system, "the potential sources of instability are institutionalized in the systems of stratification, or the allocation of rewards in society".[52] As long as there exists institutionalization, there is legitimacy to receive the redistribution. For example, "the flow of charity in modern civilization rests on institutionalized values concerning the relations between the haves and have-nots in a society with unequally distributed rewards".[53] Therefore, by this type of exchange, society could secure stability and could avoid deviation. In that sense, society could have cost saving effects.

In a mobilization system: "The stability or instability of the mobilizative type of exchange depends primarily on the fortunes of those pursuing the collective goals of society, such as wars, maintenance of the state, etc."[54] Examples of this system are cases such as mobilizing resources for economic development and securing raw materials, food and energies for sustained economic growth and for national security.

Smelser developed this further by indicating that the functions of types of exchange in fact correspond to the AGIL scheme. This is summarized in this section by focusing our attention upon the correspondence.

In the social system, an adaptation sub-system has the function of "the supply of facilities by which a variety of goals may be pursued".[55] From a macroscopic viewpoint, economic units take these adaptive functions. In the light of the types of exchange, as these adaptive functions are taken by units specializing in the market mechanism, needless to say market exchange corresponds to this system. Therefore, we can say (focusing our attention upon A_A function) as:

(1) When A_A is dominant, market exchange becomes the dominant type of exchange.

The sub-system of latent pattern-maintenance and tension-management has the function "to preserve the integrity of the value-system itself and to ensure that individual actors conform to it".[56] At the level of society as a whole, families, communities, religious, etc. have this latency function. Referring to this and the types of exchange, what is the type characteristic of preserving the integrity of the value-system? This means the type in which exchange is done with a shared value-system being equilibrated, that is (in focusing our attention upon the A_L function) as follows:

(2) When A_L is dominant, reciprocity becomes the dominant type of exchange.

Integration has the function "which deals with maintaining the interaction among individual units", and at "the level of society as a whole, this involves the allocation of rewards and facilities in accordance with the integrative requirements of society".[57] Therefore, in the light of the types of exchange, it indicates the movement of goods, factors and services with the integrative sub-system of society, and we can say (in focusing our attention upon the A_I function) as follows:

(3) When A_I is dominant, redistribution becomes the dominant type of exchange.

Finally, goal-attainment has the function in which "activities must be directed toward a goal or set of goals" and at "the level of society as a whole, the social units which specialize in goal-attainment are, broadly speaking, political".[58] In the light of types of exchange, activities in this sphere are classified as mobilization, and (in focusing our attention upon the A_G function) we could say as follows:

(4) When A_G is dominant, mobilization becomes the dominant type of exchange.

In the next section, we will examine correspondence between the schemes, methods to mitigate uncertainty, and schemes of international commodity agreements investigated (as shown above) by Parsons, Polanyi and Smelser. Also we will try to clarify a position of a futures market under these links.

Correspondence

In the previous sections of this chapter, we studied economic methods to mitigate uncertainty and we investigated functional exigencies with which a social system could maintain stability and with which social interactions could have less uncertainty. Also, we tried to relate the types of exchange in economic anthropology to the stability of social systems.

The results from the above investigations are as follows. The four methods to mitigate uncertainty correspond to the four functional exigencies, and the four functional exigencies also correspond to the four types of exchange. From the characteristics of the above correspondence, we could observe the close relations among the four methods, the four functional exigencies and the four types of exchange.

Table 12.1 shows the correspondence.

Table 12.1 Correspondence I

Four methods of mitigating uncertainty	Four functional exigencies	Four types of exchange
Futures market	Adaptation (A_A)	Market exchange
International commodity agreement	Goal-attainment (A_G)	Mobilization
Vertical integration	Integration (A_I)	Redistribution
Long-term contract	Latent pattern-maintenance and tension-management (A_L)	Reciprocity

As was shown previously, the A_G in which international commodity agreements are included as a particular case also has the four sub-systems, A_{Ga}, A_{Gg}, A_{Gi}, A_{Gl}. Here, we will summarize the characteristics of the four sub-systems from the viewpoints of this chapter, which are: (1) A_{Gg} has the function of regulating production goals, (2) A_{Gi} has the function of mitigating fluctuations through stock operation, (3) A_{Gl} has the function of ensuring transactions concluded between sellers and buyers in the long-term schedule, (4) A_{Ga} has the function of adapting to price fluctuations.

The methods of international commodity agreement are usually recognized as the following three: (1) export regulation schemes, (2) buffer stock schemes and (3) multilateral contract schemes. As indicated in chapter eleven, the above three schemes work as follows. Each committee sets a price range based upon which the scheme starts to work regulating the market price. The difference between market price and price range is adjusted by: (a) regulating supply quantity (export regulation scheme), (b) regulating the stock level (buffer stock scheme) and (c) ensuring trade quantity (previously determined in a long-term sense) within the price range regardless of market price level (multilateral contract scheme).

We can recognize, therefore, the following relations:

(a) A_{Gg} includes a function of export regulation scheme as a particular case.

(b) A_{Gi} includes a function of buffer stock scheme as a particular case.

(c) A_{Gl} includes a function of multilateral contract scheme as a particular case.

The above means correspondence between schemes of international commodity agreement and functional exigencies. Taking into consideration correspondence between functional exigencies and the types of exchange, we could have the incomplete correspondence as shown in table 12.2

Then, what is necessary to complete table 12.2, and what is a concrete scheme to fill the blank space?

As is recognized in table 12.2, the blank part corresponds to adaptation in the functional sense and corresponds to market exchange in the sense of types of exchange. This means that the blank part might be dominant in efficiency seeking from the viewpoint of functional exigencies and be dominant in a market mechanism from the viewpoint of types of exchange.

When we find the correspondent scheme of adaptation and of market exchange scheme from table 12.1, we could recognize it as a futures market.

In seeking the appropriate scheme for an international commodity agreement, it is more efficient to utilize the market mechanism, whose scheme includes a function of the futures market. The above mentioned scheme might fill the blank in table 12.2.

Table 12.2   Correspondence II

Four methods of international commodity agreement	Four functional exigencies	Four types of exchange
	Adaptation (A_{Ga})	Market exchange
Export regulation scheme	Goal-attainment (A_{Gg})	Mobilization
Buffer stock scheme	Integration (A_{Gi})	Redistribution
Multilateral contract scheme	Latent pattern-maintenance and tension-management (A_{Gl})	Reciprocity

At this stage after the above investigations, we can recognize McKinnon's idea which satisfies each appropriate condition to fill the blank in table 12.2. We would call it a futures market scheme with which table 12.2 could be completed. This is shown in table 12.3. We will enlarge a little further upon the origin of McKinnon's proposal.

The international commodity agreement might be dominant in the A_G function, particularly in the A_{Gg} or A_{Gi} function. Thus, it is inevitable that the international commodity agreement would be less efficient. It would be better to look for a scheme with more A mechanism for the A_G function. If not directly toward the A_A function, which means a function of the futures market, it should employ a relatively more efficient scheme to assign the spot market to the A function and futures market to the G function. We can recognize the above scheme as appropriate to McKinnon's proposal.

As mentioned previously, at the 1995 International Natural Rubber Agreement: "For the purpose of the efficient operation of the Buffer Stock, the Council, under the 1995 Agreement, may decide by consensus to allow the Buffer Stock Manager to purchase futures contract up to a maximum of two months forward on the strict and absolute condition that tenders are taken up on maturity."[59] The modification made in the 1995 Agreement was interesting because it partly overlapped with McKinnon's proposal. The 1995 International Natural Rubber Agreement itself came to an end without any helpful experience, because when negotiations for the 1995 International Natural Rubber Agreement took place, main producing countries like Thailand and The Federation of Malaysia were dissatisfied with the floor price level, and from past experience the agreement usually suffered from a shortage of buffer stock funds to support the floor price level. This might show that international commodity agreements usually hold buffer stock (but suffer from a shortage of funds) but the effective scheme is quite limited to such quantity control as export regulation (which means that it is necessary to persuade producing countries to cooperate with cartel resembling behaviors). On the one hand, and after all, it is necessary to pay attention to the corresponding framework, basically depending upon a function to collect information, etc., on the other hand.

Table 12.3 Correspondence III

Four methods of international commodity agreement	Four functional exigencies	Four types of exchange
Futures market scheme	Adaptation(A_{Ga})	Market exchange
Export regulation scheme	Goal-attainment(A_{Gg})	Mobilization
Buffer stock scheme	Integration(A_{Gi})	Redistribution
Multilateral contract scheme	Latent pattern-maintenance and tension-management (A_{Gl})	Reciprocity

The purpose of this chapter is to examine the correct position of futures markets. We started by proposing the frameworks of sociology and anthropology in order to have a *raison d'être* for international commodity agreements and by investigating the criteria of their schemes. Based upon the above studies, we tried to find the position of futures markets from the viewpoints of correspondence with functional exigencies and types of exchange.

Final Remarks

In this chapter, we attempted to "embed" McKinnon's idea into sociological frameworks and anthropological findings. With the same analysis, we tried to find the *raison d'être* and explanations for schemes of international commodity agreements, and to find the position and function of futures markets.

Putting forward this chapter's analysis, applying the boundary interchange of the AGIL scheme to the issues in this chapter can help for investigating the interactions between economic units in the context of different types of exchange. In particular, they might supply effective approaches to understanding the different schemes with different dominancies that transition economies have.

The analysis in this chapter seems to be a milestone for further investigation. As a matter of fact, we could easily imagine that, in the reform processes for economic transition and in introducing commodity futures market as a reform measure, one has to consider inappropriate correspondence of methods to mitigate uncertainty, functional exigencies, types of exchange etc. It might be the right time to examine appropriate correspondence among them ten years after transition, and also ten years after establishing the Budapest Commodity Exchange and five years after establishing the Warsaw Commodity Exchange.

Notes

1   See, for example, Morita (1981).
2   McKinnon (1967), p.858.
3   On the arguments see, for example, Morita (1981).
4   Hicks (1946), pp.133-135.
5   See Hicks (1946), p.134.
6   Hicks (1946), p.135.
7   Hicks (1946), p.135.
8   Hicks (1946), p.135.
9   On the details see for example Sekino (1976).
10 Scherer (1970) p.248.
11 To clarify from the chapter we would say that (1)-(4) above have differences in terms of weight they give to which function, and needless to say it would be impossible to say which is better or worse as far as there are no priorities for the functions.
12 Concerning devices to mitigate uncertainty see, for example, Harris et al. (1978).
13 Tominaga (1965) p.72.
14 Tominaga (1965) p.79, see also Tominaga (1999) on the current of contemporary sociology.
15 Tominaga (1965) p.77. On this attempt by Parsons, Tominaga (1999) mentioned that the issue described by Weber to approach relations between economy and society from viewpoint of sociology was followed by Parsons after more than 30 years. Parsons recognized the relations between economy and society to be like relations between the economic system and social system by understanding that, following Weber's theory of action with combining it to a theory of system, economic system is to be a system of economic behavior and social system to be a system of social action. We should be careful that the social system is not the same level of concept as the economic system, but the economic system is a sub-system of the social system (see p.205). Moreover, Tominaga (1999) argued, with regard to the question of what meaning the concept of

social action including economic behavior has, that no social relation of universalism generally comes into existence and the social relation of particularism is rather usual in lots of social action (pp.206-207).

16 See Tominaga (1965) pp.82-83. In Tominaga (1965), it was said to have been added that before that procedure mentioned there was a procedure for establishing a conceptual framework and after that procedure there was a procedure for formulating processes of structural change. Needless to say, however, the main theme was a decision of structure and a decision of functional mechanism, which seem to be enough from the viewpoint of this chapter.

17 On the detail, see, for example, Parsons and Smelser (1956). The following part of this chapter mainly borrows from the fourth chapter of Parsons and Smelser (1956).

18 The following is based upon Shiobara and others (1969) p.48.

19 For example, see Parsons and Smelser (1956).

20 Parsons and Smelser (1956), p.196.

21 Parsons and Smelser (1956), p.200.

22 Parsons and Smelser (1956), p.202.

23 Parsons and Smelser (1956), p.202.

24 In this chapter we will not refer to the border relations.

25 Parsons and Smelser (1956), p.202.

26 Parsons and Smelser (1956), p.202.

27 Parsons and Smelser (1956), p.204.

28 Parsons and Smelser (1956), p.204.

29 Parsons and Smelser (1956), p.205.

30 Parsons and Smelser (1956), p.204.

31 Parsons and Smelser (1956), p.204.

32 Parsons and Smelser (1956), p.203.

33 Parsons and Smelser (1956), p.204.

34 Parsons and Smelser (1956), p.199.

35 Parsons and Smelser (1956), pp.199-200.

36 Parsons and Smelser (1956), p.200.

37 Parsons and Smelser (1956), p.200.

38 See Polanyi (1977).

39 Tominaga (1999), p.207.

40 See Polanyi (1977).

41 The substantial meaning of "economic" was defined to be institutionalized procedure of the interaction between human being and the environment (see Polanyi et al. (1957)).

42 See Polanyi et al. (1957). Needless to say, the three forms are not exhaustive.

43 This was summarized in a table in Smelser (1959), p.178.

44 See Polanyi et al. (1957).

45 Something similar was covered in Nishibe (1975), p.87.

46 In investigations into scarcity by Smelser (1959), there were very interesting opinions about relations between society and uncertainty.

47 Smelser (1959), p.179.

48 Smelser (1959), p.177.

49 The following is dependent on Smelser (1959), pp.180-181.

50 Smelser (1959), p.180.

51 It would be helpful to refer to Blau (1964) in which Blau had a more detailed investigation into differences between social exchange and economic exchange. According to Tominaga's explanation (1999, p.347), it is as follows: what was emphasized by Blau in particular was that social exchange was different from

economic exchange, as social exchange was accompanied with unspecified obligation. Economic exchange finishes temporarily, but because social exchange has a tendency to awaken such feelings as personal obligation, gratitude, reliance, etc., reciprocal relations among exchange parties concerned have a tendency to be long-lasting. Blau explicitly illustrated this using the distinctions of internal reward with external reward. Physical benefit is external reward and love, respect, approval, etc. are internal reward. Economic exchange is the exchange of external reward and social exchange is the exchange of internal reward. Social exchange is, therefore, on the condition of long-lasting social relations.

52 Smelser (1959), p.180.
53 Smelser (1959), p.180.
54 Smelser (1959), p.180.
55 Smelser (1959), p.181.
56 Smelser (1959), p.181.
57 Smelser (1959), p.181.
58 Smelser (1959), p.181.
59 International Natural Rubber Organization, negotiation for the International Natural Rubber Agreement, 1995. (Homepage contents of International Natural Rubber Organization, see http://www.inro.com.my/inro).

Chapter 13

A Political Economy of
the Futures Market

Introduction

The purpose of this chapter is to examine the function of international commodity agreements and futures markets from the viewpoint of international political economy.

In chapter eleven price level adjustment functions of international commodity agreement were examined from an economics point of view, and in chapter twelve we tried to find the *raison d'être* and function of international commodity agreements and futures markets. This chapter, therefore, is a sequel to the above investigations. (There may be some repeated explanations, but the author has tries to avoid excessive repetition.)

As in the previous chapters, the topics in this chapter consider the *raison d'être* and devices of international commodity agreements, and the adequate position of futures markets within a conceptual framework.

The intergovernmental arrangement of commodity agreements has been, as is well known, pursued since the 1970s and 1980s. As foreign debt issues in developing countries have become more serious, international commodity agreements have become less popular, but important situations in international commodity agreements for North-South issues mean that using intergovernmental agreements to solve serious economic problems in developing economies is unchanged.

Analytical tools in the field of the international political economy have been developed since the end of the 1970s with international regime theory as the leading interest. One of the main reasons for this is that, although the national power of the hegemonic country, the US, has relatively been reduced since the end of 1960s, international order has not collapsed but has been maintained and thus what was the main explanation for the *raison d'être* (of the international order)? Needless to say, there have been doubts against the plausibility of regime theory,[1] and undoubtedly it could be recognized that the national power of the US has increased relatively since the collapse of the Cold War (often called "globalization"). However, for example, in 2001, it was easy to point out the rather serious situation arising from the prevention of an international agreement like the Kyoto Protocol on environment issues. Therefore, it would be meaningful to ask what is the international order and what is a reasonable explanation of the *raison d'être* of international order. What we would like to confirm here is that studies in the field of international regimes are for trying to find explanations of the *raison d'être* of international order. Needless to say, an agreement concluded internationally like an international commodity agreement is an international regime for bringing order in international economic relations. It seems to be reasonable enough to apply international regime theory to finding the *raison d'être* of international commodity agreements and to examine the adjustment function of futures markets.

In this chapter, we will describe international regime theory in the first section. In the second section we look at the correspondence with sociological and anthropological types. In the third section, we will examine the correspondence with schemes of international commodity agreement. Finally in the fourth section, based upon the investigations in the previous sections, we will study the topics of international commodity agreement and futures markets from the viewpoint of political economy.

International Regime Theory

What is an International Regime?

It goes without saying, in the field of international political economy, there have been various ways of thinking and it would be rather difficult to put forward widely approved analytical frameworks.[2]

There are various differences depending upon relative importance in political and economic affairs, etc.

In this chapter, we will focus our attention upon the framework called "international regime" out of various frameworks in the international political economy, because from the viewpoint of the analytical purpose of this chapter, the "center-periphery" approach based upon the assertions of A.G. Frank and I. Wallerstein etc., is inappropriate because it pays more attention to the systemic sphere. Also the "political economy" approach based upon the arguments of S. Strange, R. K. Ashley etc., might be difficult, as the viewpoint is too wide and relations between nations and international systems might be rather vague.

However, the term "international regime" has various definitions.

For example, John Ruggie (1975) defined a regime as "a set of mutual expectations, rules and regulations, plans, organizational energies and financial commitments, which have been accepted by a group of states".[3] Keohane (1984) defined international regimes as "sets of implicit or explicit principles, norms, rules, and decision-making procedures around which actors' expectations converge in a given area of international relations".[4]

The analytical target in this chapter is not the definition of international regime, and we define the term here as Keohane (1984) did. The main topics in this chapter investigate what kind of types of international regimes there are and study how international regimes are differentiated.

In order to find the classification of international regimes, we need criteria to classify their characteristics.

From the viewpoint of this chapter and within the framework of international regimes, one criterion is the nature of benefit from a regime and the other criterion is the nature of the necessity to move toward a regime.

The argument on the nature of the benefit of moving to a regime is as follows. According to the realist's view, a nation state is independent and behaves based on its self interest. An international regime would be formed with the self interest which the nation state has independently.[5] According to the institutionalist's view, compared to the realist's view, the interdependent relations among nation states by which the institutional framework is formed (with some reasons), and the shared interest provided by the institutional framework is given great importance. The international regime would provide the order based upon the shared interest. The institutionalist's view gives reasons for maintaining a regime, but it does not give reasons for why a regime is formed. Also the realist's view gives reasons for why a regime is formed, but it does not explain reasons for maintaining a regime (that is, order could exist in international political economy for the long term). Therefore, according to the functionalist's view, they take the realist's view in forming a regime and the institutionalist's view in maintaining a regime, and integrate both views.[6]

We will not discuss this point further. It is enough for us here to confirm that great importance would be attached to self interest and shared interest in forming and maintaining an international regime to different degrees. The importance for this chapter is that the benefit of moving to a regime are self interest and shared interest. This is one criterion that characterizes the international regime.

The argument on the nature of the necessity to move to a regime is as follows (the following figures and schemes come from A. A. Stein (1986)). The "prisoners' dilemma" type scheme is as shown in figure 13.1. It is well known and we will not go into the details, but the essence of the scheme is that, for the actor A, when the actor B prefers B_1, A prefers A_2 as $4 > 3$, and also when B prefers B_2, A prefers A_2 as $2 > 1$. For the actor B, when the actor A prefers A_1, B prefers B_2 as $4 > 3$, and also when A prefers A_2, B prefers B_2 as $2 > 1$. This indicates that the actor A always prefers A_2 when A behaves based upon self interest, and that the actor B always prefers B_2 when B behaves based upon self interest. Therefore, when actors behave based upon self interest, the equilibrium always reaches *(A₂, B₂)* and the outcome is $(2,2)$. However, it is easy to recognize that for a society as a whole and for each actor the outcome $(3,3)$ coming from the equilibrium *(A₁, B₁)* would be better. In such a situation, in order not to reach the prisoners' dilemma equilibrium *(A₂, B₂)* it might be necessary to have an international regime.

The "dilemma of common aversion" type scheme is as shown in figure 13.2. The essence of the dilemma is as follows.[7] For the actor A, when the actor B chooses B_1, A chooses A_2 as $4 > 2$, and when the actor B chooses B_2, A chooses A_1 as $3 > 1$. Therefore, when B_1, A chooses A_2, and when B_2, A chooses A_1. For the actor B, when the actor A chooses A_1, B chooses B_2 as $4 > 2$, and when the actor A chooses A_2, B chooses B_1 as $3 > 1$. Thus, when A_1, B prefers B_2, and when A_2, B prefers B_1. As the result of independent behavior by A and B searching for self interest, either (A_1, B_2) or (A_2, B_1) exists. If a regime in which the results (A_1, B_2) and (A_2, B_1) might happen with $\frac{1}{2}$ probability is introduced, the expected profit for both A and B would become $\frac{7}{2}$. In that case, therefore, both A and B cooperate to introduce the regime.

The main difference between the prisoners' dilemma and the dilemma of common aversions is whether or not voluntary cooperation could exist. This means that in the former case, in which each actor calls for self interest, the scheme could reach a unique equilibrium with no Pareto optimum, and in the latter case, in which there could be no unique equilibrium, it might be possible to have more expected profit if a cooperated regime could be introduced. It could be also said that the prisoners' dilemma type scheme is a case in which calling for self interest might not be consistent with shared interest, but the dilemma of a common aversions type scheme is a case in which calling for self interest might be consistent with shared interest.

It could be said in another way that in cases of the dilemma of common aversions it would be easier to be consistent with rules than in cases of the prisoners' dilemma. In this chapter, we can call the former case "rule consistency" and the latter case "rule confrontation". Rule confrontation means that it is relatively difficult to reach a unified rule, and does not mean that actors are hostile to a rule.

Actor *B*

	B_1	B_2
Actor *A*		
A_1	3 , 3	1 , 4
A_2	4 , 1	2 , 2

Figure 13.1 Prisoners' dilemma

Source: Stein (1986), p.122.

Actor *B*

	B_1	B_2
Actor *A*		
A_1	2 , 2	3 , 4
A_2	4 , 3	1 , 1

Figure 13.2 Dilemma of common aversions

Source: Stein (1986), p.126.

We will not investigate the nature of "games" further. What is more important for this chapter is to recognize that the nature of necessity to move to an international regime has the two cases of: (1) rule consistency and (2) rule confrontation. It is another criterion for characterizing an international regime.

There are also some benefits in forming an international regime focusing our attention upon more specific points. We would like to mention the following four natures of benefit.

The first benefit is to mitigate uncertainty. In this chapter, we should first clarify the nature of mitigating uncertainty. It might be a good way to recognize the nature of mitigating uncertainty in examining a typical "insurance regime".[8] An example of an insurance regime is a STABEX scheme (export earnings stabilization scheme), which is a scheme that includes fund pooling for preparing for export earnings' reduction. The effect of mitigating uncertainty is to increase the expected benefit for individual actors by providing shared interest for a shock absorbing mechanism.

The second benefit is to reduce the cost of gathering information. The main ways for the regime to reduce information gathering costs are the following two. One is the way of establishing the organization to gather information, to analyze information and to provide information so that functions that deal with information are improved. The other is the way of promoting a contract agreement and transaction because the regime formation would try to remove asymmetric information and to make negotiation and transaction easier.[9]

The third benefit is to introduce stability. As was shown as a definition of the regime, it means sets of implicit or explicit principles, norms, rules, and decision-making procedures around which actors' expectations converge in a given area of international relations. We could recognize that a regime has principles, norms, etc. The third benefit is closely related to the mechanism to converge the actors' expectations and behaviors in a given area of international relations. That is to say, violation and destruction of the principles and rules of a regime would cause other countries to retaliate and would disgrace the international reputation of the country. In order to avoid the above costs, expectations and behaviors would converge in a given area of international relations toward principles, norms, rules, etc. The mechanism toward convergence results in the third benefit of stability by setting a regime.

The fourth benefit is to reduce transaction costs. The benefit of a regime is less transaction costs for the following two reasons. One is that, as mentioned, the existence of a regime could save the cost of negotiation when nations need to negotiate over some specific issues because a regime provides common sets of implicit or explicit principles, norms, rules, and decision-making procedures. In other words, a regime could absorb the portion of fixed cost and countries in negotiation could reduce the marginal cost for negotiation and transaction. The other reason is that, as a regime provides principles and norms etc., multiple issues in different fields could be linked. That is to say, unless a regime existed, each country would separate each issue and have to start by establishing principles, norms, rules, etc. for each issue. By absorbing the problems and waste, a regime could reduce marginal costs for negotiations and transactions. That is the effect of reducing transaction costs.

As mentioned earlier, and in the fourth section, we have a standard view on the change of international regime.

The following are three explanations on the change to international regime.[10]

The first explanation is realism. Needless to say, as mentioned above, the realist's view emphasizes self interest. From the viewpoint of realism, therefore, self interest combined with national power comprise the power distribution, and with a change in the power distribution a regime would change.

The second explanation is functionalism. The functionalist's view emphasizes shared interest concerning the change to a regime. From the viewpoint of functionalism, therefore, depending upon the nature of shared interest and the preference of the actors, the regime employed would be decided on and changed.

The third explanation is epistemology. From the viewpoint of epistemology, a regime would be formed by ideology and knowledge, and therefore the change of value consciousness and recognition would lead to a change of regime.

(In this chapter, we will not theoretically investigate more about the change to international regime. As considered in the fourth section of this chapter, our investigations will be limited to applying the framework to interpret international commodity agreements.)

Classification of International Regimes

Based upon the investigation in the previous section, the purpose of this section is to recognize how to classify international regimes, which is also a basis for the investigations in the next sections.

As studied earlier, the two criteria to characterize a regime are: (1) a criterion of self interest and shared interest to move toward the formation of a regime, and (2) a criterion of rule consistency and rule confrontation leading to a necessity to form a regime. According to the two criteria, there could be four quadrants as shown in figure 13.3. Also the nature of the four benefits could correspond to the four quadrants. The purpose of this section is to investigate the correspondence between the four benefits and the four quadrants.

Quadrant I is the area in which self interest and rule consistency are dominant. In the four benefits described earlier, the effect of mitigating uncertainty, like the case of an insurance regime, provides a mechanism against probable risks and has the function of increasing self interest measured by expected benefit. This effect could come under the classification of rule consistency, meaning putting more weight upon self interest consisting with shared interest. Therefore, we could say that:

The effect of mitigating uncertainty is a function in quadrant I.

Quadrant II is the area in which shared interest and rule consistency are dominant. This area indicates the case where it is difficult to cover the costs only by benefit seeking behavior and which has a characteristic compatible with rationality seeking self interest. The effect which comes under this characteristic in the four benefits might be the effect of reducing the information gathering cost. That is to say, the effect of contributing shared interest for regime members through providing information and of making transactions more active by eliminating asymmetry of information has a characteristic common with self interest. Therefore, we can say that:

The effect of reducing information collecting costs is a function in quadrant II.

Quadrant III is the area in which shared interest and rule confrontation are dominant. This area shows the case in which is difficult to cover the costs only by self interest seeking behavior and which would reach the non-Pareto optimum unique equilibrium. This means it is rather more difficult to provide shared interest than in other quadrants. In the four benefits, the effect that comes under this characteristic might be stability through binding force by a regime. That is to say, the effect indicates order and stability by arranging a mechanism through forming a regime to prevent such costs as a decline of international trust, when it would be difficult for an individual actor to voluntarily adjust to destruction and disorder, etc. by self interest. Therefore, we can mention that:

The effect of having stability is a function in quadrant III.

Quadrant IV is the area in which self interest and rule confrontation are dominant. Although self interest has put more weight upon it, with only self interest they would reach non-Pareto optimum equilibrium and it is necessary to avoid this situation by forming a regime. In the four benefits, the effect of reducing transaction costs might be most appropriate to this area. That is to say, when in negotiations and transactions for goods and services, it could make self interest of individual actors much more important by forming a regime in combining negotiation and transaction issues. In such an example as raising tariff barriers for optimum tariffs for countries concerned, forming a regime of international free trade and reducing transaction costs shows the effect. Therefore, we could say that:

The effect of reducing transaction costs is a function in quadrant IV.

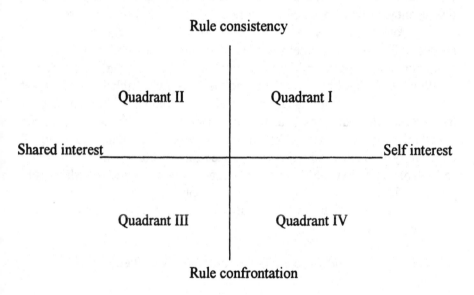

Figure 13.3 Four quadrants

As indicated above, we can see the four quadrants constructed by two axes: (1) the axis of benefit shown by self interest and shared interest, and (2) the axis of cooperation indicated by rule consistency and rule confrontation. Also we can see the four benefits of forming a regime which corresponds to the four quadrants based upon dominance. This makes the four classifications of international regimes clear.

The Correspondence

The purpose of this section is to investigate the four types of international regime, the four schemes for mitigating uncertainty in economics, the four functional exigencies in sociology, the four types of transaction in anthropology, and to examine the correspondence between them (we will not, however, describe them in detail as we mentioned previously).

Correspondence to the Four Schemes in Economics

In consumers' and producers' behavior, between expected and realized prices occurs for several reasons. The reason why it is difficult to adjust the discrepancy is that "people may foresee their own wants incorrectly, or make wrong estimates of the results of the technical processes of production".[11] A way to alleviate the risk coming from such discrepancy is transactions in futures markets. That is to say, a futures market is a device to alleviate disequilibrium in the spot market by establishing a market intertemporarily and by adapting to the environment through market transaction. In that sense, a futures market is a device to mitigate uncertainty through the market. In other words, a device to mitigate uncertainty through the market is a device in rule consistency to increase self interest in an expected sense through a function of a regime which is to provide shared interest, putting more emphasis upon self interest of individual actors. Therefore, we can say concerning quadrant I in the previous section that:

Quadrant I corresponds to a function of a futures market.

In utilizing the futures market, it is necessary to pay deposit money, particularly when there could be great uncertainty and a big risk. In order to eliminate such costs, in general, the following two devices would be established.

One is a device based upon shared interest provided by a regime. This means that buyers and sellers decide the transactions between themselves by forming a regime to mitigate uncertainty. Such a device is for tension management leading to the implementation of a contract by mitigating uncertainty through shared interest between actors based upon self interest equilibrium (reciprocity).

The device to mitigate uncertainty by long-term contract undoubtedly indicates a rule consistent scheme, making the increase in self interest compatible with attaching much importance to the shared interest provided by a regime. Therefore, concerning quadrant II, it could be said that:

Quadrant II corresponds to a function of long-term contract.

The other is a device based upon self interest provided by a regime. This indicates that it might not be probable to keep a contract because of price fluctuation and long negotiation being in a stalemate position, etc., for buyers and sellers to be in reciprocity, even if they have a long-term contract.[12] It is a case in which a regime of long-term contract does not work effectively. In such a case, it might be more effective to have a device putting more weight upon self interest, although it is rule confronted, to mitigate uncertainty and to eliminate cost burden. This could be a case in which, on the initiative of either buyer or seller, they are integrated and various resources are redistributed. Through the redistribution, the overall benefit could be increased by alleviating uncertainty. We call the case vertical integration. Thus, it could be said that in quadrant IV:

Quadrant IV corresponds to a function of vertical integration.

The devices mentioned above are established by individual actions to form a regime.

However, there could be the case in which reasonable action by individual actors would not create enough solutions. The nature of such a case is rather rule confronted, for which government intervention could be used as a get out. Also government intervention could be used to get shared interest of goal attainment. The international commodity agreement would be used as a device for government to mobilize resources for mitigating uncertainty. Therefore, it could be said that for quadrant III shared interest and rule confrontation are dominant:

Quadrant III corresponds to a function of international commodity agreement.

Correspondence to the Four Functional Exigencies

Next we will examine the correspondence to the four functional exigencies. As mentioned previously, and we will not go into details here, a sociological answer to the question of what is a function for keeping a society which is interdependent system constant, is the four functional exigencies known as the AGIL scheme as shown earlier. A macroscopic way of describing the functional exigencies is as follows: a sub-system taking A is economy, G is polity, I is the integrative sub-system, and L is the pattern-maintenance and tension-management sub-system.

We focus our attention here upon the A sub-system. Particularly we will examine more specific sub-sytems within the A sub-system called here A_A, A_G, A_I, A_L.

A_A is known as a function for adapting to a demand for current production. In other words, it is a function to maximize profit opportunity efficiently by adapting flexibly for uncertainty. Therefore, in this function, individual actors behave to maximize self interest to adapt the rule consistently.

Quadrant I corresponds to the A function.

A_L is a function to provide, keep and renew a motivation pattern which is indispensable in order for a system to interact. In a sub-system like this, there could be functions of commitment to long-term productivity, commitment to productivity, commitment to planned allocation of resources, and economic values. Therefore, under the functions, individual actors would behave in a rule consistent way and put more weight upon shared interest provided by a regime.

Quadrant II corresponds to the L function.

A_G is a function of the production sub-system. Thus, the policy would be determined to attain particular goals. For example, having a goal to regulate the production volume for keeping the price level stabilized, and regulating the production level to implement the goal would be included as the function of this sub-system. Individual actors would behave, therefore, as attaching more importance to shared interest in the rule confrontation situation.

Quadrant III corresponds to the G function.

A_I is a function of an entrepreneurial sub-system. As the I function has a function of social integration, the A_I sub-system has an entrepreneurial function. This means that the A_I function has an enterprise function of redistributing production factors to adjust market demand, and has a function of introducing new ways of combining production factors with market demand (this is usually called vertical integration). Therefore, under the function of A_I, individual actors accept the prerequisite of social integration, even in rule confrontation under which they attach more importance to self interest.

Quadrant V corresponds to the *I* function.

Correspondence to the four exchange types

How about the correspondence to the four exchange types? As shown in the previous chapter, the term "exchange types" refers to the concept based upon both Polanyi's way of classification, which classified economies according to dominant integration type, and Smelser's further analysis. According to that, (positive) functions of exchange types could be interpreted to give the social structure concerned permanency, and finding factors to make exchange types stable could contribute to recognizing the framework of a regime. Hereinafter, we will study exchange types according to Smelser (1959) and investigate the correspondence.

The first type of exchange is a system of exchange through the market. We do not need to explain the details about this first type. Structural stability of the society concerned could be achieved through the adjustment function of markets. Needless to say, the situation in which market exchange works well indicates a case of rule consistency and importance is attached to self interest of individual actors. Therefore, we could say that:

In quadrant I, market exchange is a dominant type of exchange.

The second type of exchange is a system of reciprocity. Under the reciprocal system, exchange would be done based upon the principle which says that the exchange of goods and services should be in reciprocative equivalence. In other words, if this type of exchange collapses, it would not happen in the short-term but occur slowly through the collapsing of the shared value system among individual actors. It could be recognized, therefore, that the existence of a reciprocal principle sharing value system provides shared interest, absorbing information about collecting costs and could be compatible with rule consistent behavior.

In quadrant II, reciprocity is a dominant type of exchange.

The third type of exchange is a system of mobilization. Under the mobilization system, pursuing the collective goals of society which are not provided by self interest would be dominant and public authority mobilizes resources to achieve the goals. An example of this type of exchange is the mobilization of resources by government to industrialize and grow the economy. Therefore, more importance is attached to shared interest of pursuing the collective goals, which could not be achieved by self interest, and which means it is rule confronted.

In quadrant III, mobilization is a dominant type of exchange.

The fourth type of exchange is a system of redistribution. This redistribution system indicates the institutionalization of the allocation of rewards in society. Under this type of exchange, the flow of goods and services by charity could be done with the institutionalized values (for example, the relations between the haves and have-nots - the haves should give to the have-nots - contribute to the stability of society). This type of exchange enables the society to secure stability and to avoid social deviation. When compared with the reciprocal system, it is clear that this system does not have reciprocative equivalence and individual actors are not rule consistent. It might be necessary, therefore, for social stability with this type of exchange to combine with increasing self interest (or the expected self interest). In that sense, this system is rule confronted and attaches more importance to self interest.

In quadrant IV, redistribution is a dominant type of exchange.

In this section, as mentioned above, we are examining the correspondence of quadrants I-IV to the four devices to mitigate uncertainty, the four functional exigencies and the four types of exchanges. We will summarize them here. Quadrant I (which is rule consistent and attaches more importance to self interest) corresponds to the function of mitigating the effect of uncertainty through a regime and corresponds to the function of a futures market, and also corresponds to the A (adaptation) function. In quadrant I, market exchange is dominant in the type of exchange. Quadrant II (which is rule consistent and attaches more importance to shared interest) corresponds to the function of declining costs of information collecting and to the function of long-term contract. Quadrant II also corresponds to the L (latent pattern-maintenance and tension-management) function, and reciprocity for the type of exchange is dominant. Quadrant III (which is rule confronted and attaches more importance to shared interest) corresponds to the function of the stabilization effect and to the function of international commodity agreements. Quadrant III also corresponds to the G (goal-attainment) function and mobilization of the exchange type is dominant. Quadrant IV (which is rule confronted and attaches more importance to self interest) corresponds to the function of reducing transaction costs through a regime and to the function of vertical integration. Quadrant IV also corresponds to the *I* (integration) function and redistribution of the type of exchange is dominant.

Correspondence to the Schemes of International Commodity Agreements

In the previous two sections, we classified international regimes into four types and four quadrants. Also we investigated the correspondence to four devices to mitigate uncertainty, four functional exigencies and four types of exchange.

The purpose of this section is to expand the correspondences to schemes of international commodity agreements and to examine the function of futures markets.

First we will recapitulate here the schemes of international commodity agreements (see chapter eleven for details). Usually the following three schemes are employed: (1) multilateral contract, (2) export regulation, and (3) buffer stock. First the agreement sets floor and ceiling prices which creates a price range. When a market price level differs from the price range, the stabilizing scheme starts to operate.

The buffer stock scheme operates to make a market price within the price range by buying and selling operations of stocks through the authority's intervention.

This scheme has advantages compared with other schemes because there is no obligation for the authority to directly intervene in the trade and there are no serious obstacles to the outsider problem. However, actually, it is difficult to solve such problems as the size of buffer stock and who finances the cost and who operates it. It has been said that the scheme has been most discussed and least realized.[13] The buffer stock scheme was operated in the International Tin Agreement, International Cocoa Agreement, International Natural Rubber Agreement, etc., and it was jointly operated with the export regulation scheme in the International Tin Agreement and International Cocoa Agreement. In the case of the International Tin Agreement, which was evaluated as successful because of the price stabilization, it could be said that the main reason for the price stabilization was the strategic stockpile behavior of the US.[14] (As well known, however, the international agreement was in serious crisis throughout the 1985 tin case). That is to say, even if it is considered to have a superior mechanism, it seems that it is not easy to operate well with the scheme.

When a difference between the market price level and price range level is observed, an export regulation scheme can be used to adjust the difference by regulating the export (or production) quantity. An export regulation scheme was operated in the International Sugar Agreement, International Coffee Agreement, International Tin Agreement, International Cocoa Agreement, etc., and was most often operated as a quantity regulation mechanism.[15] However, in fact, when the market price level was above the ceiling, the only operation was to stop the quantity regulation. It could be argued that the regulation of ceiling level and floor level is extreme asymmetry. The scheme has, therefore, various problems like market distortion, free riders' benefit for non-member countries, etc. Generally speaking, an international commodity agreement is actually operated through an export regulation scheme. (In other words, when the export regulation scheme is not successfully operated, it is difficult to make the agreement work.)

The multilateral contract scheme has a mechanism in which a guaranteed quantity of overall transaction is decided and, limited to the guarantee part, the difference between the market price level and price range level is adjusted by the burden of either export countries or import countries. When market price is above the ceiling level, the difference must be adjusted by the export countries and when below the floor level, by the import countries. Needless to say, the quantity outside the guaranteed part is traded in the market. As investigated in chapter eleven, this scheme was operated in the International Wheat Agreement in the 1949 agreement to the 1956 agreement, and in the 1959 agreement to the 1967 agreement.

Chiba (1987) expressed the view that, in the future, the multilateral contract scheme would neither be operated by the wheat agreement nor by other commodity agreements.[16] It could be said that this scheme is compatible with a market mechanism, but it would be necessary to have various technical conditions and economic conditions. Moreover, as mentioned in chapter eleven, the history of the International Wheat Agreement suggests that the actual mechanism working for the international agreement was not a multilateral contract scheme but an export regulation scheme.

The three schemes of international commodity agreements include the above mechanisms, in which an export regulation scheme would actually work for most of the international commodity agreement operations.

Then, what are the criteria for employing a particular scheme for a commodity agreement? (See chapter eleven for details of the criteria, here we give a summary.)

The multilateral contract scheme is mentioned above, which means that when the market price is above the ceiling price, export countries adjust the difference to make the market price fall within the price range, and when the market price is below the floor price, import countries adjust the difference to make the market price increase within the price range. It could be said that a penalty rule is introduced so that transactions not within the price range are penalized (needless to say the transaction is implemented). Therefore, the criterion for a multilateral contract scheme is whether or not the transaction is carried on even if it is penalized. It would be necessary that, when the transaction was significantly different from the price range, a more severe penalty is applied. When the penalty is too severe, the transaction could not be carried on and the function of the multilateral contract scheme would not work. In other words, how much the penalty is or how much the fluctuation of the market price is, is the criterion for a multilateral contract scheme to be operated. Therefore, we can say that "it might be in the case of relatively stable market prices that the multilateral contract scheme could be employed". From the viewpoint of this chapter, we could say that market price is relatively stable and individual actors are rule consistent in a multilateral contract scheme. It could be recognized also here that the scheme gains shared interest by stabilizing prices, not causing a tension between transaction parties and being reciprocal of the burden between export countries and import countries. Therefore, we can say that:

The multilateral contract scheme corresponds to quadrant II.

The facts about the multilateral contract scheme might show that the penalty would be too severe and the multilateral contract scheme could not function, and as Chiba (1987) suggested, the multilateral contract scheme would not be employed for commodity agreements. In that case, the mechanism to adjust the difference between the market price level and price range level through the transactions of export and import countries could not work.

Then how could the difference (the disequilibrium) be adjusted?

There are two ways, as follows: (1) with the market, and (2) without the market. (1) means a buffer stock scheme and (2) indicates an export regulation scheme. What are the criteria for employing a buffer stock scheme and an export regulation scheme? Also, in the case of buffer stock, whether to impose a stock burden on consuming countries or producing countries would depend on the market.

The case for consuming countries to bear the burden is of adjusting the excess supply without a price mechanism. It might be the same situation as when consumers are in an all or nothing demand curve with a fixed price. Another way of saying this is that it could not exist if the all or nothing demand curve did not exist. Therefore, we can say that the case for employing a buffer stock scheme with more burden for consumer countries only occurs when producing countries have enough market control and the excess supply volume is less than the demand volume at the floor price.

The case for producing countries to bear the burden is as follows. In adjusting the excess supply under a fixed price, when producing countries impose the adjustment cost (that is, the stock management cost), the real level of floor price is reduced and the benefit for producing countries is reduced. If an all or nothing demand curve exists, however, the portion above the normal demand curve is transferred from consuming countries to producing countries and the benefit for producing countries is increased. When keeping the price level and the excess supply fixed, the net value comparing increased portion with decreased portion depends upon the real level of floor price, which means the stock management cost. Therefore, we can say that the case for employing a buffer stock scheme with more burden for producing countries only occurs when the unit cost for managing the stock is relatively small.

As indicated above, the buffer stock scheme crucially depends upon the size of stock and the burden sharing and the scheme is a case of rule confrontation for individual actors. It could be reasonably said that when the buffer stock mechanism is successfully managed and when the price stabilization effect is recognized, it means buffer stock management is profitable. On the contrary, however, when buffer stock management destabilizes the price level, it indicates that the buffer stock management produces a loss and a new cost burden. In other words, the buffer stock mechanism would attach more importance to self interest. That is to say:

The buffer stock scheme corresponds to quadrant IV.

Once again the facts are as mentioned previously that the buffer stock scheme was discussed most often and was the realized mechanism. The main reason for it might be the difficulty of adjusting the stock managing cost.

When the price level fluctuates heavily and the stock management cost is fairly high, it would be reasonable for the government to intervene rather than leaving it to the market mechanism,[17] which is an export regulation scheme. The reasons why an export regulation was most often employed in international commodity agreements are difficulties in satisfying the criteria for a multilateral contract scheme and a buffer stock scheme and the final dependence would be upon the export quantity regulation among member countries. This is the criterion for employing an export regulation scheme. This means therefore that the export regulation scheme puts more weight upon shared interest, the stabilization of price levels through quantity regulation of export countries. It can easily be recognized in the nature of rule confrontation what the allocation to regulate quantity among export member countries is, what the regulation against non-member countries is, and what the adjustment of claims among import member countries is, as it is difficult to keep the ceiling price level.

Therefore, we could say that:

The export regulation scheme corresponds to quadrant III.

In this section, we examined the correspondence between schemes of international commodity agreement and the quadrants investigated in the first section, showing that the multilateral contract scheme corresponds to quadrant II, the export regulation scheme corresponds to quadrant III and the buffer stock scheme corresponds to quadrant IV.

A Political Economy of International Commodity Agreements

The purpose of this chapter is to clarify the correspondence between international commodity agreement schemes and the types of international regime in political science, the devices to mitigate uncertainty in economics, the functional exigencies in sociology and the types of exchange in anthropology. The reason for examining the correspondence is to have a clearer view with regard to the questions investigated in this book. The main purpose of this chapter based upon the above investigations is to explain the *raison d'être* of the international commodity agreement and to find the appropriate position of a futures market, and also to interpret the trends in international commodity agreements.

In this chapter's explanation, the trends in international commodity agreements are to interpret why the actual devices of international commodity agreements were in quadrant III and why the change from quadrant III to quadrant II happened.

The Correspondence

First of all, table 13.1 summarizes the correspondence investigated previously.

The schemes of international commodity agreement corresponding to quadrant I (which was not examined in the previous section) are considered as follows. The devices to mitigate uncertainty correspond to the nature of futures markets, and functional exigencies correspond to adaptation to search efficiency, and also the types of exchange correspond to market exchange. Needless to say, quadrant I is classified as a region with self interest and rule consistency in the nature of a regime. Also the benefit of forming a regime is the effect of mitigating uncertainty. Based upon the above characteristics, the schemes of international commodity agreement which correspond to quadrant I might be a mechanism for introducing a function of futures markets and for mitigating uncertainty through searching efficiency, which is called a device of futures markets in table 13.1 (see also chapter twelve).

As pointed out previously, the international regime is an institution which is defined as "sets of implicit or explicit principles, norms, rules and decision-making procedures around which actors' expectations converge in a given area of international relations."[18] Regardless of the definitions, the international commodity agreement, which is the subject of this chapter's analysis, is undoubtedly included as an international regime. We mentioned the reasons why an international regime would be formed and would be maintained in the first section, these are the four benefits of forming a regime shown in table 13.1.

Therefore, we could say that:

The *raison d'être* of an international commodity agreement is the benefit of forming a regime.

To further the correspondences needs further investigation. As mentioned in the third section, the most usual international commodity agreement scheme is export regulation. (During the period mentioned in chapter eleven) the International Wheat Agreement was actually working under an export regulation scheme. The International Tin Agreement and The International Cocoa Agreement also had an export regulation scheme. What are the reasons for this?

This could be explained using the correspondences shown in table 13.1. Attaching more importance to an export regulation scheme means that the benefit of having a regime could be seen as putting more emphasis upon stability. In order to attain this goal, the authority could introduce an export regulation scheme to put emphasis on mobilization as the exchange type. It could be said that export regulation is a scheme in which shared interest is given more emphasis than self interest, by putting less emphasis upon efficiency and putting more weight upon rule confrontation. It could be interpreted therefore that selecting a regime in quadrant III means attaching more importance to stability than to efficiency, which is an export regulation scheme. This interpretation might be compatible with the economic criterion for employing an export regulation scheme in cases of more volatile market prices and of higher stock management costs.

Therefore, we could say that:

The reason for employing an export regulation scheme is to choose a regime in quadrant III for more stability but less efficiency.

However, when we look back upon the history of the international commodity agreement, we can see that the regime mainly working in quadrant III could not supply enough shared interest. The international commodity agreement has therefore shifted the emphasis toward functions of gathering, analyzing and providing information by deleting price rules and provisions of rights and duties for member countries. What can we interpret by this change and why?

In other words, the change mentioned above is a shift in the nature of the benefits of an international regime toward more effectiveness and a decrease in information gathering costs, which means a change to quadrant II from quadrant III. The nature of the regime change can be made much clearer by the correspondence shown in table 13.1. More importance would be attached to the reciprocity of types of exchange in which benefit is widely and symmetrically allocated and upon latent pattern-maintenance and tension-management of functional exigencies in which managing tensions and maintaining patterns have placed more emphasis on individual actors.

If international commodity agreements with these natures are established, it might be the multilateral contract scheme which has the long-term contract with the mechanism for flexible adjustment for situation changes. (The multilateral contract scheme mentioned here is the one with the functions described in this chapter and not the scheme included in the International Wheat Agreement. As shown in chapter eleven, the actual mechanism worked in the then International Wheat Agreement and should be recognized as an export regulation scheme.)

However, it can easily be said that there is a large cost to having an international commodity agreement in the real sense with shared interest. Based upon the reciprocity and the tension-management and putting more emphasis on functions concerning information, the real workings of an international commodity agreement could be interpreted as moving to a rather flexible (not fully corresponding to the nature of quadrant II) regime being formed with equilibrium of shared interest and cost burden.

Table 13.1 Correspondence

Quad-rant	Nature of benefit of international regime	The four devices to mitigate uncertainty	The four functional exigencies	The four types of exchange	International commodity agreement Schemes
I	Effect of mitigating uncertainty	Futures market	A (adaptation)	Market exchange	Using futures market scheme
II	Effect of decreasing information gathering costs	Long-term contract	L (latent pattern-maintenance and tension-management)	Reciprocity	Multilateral contract scheme
III	Effect of stabilization	International commodity agreement	G (goal attainment)	Mobilization	Export regulation scheme
IV	Effect to decrease transaction costs	Vertical integration	I (integration)	Redistribution	Buffer stock scheme

We can conclude, therefore:

The movement of the international commodity agreement is the regime change from quadrant III to quadrant II.

As mentioned above, this regime change is a result of the shift of advantage in the benefits of regime formation, from the effect of stabilizing to the effect of decreasing information gathering costs. That is to say:

The regime change from the area in quadrant III to quadrant II is due to the advantage shift of regime formation benefit.

Although it might be completely different from the McKinnon proposal mentioned in chapter eleven, how can we explain the International Natural Rubber Agreement allowing the buffer stock manager to have a future contract (even if only for two months)? Needless to say, the main scheme of the International Natural Rubber Agreement was the buffer stock scheme in which issues such as political negotiation regarding price range and buffer stock finance closely connected with price range setting were discussed. Thus, as the main scheme was the buffer stock scheme, it mainly corresponded to quadrant IV and the futures trading could be regarded as the secondary scheme.

Primarily, issues concerned with primary commodities have been based upon price fluctuation mainly due to various types of uncertainty. Needless to say, even if we could observe huge fluctuations in primary commodities in a statistical sense, it would be reasonable from the viewpoint of economics when demand and supply is in equilibrium. When price expectation would work, however, to expand disequilibrium caused by uncertainty, it would be necessary to have a reasonable mechanism for adjusting the disequilibrium in gathering and providing information.

As a scheme for adjusting the uncertainty, it might be plausible to assign a regime whose dominant benefit is reducing uncertainty. As shown above, a change of regime means a shift in the dominant benefit of the regime. Therefore, concerning the international commodity agreement, it might be reasonable to change a regime so that it reduces uncertainty more, even if the shift is partial and joint.

As indicated in table 13.1, the nature of quadrant I shows adaptation in the sense of functional exigencies and futures markets in the sense of reducing uncertainty. A regime shifting toward quadrant II is not a tight mechanism because of the shared interest and cost burden. When a regime is in quadrant I, as both self interest and rule consistency are dominant in the scheme, the cost burden would not be serious. The cost of reducing uncertainty through the futures market would be considered as taken by individual actors attaching importance to self interest. From the viewpoints of both the nature of the regime benefit and cost burden, a regime shift toward quadrant I would be reasonable for the international regime of the commodity agreement to adjust price fluctuation.

Therefore, we can say that:

It is reasonable that the international commodity agreement scheme is naturally in quadrant I.

This way of thinking for utilizing futures markets is considered to be based upon the rationality for more efficiency.

However, almost all the international commodity agreements did not actually have a reasonable scheme. This was mainly due to the differences of dominance on the nature of regime benefit, functional exigencies, type of exchange, etc. as well as the necessity to set up the futures market. If one puts more weight upon fair distribution than efficiency, it would show the dominance on social integration in functional exigencies, on redistribution in types of exchange, on buffer stock in international commodity agreement schemes. In the International Natural Rubber Agreement negotiation process, what Thailand and Malaysia requested as the dominant factor was redistribution through the buffer stock scheme (to producing countries). Therefore, even if we could partially observe a regime function in quadrant I, it could be considered reasonable that such functions as shown in quadrant I could not have dominance.

Conclusion

The purpose of this chapter is to examine the appropriate position of the adjustment schemes for price fluctuation in international commodity agreements, and to consider the position of futures markets in connection with the international commodity agreements mainly based upon the natures of the regimes. In this chapter, as well as in the previous chapters, when and almost only when we can recognize some effects in schemes of intergovernmental agreement, it might be case for such authorities as an international commodity committee to be able to have conditions for quantity regulation. In most international commodity agreements, however, it would be extremely difficult to have effective regulation on the price range through spot market intervention. The question of why such agreements which are recognized as difficult could exist was examined, and the question of whether there could be more efficient schemes and what they could be were considered. The above questions investigated in this chapter are based upon the nature of regime benefits. Table 13.1 is the result of this.

Both in this chapter and in chapter twelve, what we have in mind is how the mechanism of futures markets is placed in the framework concerned. (As mentioned in the book referred to as the "McKinnon Proposal") a scheme based on a futures market is undoubtedly the most efficient. However, it might be that a scheme in which the function works well in quadrant I might not be realized. Table 13.1 indicates the reason why the best scheme might not be realized. As mentioned previously, one of the fundamental reasons is the immaturity of futures markets, not the establishment of new international organizations, nor the issue of domestic economic policies, etc. (Needless to say, setting up futures markets is the role of authority, however, the main issue is not the policy itself but the function of the market).

As we have investigated in this book, it would not be easy to effectively adjust through spot market intervention (by international organizations and domestic authorities) against capital movement (toward commodity, currency, and other types of monetary asset) for profit from risk taking.

For several decades, the Central European economies attached more importance to dominant functions allocated to quadrant III (described earlier). If we define the economic reforms toward more market mechanism assigned to quadrant I in this chapter as the "transition", it would undoubtedly be reasonable to reform the economy with the type of benefits in quadrant I. As examined in the first part of the book, commodity futures markets in Central Europe are still immature. In order to develop the commodity futures markets, the main policy should be not government intervention but for better works of the market mechanism (and of listing new commodities).

Notes

1 See, for example, Strange (1998).
2 For example, Kousaka and Kumon (1983) mentioned that "understanding phenomena in international political economy could be fine if you have 'rather advanced common sense'. When you have 'flexible and well worked common sense', you can recognize almost all the phenomena. When you could have stocks of them, you have your own views on international political economy" (Introduction). Although it might not be easy to understand what the "rather advanced common sense" and "flexible and well worked common sense" are, we could recognize that several ways of thinking in the field of international political economy could exit. Upon the classification and upon the field of international political economy, the article by Sueuchi (1990) has been useful.
3 Ruggie (1975).
4 Krasner (1983).
5 See, for example, A. A. Stein (1983).
6 Keohane (1984), p.193.
7 See A. A. Stein (1983), pp.125-127. Stein (1983) mentioned the "common indifference" case as well as the "divergent interests" case explained in this chapter. However, it would be enough here to investigate the "divergent interests" case.
8 Keohane (1983), pp.167-170 and also see Keohane (1984), p.193.
9 As is well known, this is the same topic discussed by Akerlof (1970).
10 Regarding the change of regime, the author owes much to Yamazaki (1989).
11 Hicks (1946), p.134.
12 See Scherer (1970), p.248.
13 Chiba (1987), p.219.
14 See Smith and Schink (1976).

15   Chiba (1987), p.214. Needless to say, in a case such as the International Coffee Agreement, this existed basically without price range.

16   Chiba (1987), p.213.

17   Needless to say, if the market is in a monopoly condition, regulation by the authority (in order to stabilize price level) is not necessary at all. In such a situation, the necessity to establish an international commodity agreement to regulate price level does not exist.

18   Keohane (1983), p.57.

Chapter 14

A Destabilizing Effect of Commodity Market Intervention

Introduction

In the previous chapters in part three of this book, we discussed excessive speculation, corner markets, early stage discovery of destabilized speculation, stabilization schemes for volatile commodity prices, etc., related to flexible capital movement. Based upon the above investigations, this chapter will contribute by examining the open-macro-economic effect of stabilized intervention by an intergovernmental scheme (known here as a buffer stock operation).

Since the beginning of the 1970s, the international economic system has experienced several serious problems that need to be resolved. One of the pressing issues is the primary commodity problem, which has mainly been the arena of the United Nations Conference on Trade and Development (UNCTAD). Intergovernmental cooperation such as The Integrated Program for Commodities (IPC) was then, for example, one of the first steps in developing a new system. While we have never had enough knowledge to determine the possibilities of success for the program, examination of some functions of the international commodity agreement still might be an important step in finding avenues of mutual interest to both the developed and developing economies.

Although a vast literature analyzing the workings of the international commodity agreement exists, little of it explores problems from an open-macro-economic point of view, in particular with relation to asset market behavior. The purpose of this chapter, therefore, is to meet the need for studies on the broader-based effects of intervention through buffer stock operation. We start with a fairly suitable analytical tool to accomplish this, that is, the method devised by Carl Van Duyne (1979). While his own work did not directly deal with this kind of intervention, application of his theoretical framework in the analysis of the effects of such operations has proven fruitful.

This chapter is divided into two sections: in the first section, a modified Van Duyne model is presented and in the second the model is used to ascertain the intervening effects from an open-macro-economic point of view.

The Model

The model in this chapter deals with two countries, two goods, and three assets. One country perfectly specializes in primary commodity production and the other in manufactured good production, with full employment prevailing everywhere. We assume that the home country produces the manufactured good and the foreign country the primary commodity. We also assume that the manufactured good is a fix-price good and the primary commodity is a flex-price good in the Hicksian sense.

Commodity stocks, domestic money, and foreign exchange are the three assets which are imperfect substitutes in asset holders' portfolios. Only the home country has asset markets and asset holders. The nominal yield on domestic money and foreign currency as well as the strong cost of commodity stocks, are all assumed to be zero.

Asset Markets

We consider first the working of asset markets. The equilibrium system of an asset market is represented with the following equations:

$$F = f(\dot{\pi}e, \dot{p}e) \cdot W \tag{1}$$

$$pC = c(\dot{\pi}e, \dot{p}e) \cdot \pi W \tag{2}$$

$$M = m(\dot{\pi}e, \dot{p}e) \cdot \pi W \tag{3}$$

$$W = F + \frac{p}{\pi}C + \frac{1}{\pi}M \tag{4}$$

$$\pi = \frac{\dot{\pi}e}{\theta} + \bar{\pi}, \quad \theta < 0 \tag{5}$$

$$p = \frac{\dot{p}e}{\delta} + \bar{p}, \quad \delta < 0 \tag{6}$$

$$f + c + m = 1 \tag{7}$$

Where

Where

F :   domestic money,

C :   commodity stocks,

M :   foreign currency,

W :   nominal value of net wealth,

π :   spot exchange rate expressed as the foreign currency price of foreign exchange,

p :   the spot foreign currency price of primary commodity,

$\dot{\pi}^e$:   the expected rate of change in π

$\dot{p}^e$:   the expected rate of change in p

f, c, m :   the fraction of aggregate portfolios held in each of the three assets and their functional forms, and

θ, δ :   the adjustment rate.

Participants in the markets for domestic money and the primary commodity are assumed to know the long-run equilibrium prices, i.e., $\bar{\pi}$ and $\bar{p}$ With respect to f, c and m, the following properties are assumed to hold:

$$\frac{\partial f}{\partial \dot{\pi}^e} = f_1 > 0, \qquad \frac{\partial f}{\partial \dot{p}^e} = f_2 < 0$$

$$\frac{\partial c}{\partial \dot{\pi}^e} = c_1 < 0, \qquad \frac{\partial c}{\partial \dot{p}^e} = c_2 > 0$$

$$\frac{\partial m}{\partial \dot{\pi}^e} = m_1 < 0, \qquad \frac{\partial m}{\partial \dot{p}^e} = m_2 < 0$$

In equations (1), (2), and (3), asset holders in the aggregate are constrained by net wealth at any moment in time, so the sum of responses of all assets to changes in $\dot{\pi}^e$ and $\dot{p}^e$ must be zero:

$$f_1 + c_1 + m_1 = 0 \tag{8}$$
$$f_2 + c_2 + m_2 = 0 \tag{9}$$

In what follows, we also assume for convenience that asset holders face just the portfolio choice between the commodity and domestic money, with M and m being constant and very small. In the following discussion, we then drop equation (3). Since m is not zero but positive and very small, instead of equations (7), (8), and (9), we have,[1]

$$f + c = 1$$

$$f_1 + c_1 > 0 \tag{8`}$$

$$f_2 + c_2 > 0 \tag{9`}$$

This system works as follows. We first assume a disturbance concerning domestic money, whereby the existence of a divergence from the initial long-run equilibrium is reflected in the differences between the desired and existing levels of the two assets, with domestic money being in excess and the primary commodity short. Asset holders then expect π^e and p^e on the basis of correctly calculated $\bar{\pi}$ and $\bar{p}$. (In this model, π^e and p^e are assumed to be given.) We assume asset holders' behavior is such that when the difference between the desired and existing levels of C is negative, i.e., the desired level is above the existing level, they expect that holding more C will give rise to capital loss since they know that market prices will settle at the level of $\bar{\pi}$ and $\bar{p}$ respectively at the time when adjustment in real terms is completed despite a sharp initial rise in market prices. Therefore, when the difference dC is negative, p^e becomes negative. This assumption guarantees that p will not become initially large. Similarly, π^e becomes positive when there are excess holdings.

Through the above process, f in question (1) becomes larger and c in equation (2) becomes smaller. Prices change to the level described by the right-hand side of equation (5) and (6). Thus the values of endogenous variables, π, p, f, c, F, C, and W are determined by equations (1) through (7`), excluding equation (3) and including one redundant equation.

To examine the effects on p and π of differences of C and F from the long-run equilibrium level, we assume that equilibrium conditions are satisfied initially, and prices are set equal to unity. We derive the effects by totally differentiating equations (1) and (2). (The terms $d\pi$, dp, dF, and dC below should be interpreted as deviations from prices and stocks that will be obtained in the long-run equilibrium.)

By totally differentiating equations (1), (4), (5), and (6), we obtain,

$$dF = fdW + W \cdot \left(f_1 d\pi^e + f_2 dp^e \right)$$
$$dW = dF + cWdP - cWd\pi + dC$$
$$d\pi^e = \theta d\pi$$
$$dp^e = \delta dp$$

With these derivatives and (7`), we have,

$$W\{(fc - f_1\theta)d\pi + (-fc - f_2\delta)dp\} = -cdF + fdC \tag{10}$$

Similarly, by totally differentiating equation (2) and substituting the derivatives into it, we obtain,

$$W\{(-fc - c_1\theta)d\pi + (fc - c_2\delta)dp\} = cdF - fdC \tag{11}$$

Thus, we have,

$$W\begin{bmatrix} fc - f_1\theta & -fc - f_2\delta \\ -fc - c_1\theta & fc - c_2\delta \end{bmatrix}\begin{bmatrix} d\pi \\ dp \end{bmatrix} = \begin{bmatrix} -c & f \\ c & -f \end{bmatrix}\begin{bmatrix} dF \\ dC \end{bmatrix} \tag{12}$$

or,

$$\tilde{D}\begin{bmatrix} d\pi \\ dp \end{bmatrix} = \tilde{B}\begin{bmatrix} dF \\ dC \end{bmatrix} \tag{13}$$

The inverse matrix of D is expressed as,

$$\tilde{D}^{-1} = \frac{W}{\Delta}\begin{bmatrix} fc - c_2\delta & fc + f_2\delta \\ fc + c_1\theta & fc - f_1\theta \end{bmatrix}$$

Where

$$\Delta = (fc - f_1\theta)(fc - c_2\delta) - (-fc - f_2\delta)(-fc - c_1\theta)$$

With the help of equations (5) through (9'), Δ is found to be unambiguously positive.

Next we used to determine the signs of the elements of the following coefficient matrix A,

$$\begin{bmatrix} d\pi \\ dp \end{bmatrix} = \tilde{D}^{-1}\tilde{B}\begin{bmatrix} dF \\ dC \end{bmatrix} = \tilde{A}\begin{bmatrix} dF \\ dC \end{bmatrix} = \begin{bmatrix} a_{11} & a_{12} \\ a_{21} & a_{22} \end{bmatrix}\begin{bmatrix} dF \\ dC \end{bmatrix} \tag{14}$$

Excluding W and Δ for convenience, the element a_{ij} is expressed as,

$$a_{11} = (fc - c_2\delta)(-c) + (fc + f_2\delta)c$$
$$= \delta\{c(f_2 + c_2)\}$$
$$a_{22} = (fc + c_1\theta)f + (fc - f_1\theta)(-f)$$
$$= \theta\{f(f_1 + c_1)\}$$
$$a_{12} = (fc - c_2\delta)f + (fc + f_2\delta)(-f)$$
$$= -\delta\{f(f_2 + c_2)\}$$
$$a_{21} = (fc + c_1\theta)(-c) + (fc - f_1\theta)c$$
$$= -\theta\{c(f_1 + c_1)\}$$

Then we have the following unambiguous signs of a_{ij} : a_{11} and a_{22} are negative, and a_{12} and a_{21} are positive.

The signs obtained above indicate the effects on the terms of trade of the price changes necessary to adjust the disequilibrium caused by the initial shock in asset markets in the home country. As assumed, the home currency price of the manufactured good in the home country is fixed in the Hicksian sense, but the foreign currency price of the manufactured good varies directly with the exchange rate. Let p_m and p_m^* denote the home currency price and the foreign currency price, respectively. If units are chosen so that $p_m = 1$, then $p_m^* = \pi$. Thus, the terms of trade to the foreign country is expressed as $\frac{p}{\pi}$, since $\frac{p}{p_m^*} = \frac{p}{\pi}$. On the basis of the previous discussion, it can be easily shown that,

$$\frac{d\left(\frac{p}{\pi}\right)}{dF} = \frac{\partial\left(\frac{p}{\pi}\right)}{\partial p} \cdot \frac{dp}{dF} + \frac{\partial\left(\frac{p}{\pi}\right)}{\partial \pi} \cdot \frac{d\pi}{dF}$$

Because $p = \pi = 1$ at the initial equilibrium,

$$\frac{d\left(\frac{p}{\pi}\right)}{dF} = \frac{dp}{dF} - \frac{d\pi}{dF} = a_{21} - a_{11} > 0$$

Similarly,

$$\frac{d\left(\frac{p}{\pi}\right)}{dC} = \frac{dp}{dC} - \frac{d\pi}{dC} = a_{22} - a_{12} < 0$$

These imply that the terms of trade with the foreign country move directly with changes in domestic money holdings and inversely with changes in commodity stocks.

Goods Markets

Through such effects on the terms of trade, stocks equilibrated in asset markets in monetary terms can be equilibrated in real terms through adjustments in goods markets. The assumptions concerning the functioning of goods markets are basically similar to those of Van Duyne (1979) with several modifications essential to this chapter.

With the assumptions mentioned previously - perfect specialization and full employment - production of each good is fixed. Further, we also assume that the demand for each good in each country is a function of degree zero in nominal prices, nominal income, and nominal wealth.

The goods market is determined with the following equations:

$$\dot{C} = \bar{S} - X\left(\frac{p}{\pi}, W\right) \tag{15}$$

$$\dot{F} = \frac{p}{\pi} X - D^m(p, \pi, Y) \tag{16}$$

$$Y = p\bar{S} \tag{17}$$

Where
- X : imports,
- $\bar{S}$: aggregate production of primary commodity,
- D^m : foreign demand for manufactured good, and
- Y : national income of foreign country.

With regard to X and D^m, the following properties hold:

$$\frac{\partial X}{\partial\left(\frac{p}{\pi}\right)} = X_1 < 0, \qquad \frac{\partial X}{\partial W} = X_2 > 0$$

$$\frac{\partial D^m}{\partial p} = D_1^m > 0, \qquad \frac{\partial D^m}{\partial \pi} = D_2^m < 0, \qquad \frac{\partial D^m}{\partial Y} = D_3^m > 0$$

Equation (15) implies that the rate at which commodity stocks are accumulated equals the excess supply of the commodity. Equation (16) refers to the current account surplus or deficit for the foreign country. The dynamic adjustment process can be analyzed in the same manner as Van

Duyne (1979) does, that is, by taking a Taylor's series expansion in the neighborhood of the long-run equilibrium.

From equation (15) and (16), we obtain,

$$
\begin{bmatrix} \dot{F} \\ \dot{C} \end{bmatrix} = \begin{bmatrix} -X - X_1 - X_2 C - D_2^m & X + X_1 + X_2 C - D_1^m - \bar{S}D_3^m \\ X_1 + X_2 C & -X_1 - X_2 C \end{bmatrix} \begin{bmatrix} d\pi \\ dp \end{bmatrix}
$$
$$
+ \begin{bmatrix} X_2 & X_2 \\ -X_2 & -X_2 \end{bmatrix} \begin{bmatrix} dF \\ dC \end{bmatrix}
\tag{18}
$$

or

$$
\begin{bmatrix} \dot{F} \\ \dot{C} \end{bmatrix} = \begin{bmatrix} p_{11} & p_{12} \\ p_{21} & p_{22} \end{bmatrix} \begin{bmatrix} d\pi \\ dp \end{bmatrix} \begin{bmatrix} w_{11} & w_{12} \\ w_{21} & w_{22} \end{bmatrix} \begin{bmatrix} dF \\ dC \end{bmatrix} = \tilde{P} \begin{bmatrix} d\pi \\ dp \end{bmatrix} + \tilde{W} \begin{bmatrix} dF \\ dC \end{bmatrix}
\tag{18'}
$$

$\tilde{P}$ represents the price effects and $\tilde{W}$ the direct wealth effects of changes in asset stocks.

Substituting equation (14) into equation (18'), we obtain,

$$
\begin{bmatrix} \dot{F} \\ \dot{C} \end{bmatrix} = \tilde{P}\tilde{A} \begin{bmatrix} dF \\ dC \end{bmatrix} + \tilde{W} \begin{bmatrix} dF \\ dC \end{bmatrix}
$$
$$
= \begin{bmatrix} p_{11}a_{11} + p_{12}a_{21} & p_{11}a_{12} + p_{12}a_{22} \\ p_{21}a_{11} + p_{22}a_{21} & p_{21}a_{12} + p_{22}a_{22} \end{bmatrix} \begin{bmatrix} dF \\ dC \end{bmatrix} + \begin{bmatrix} w_{11} & w_{12} \\ w_{21} & w_{22} \end{bmatrix} \begin{bmatrix} dF \\ dC \end{bmatrix}
$$
$$
= \begin{bmatrix} z_{11} & z_{12} \\ z_{21} & z_{22} \end{bmatrix} \begin{bmatrix} dF \\ dC \end{bmatrix}
\tag{19}
$$

To identify the signs of the element z_{ij}, we will examine the adjustment process. First, with the initial disturbance $dF > 0$, the terms of trade for the foreign country improves. As the Marshall-Lerner condition indicates, improvement in terms of trade for the foreign country makes the foreign country's trade account deficit deteriorate. The direct wealth effects work in the opposite direction, that is to say, a positive dF means that the demand for both goods increases because the level of existing stocks is above the desired level and this difference stimulates the demand. The increased demand for both goods in turn exacerbates the home country's current account deficit. As we assume that the price effects are more powerful than the direct wealth effects, the net effect on $\dot{F}$ of dF is negative and we have negative z_{11}.

Second, we study the process concerning z_{22}. The shortage of C makes the terms of trade for the foreign country improve, which implies that the demand for primary commodity in the home country decreases, $\dot{C} > 0$. The direct wealth effects make $\dot{C}$ negative because dC operates on the demand to be suppressed. With the two effects, z_{22} is negative.

Similarly, we derive the signs of z_{12} and z_{21}. With the Marshall-Lerner condition, we get the relation between dC and $\dot{F}$. The disequilibrium in commodity stocks changes the terms of trade which exacerbates the foreign country's trade account deficit, $\dot{F} < 0$. It means that the sign of z_{12} is positive. The direct wealth effects also work to make it positive, because the demand suppression by negative dC increases the foreign country's trade account deficit.

With the assumption of the dominance of price effects, we get the net relation between dF and $\dot{C}$. The excess of F changes the relative price ratio and the demand for the primary commodity decreases, $\dot{C} > 0$. This means that, from this point of view, the sign of z_{21} becomes positive. Although positive dF means that the demand for both goods increases due to the wealth effects and the resulting negative $\dot{C}$ implies a negative z_{21}, with the above assumption the net effect is a positive z_{21}.

Therefore, with signs of elements z_{ij} established, we can say that the adjustment path moves toward stability since the disequilibrium caused by the initial disturbance ($dC < 0$ and $dF > 0$) is eliminated through the adjustment ($\dot{C} > 0$ and $\dot{F} < 0$).

Economic interpretation of the above stabilizing process is as follows. Negative $\dot{F}$ means that the foreign country's trade account deficit increases and the level of π also goes up. Thus the desired level of domestic money $\bar{F}$ rises much higher and the difference between the desired and the existing level dF shrinks toward zero despite expansion of the domestic money. Similarly, positive $\dot{C}$ indicates that in the goods market excess supply of the primary commodity comes into existence and the level of p falls. Through this process, the disequilibrium disappears in real terms. As long as the level of p is above the level of $\bar{p}$, with excess supply the price continues downward and the difference between the desired and the existing levels dC also shrinks toward zero.

Effective Intervention Through the International Commodity Agreement

Price stabilization is one of the main purposes of the international commodity agreement concluded between exporting and importing countries. As is well known, the international commodity agreement has several intervening techniques to carry out its aims such as buffer stocks, multilateral contracts, and export restriction schemes.

The history of commodity trade as described by, for example, J. W. F. Rowe (1965), reveals a long struggle with price instability and the efforts to find better techniques for price stabilization. One such scheme was included in the worldwide experiment by the international commodity agreement mainly through buffer stock operation. The latter is the focus of the rest of the chapter. Under the terms of the stock scheme, participating countries contribute to the fund and so establish a buffer stock.[2] Through negotiations they decide the price range within which to keep market prices by means of buffer stock operation. The international commodity agreement releases the stock to lower the free market price when the latter rises above the ceiling level of the range, and purchases and accumulates the commodity to raise the free market price when it drops below the floor level of the range.

Before presenting our own discussion, we briefly review the arguments of H. G. Johnson (1967) and R. Komiya and A. Amano (1972) to clarify the scope and limit of this chapter at this stage. H. G. Johnson states that "the crucial difficulty in all price-stabilization scheme is to forecast the long-run equilibrium price". And as we can assume a real improvement in forecasting accuracy, it "might be sufficient by itself to evoke stabilization of markets for primary products through speculation and arbitrage by private traders, without the need for international agreement" (1967, p.149). We can find a similar assertion in Komiya and Amano (1972, p.230). They state: "If short-run price fluctuation can be stabilized by means of buffer stock operation, the primary commodity producing countries would try to implement the operations by themselves without international agreements... That is, if prices could be efficiently stabilized with the stock, the stock holding itself would be profitable so that not only an individual country but an individual private enterprise could try to do it. The reasons why they would not carry out such operations are high storing costs and difficulties to obtain an accurate price forecast and to produce necessary funds." The assertions cited above are quite reasonable, and as a matter of fact, without a solution to either the forecasting problem or the financial problem, further discussion is trivial. Likewise, if either one is satisfactorily eliminated, the problems regarding short-run price instability become tractable.

The model and the mechanism developed in the preceding section should be interpreted as a case where the first problem is successfully resolved. It was proved that the model has a stable solution under the assumptions mentioned, which means that we can leave the market to adjust itself. If so, a more realistic approach should concentrate on how to utilize information as efficiently as possible. Although we have no space to consider more on this interesting point, I wish to mention only one view expressed by L. B. Krause (1976, p.186), saying, "The manager should perform transactions in the forward as well as the spot market. Since funds or stocks on hand are not required for buying or selling forward, this will free the manager from the limitations of the existing stock in attempting to maintain the price within the range." According to him, the futures market works to mitigate forecasting and functioning problems. Recently further interesting trials along this line have also been attempted.[3]

At any rate, we have several assertions for supporting and approximating the assumption of perfect foresight. The assumption that the manager of the international commodity agreement is given the ability to work substitutionally, not complementarily with the dynamic adjustment mechanism of market[4] fits well in the scope of this chapter, which is to examine open-macro-economic effects of "successful" intervention through buffer stock operation. In this case, however, the more efficiently the manager intervenes, the more inefficient the open-macro-economy becomes, which can be clearly shown with the help of the model developed in the previous section. The assumptions about international commodity agreement intervention are summarized below.

(1) The manager has full knowledge about the long-run equilibrium prices.

(2) The manager promptly intervenes as soon as the free market price goes out of the set price range.

With these two assumptions it is ensured that the agreement can intervene successfully to maintain prices within the range arranged at the level of the long-run equilibrium. We also assume:

(3) The international commodity agreement cannot afford enough stocks to instantly eliminate the initial disequilibrium in real terms.

Therefore, the prompt intervention of the manager is just the beginning of this analysis. If the international commodity agreement can maintain sufficient stocks, the problem we are attempting to analyze here will completely disappear.[5]

In addition to them, to make the discussion precise, we add another two

assumptions:
   (4) The manager behaves as an individual asset holder in the asset
        market.
   (5) The major reason for the price changes examined here is due to asset
        market behavior, that is, the shift from monetary to real assets, the
        dominant factor of which is disequilibrium in monetary assets.
    The next step is to incorporate the above assumptions in the model
prepared in the preceding section. The first assumption implies that the
price range can be arranged at the level where the economy is in the
long-run equilibrium. The second assumption states that, as soon as market
prices move away from the level $\bar{p}$, the difference will be promptly
eliminated by successful intervention. Based on this assumption we can say
that p is always equated to $\bar{p}$ and that because this economy has three assets
of which one is assumed to be negligible, the price of another asset would
also be assumed to be equated to the long-run equilibrium level, $\pi = \bar{\pi}$.[6]
According to the third assumption, stock disequilibrium in real terms can
be adjusted only through the function of the goods markets, and not
through intervention.[7]
    Therefore, if we incorporate buffer stock operation in the model by the
first two assumptions we always have

$$\begin{cases} dp = 0 \\ d\pi = 0 \end{cases} \tag{20}$$

And by the third assumption, we have

$$\begin{cases} dC \neq 0 \\ dF \neq 0 \end{cases} \tag{21}$$

Furthermore, the fifth assumption gives us the following additive
information. Since the domestic money disequilibrium dominates over the
commodity stock disequilibrium through the adjustment, we have the
following inequality throughout,[8]

$$dC < dF \tag{22}$$

Therefore, intervention changes the adjustment path from the one described
in equation (18') or (19) to the following:

$$\begin{bmatrix} \dot{F} \\ \dot{C} \end{bmatrix} = \begin{bmatrix} w_{11} & w_{12} \\ w_{21} & w_{22} \end{bmatrix} \begin{bmatrix} dF \\ dC \end{bmatrix} \tag{23}$$

Equation (23) is easily obtained by substituting equations (20) and (21) into (18'). In equation (23) the terms to express the price effects are excluded, and only the terms to express the direct wealth effects remain.

As described as the inequality (22), dF has a dominant effect over dC throughout the process. Thus, according to the adjustment mechanism expressed by equation (23) with inequality (22), we have $\dot{F} > 0$ and $\dot{C} < 0$. In the home country, the disequilibrium initially disturbed indicated the excess of F and the shortfall of C. Therefore, in order to eliminate the disequilibrium and to move toward long-run equilibrium it is necessary for F to decrease, and/or for C to increase. In a stable system as described in the previous section, the excessive F and the short C both disappear through the adjustment processes, i.e., $\dot{F} < 0$ and $\dot{C} > 0$. But the process obtained in this section with buffer stock operation is not stable. The system including such an intervening mechanism makes the disequilibrium expand, i.e., $\dot{F} > 0$ and $\dot{C} < 0$. It is unstable. Needless to say, the system examined in this chapter becomes unstable due to the intervention.

Economic interpretation of the unstable adjustment is similar to the adjustment mentioned in the previous section. Positive $\dot{F}$ implies that the surplus in the foreign country's trade account increases and the value of domestic money declines. Although the quantity of domestic money may shrink, as the desired level of domestic money $\bar{F}$ drops lower, the difference between the desired and the existing level dF continues to expand. Negative $\dot{C}$ indicates that excess demand for the primary commodity in the goods market appears and that the stock disequilibrium in real terms deteriorates. This excess demand makes the desired level of the primary commodity $\bar{C}$ much higher. Therefore the difference dC continues to expand.

Moreover, the above process may increase the tendency that p will go up and π will go down much further. If so, the international commodity agreement will have to intervene in the market constantly.

Notes

1   Obviously, (7'), (8'), and (9') are not consistent. But loss of rigor seems small compared to the increase in clarity and ease of application.
2   We assume in this chapter that the quantity of the stock is exogenously given. It is also assumed that the international commodity agreement uses the commodity as the

intervening means.

3   See, for example, G. Goodwin and J. Mayall (1979).

4   Without this assumption, assertions by H. G. Johnson (1967) and R. Komiya and A. Amano (1972), etc. can hold.

5   Problems may move to another dimension, but, of course, they are still not resolved. One thing that is clear is that problems will move from more economic areas to less economic (or more political) ones.

6   The reader should note that when π moves freely with $dp = 0$ (as result of trade balance) the following conclusion is strengthened. When dF and dC are positive and negative respectively, $d\pi$ and dp are negative and positive respectively (and vice versa), and with the sign of each element and the assumption of freely moving π, it is easily shown that in the case of $d\pi \neq 0$ the result obtained in section two remains unchanged (and rather strengthened), because in this case, we have the following equations:

$$\begin{bmatrix} \dot{F} \\ \dot{C} \end{bmatrix} = \begin{bmatrix} - & + \\ + & - \end{bmatrix}\begin{bmatrix} d\pi \\ 0 \end{bmatrix} + \begin{bmatrix} + & + \\ - & - \end{bmatrix}\begin{bmatrix} dF \\ dC \end{bmatrix}$$

Therefore, in that sense, the assumption is just for simplification.

7   This means that asset holders' expectation is still unchanged throughout the intervention. With improvement in expectation formation theory, this assumption should be replaced by a much stronger one.

8   The result obtained in the second section largely depends upon this inequality (22). Needless to say, this assumption tells us other possible stories. For example, if the opposite assumption describes the situation more realistically, the result in the second section will have no power to interpret the real world. But the reader should note that it does not bear any relation to the result in the first section.

Concluding Remarks

We have mentioned a variety of arguments in the 14 chapters of this book. They are economic reforms in Central Europe, some considerations of the need and functions of commodity futures markets in Central Europe, the nature of risk in Central Europe, existence of some barriers against capital movement, several problems with instability due to speculative capital movement, and international commodity agreement as a measure to deal with the unstable price movement related to speculation, etc.

As indicated in the Preface, it might be rather difficult for readers to get a consistent view of such a variety of topics.

However, what becomes clear through this book is actually fairly simple. That is to say: (1) the existence of risk characteristic of the transition of former centrally planned economies to a market oriented economy, and (2) the existence of a disturbing factor called speculative transactions which occurs as a result of international economic regimes and is also accompanied by systemic transformation and (3) the way to adjust the disturbing factor.

This book started by discussing the needs and functions of a commodity exchange focusing our attention upon the Warsaw Commodity Exchange which aimed to decrease budget deficit, particularly in the agricultural sector, which was the main sector with a large budget deficit, by introducing a search mechanism for equilibrium prices of agricultural products. This is easy to understand because the transition toward a market oriented economy started to reduce the huge amount of budget deficit (accumulated in the centrally planned system). Also through an examination of the efficiency of the Budapest Commodity Exchange, which was established with the aim of having the convenience of 24-hour transactions, we inquired into the actual efficiency situation and studied the environment of being destabilized by capital movements.

At the same time, although expected from the beginning of the transition, we can see the current situation of the delayed effectiveness of structural reforms and the lack of transparency and trust in the policy on the part of receiving countries.

We have to point out that the major reasons for bad economic performance in the centrally planned systems of the transition countries were lack of enough incentive for technological innovation and lack of convertible currency. Also we therefore have to point out the inefficiency of a centrally planned system which does not have the flexible adjustment mechanism of demand and supply through the spot market (this might make it inevitable, thus, that part of the adjustment mechanism was left to the informal sector, or the "second economy" or "black economy", etc.). This means that having advanced technology and more capital might be very important for a successful transition toward a more efficient economy. However, we should make it clear that several difficult barriers hindering capital movement exist.

It could undoubtedly be said that the nature of capital movement in foreign direct investment is not the same as in portfolio investment. Also the nature of short-term capital movement is different from long-term capital movement. However, as far as the current environment of transition economies is concerned, it is immature for transition economies to recognize which and how risks are and which information indicates correct situation, etc. It is meaningful therefore to investigate the problems which companies and governments of (Western) advanced economies have faced and have adjusted to. Such an investigation into risk seems to be helpful in examining commodity futures markets which are not well equipped enough such as the Warsaw Commodity Exchange (as of the year 1999), to evaluate the current environment exactly. Needless to say, once the economic transitions are taken further and they have a fully equipped market mechanism, it will be necessary to correctly analyze the risk accompanied by capital movements in the short-term and in profit orientation. Unfortunately, however, (we have to say in final remarks) it is too early to do this sufficiently well.

The existence of risk means the existence of profit opportunity. To gain profit from risk a well organized market infrastructure is necessary. Then what does "well organized market infrastructure" indicate? For example, when speculation has destabilizing effects, what would be reasonable to adjust it? Is it reasonable to have any price limit in regulation?

As mentioned in this book, it was correct for the Budapest Commodity Exchange to increase the volume of trade in the financial sector. However, at the time it was also correct to say that the Budapest Commodity Exchange was affected by serious problems. Faced with the serious issue of the instability of the international monetary system, it is not easy to come up with a general framework. In this book, we have tried to put forward ideas for breaking out the difficult situations through such case studies as excessive speculation, futures market intervention, schemes of intergovernmental intervention, etc. It is understandable that, because it is not meaningful to say that the Budapest Commodity Exchange is less efficient than the Tokyo Grain Exchange (except for a few commodities), similar problems in the commodity exchanges of transition economies to those in the commodity exchanges in developed countries, such as Chicago, London, New York, Tokyo, etc. It should be understood that, as the volume of trade in commodity exchanges in Central Europe is generally thin, the working mechanism would be comparatively vulnerable. (However, in this book we cannot refer to any research into economic welfare related to price stability and instability which have been improved by economists, including the author of this book. This could be attempted in another venture.)

This vulnerability might have the same origin as the factors hindering inward investment. Mitigating such factors that hinder investment means alleviating the vulnerability. However, even if such vulnerability means that it can be easily distorted (as the size of market is small), it would not be free from speculative instability. It would start to reach the markets in Chicago, London, New York, Tokyo, etc.

By investigating several problems in economic transition and capital movement in Central Europe, and with examination of some issues arising from speculation and intergovernmental schemes of intervention, we seem to be reaching key issues such as: (1) what risks are and how to adjust them, (2) what characteristic risks for transition economies are and how to adjust them, (3) how speculative phenomena are approached and whether or not reasonable adjustment schemes can be introduced, (4) what plausible criteria there could be besides an efficient market hypothesis. Similar issues would be seriously analyzed in Budapest and Warsaw (and in Moscow, Prague, and in other Central and Eastern European countries). Then we would hope that the analyses in this book on the issues that accompany economic transition, with the risk characteristics, adjustment schemes against speculative instability, etc., could be useful. Therefore, in that sense, the analyses in this book can be understood as providing an effective framework to deal with the problems which would occur in the long-term taking past circumstances and future prospects into account.

As was mentioned at the beginning of this book, we should have investigations as fourth and fifth parts based upon analyses in the three parts of this book. As also mentioned earlier, both topics of economic transition and capital movement in Central Europe, particularly of speculative behavior in futures markets in Central Europe, are now changing rapidly which clearly show that further consideration in the future will be necessary. We hope that, with the progress of theoretical frameworks of economic transition and of financial engineering, etc., and based upon the theoretical frameworks analyzed in this book, effective scientific frameworks can be developed to resolve the problems.

Bibliography

Akerlof, G. A. (1970), "The market for lemons: Qualitative uncertainty and the market mechanism", *Quarterly Journal of Economics*, Vol.84, pp.488-500.

Akiyama, T. and P. N. Varangis (1990), "The Impact of the International Coffee Agreement on Producing Countries", *World Bank Economic Review*, Vol.4, No.2 (May), pp.157-173.

Anderson, R. W. and C. L. Gilbert (1988), "Commodity Agreements and Commodity Markets: Lessons from Tin", *Economic Journal*, Vol.98 (March), pp.1-15.

Aoki, M., and M. Okuno (eds) (1996), *Keizai Shisutemu no Hikaku Seido Bunseki (Comparative Analyses of Institution of Economic Systems)*, Tokyo, Tokyo University Press.

Arrow, K. J.(1975), "Vertical integration and communication", *The Bell Journal of Economics*, Vol.6, No.1, pp.173-183.

Artisien, P., M. Rojec and M. Svetlicic (1993), *Foreign Investment in Central and Eastern Europe*, New York, St.Martin's Press.

Ashley, R. K. (1980), *The Political Economy of War and Peace: The Sino-Soviet-American Triangle and the Modern Security Problematique*, London, Frances Pinter.

Bakos, G. (1992), "Japanese capital in Central Europe", *Hitotsubashi Journal of Economics*, Vol.33, No.2 (December), pp.149-168.

Bakos, G. (1994), "Hungarian transition after three years", *Europe-Asia Studies*, Vol.46, No.7, pp.1189-1214.

Balcerowicz, L. (1995), *Socialism, Capitalism, Transformation*, Budapest, Central European University Press.

Becker, G. S. (1971), *Economic Theory*, 1st ed., New York, Alfred A. Knopf.

Beckerman, W. and T. Jenkinson (1986), "What stopped the inflation? Unemployment or commodity prices?", *Economic Journal*, Vol.96 (March), pp.39-54.

Bednarski, M. (1995), "Outcome and effects of ownership reforms", IPiSS, *Social Policy in 1993-1994 : Main Problems in Transition Period*, Warsaw, Institute of Labour and Social Studies, pp.86-101.

Bednarski, M. and R. Kokoszczynski (1988), "Nieoficjalna gospodarka I jej spoleczna nastepstwa (Unofficial economy and its social result)", *Ekonomista*, Nr.3-4, pp.701-719.

Bevan, D., P. Collier and J. W. Gunning (1993), "Trade shocks in developing countries: Consequences and policy responses", *European Economic Review*, No.37, pp.557-565.

Blau, P. (1964), *Exchange and Power in Social Life*. New York, Wiley.

Bleaney, M. and D. Greenaway (1993), "Long-run trends in the relative price of primary commodities and in the terms of trade of developing countries", *Oxford*

Economic Papers, Vol.45, No.3 (July), pp.349-363.

Blizniak,D. and L. Gontarski (1996), *Gielda Towarowa (Commodity Exchange)*, Warsaw, Fundacja Na Rzecz Gieldy Zbozowo-Paszowej (Foundation for Exchange of Corn-Feeding Stuff).

Blizniak,D. and L. Gontarski (1997), *Towarowe Rynki Terminowe (Terminal Markets)*, Warsaw, Fundacja Na Rzecz Gieldy Zbozowo-Paszowej (Foundation for Exchange of Corn-Feeding Stuff)..

Bozyk, P. (1989), *Marzenia i Rzeczywistosc: Czy Gospodarke Polska Mozna Zreformowac (Dream and Reality: Is it possible to reform Polish economy)*, Warsaw, PIW.

Bozyk, P. (1991), *Droga do nikad? Polska i jej sasiedzi na rozdrozu (Road to nowhere? Poland and Its Neighbors at the crossroad)* , Warsaw, BGW.

Bozyk, P. (1992), *Kto Winien?(Who is responsible?)*, Warsaw, PAE.

Bozyk, P. (1993), "Ewolucyjni wariant transformacji powiazan zewnetrznych" (The evolutionary variant of transformation of external relations)", *Ekonomista*, No.3, pp.283-300.

Bozyk, P. (1994a), *Ktoredy do Europy? (Which Way to Europe?)*, Warsaw, Graf-Punkt.

Bozyk, P. (1994b), "An Evolutionary Mode of Transformation of External Relations", paper presented at the 16th World Congress of IPSA, Berlin, 15-21 August.

Bozyk, P. (1995), *Polityka Gospodarcza Polski 1985-2000 (Political Economy in Poland 1985-2000)*, Warsaw, PWSH.

Bozyk, P. (1999), "Gradualism versus shock therapy", Hare, P. G. (ed) (1999), pp.25-38.

Burger, K. and H. P. Smit (1989), "Long-term and short-term analysis of the natural rubber market", *Weltwirtschaftliches Archiv*, Vol.125, pp.718-746.

Chiba,Y. (1966), *kokusai komugi kyoutei no kaiko: 1933-1966 (Retrospection of International Wheat Agreement: 1933-1966)*, yunyu shokuryou kyougikai Jimukyoku.

Chiba,Y. (1977), *Kokusai Shohin Kyoutei (International Commodity Agreements)*, Nihon kokusaimondai kenkyujyo.

Chiba, Y. (1987), *Kokusai Shohin Kyoutei to Ichiji Sanpin Mondai (International Commodity Agreements and Primary Commodity Issues)*, Tokyo,Yushindou.

Cho, Y. J. (1986), "Inefficiencies from financial liberalization in the absence of well-functioning equity markets", *Journal of Money, Credit,and Banking*, Vol.18 (May), pp.191-199.

Coase, R. H. (1960), "The Problem of social cost", *The Journal of Law and Economics*, Vol.3 (October), pp.1-44.

Deaton, A. and G. Laroque (1992), "On the behaviour of commodity prices", *Review of Economic Studies*, No.59, pp.1-23.

DeBroeck, M., and V. Koen (2000), "The 'Soaring Eagle': Anatomy of the Polish take-off in the 1990s", IMF Working Paper/00/06, Washington, DC, International Monetary Fund.

Dlay, W. H. L. (1976), "The advantages of exclusive forward exchange rate support", *IMF Staff Papers*, Vol.23, pp.137-163.

Duncan, R. C. and B. Borrell (1992), "A survey of the costs of world sugar policies", *World Bank Research Observer*, Vol.7, No.2 (July), pp.171-194.

Dunning, J. H. (1979), "Explaining changing patterns of international production: In defence of the eclectic theory", *Oxford Bulletin of Economics and Statistics*, Vol.41, pp.269-295.

Dunning, J. H. (1993), "The Prospects for foreign direct investment in eastern europe", P. Artisen and others (eds) (1993), pp.16-33.

Dunning, J. and M. Rojec (1994), "Foreign Privatization in Central and Eastern Europe", The Central and Eastern European Privatization Network Technical Paper Series, No.2.

Duyne, C. V. (1979), "The macroeconomic effects of commodity market disruptions in open economies", *Journal of International Economics*, Vol.9, No.4 (November), pp.559-582.

EBRD (1999), *Transition Report 1999*, London, European Bank for Reconstruction and Development.

Fama, E. F. (1970), "Efficient capital market: A review of theory and empirical works", *Journal of Finance*, Vol.25, No.2 (May), pp.383-417.

Farkas, P. (1997), "The effect of foreign direct investment on research, development and innovation in Hungary", Working Paper No.81, Institute of World Economy, Budapest, July.

Farnsworth, H. C. (1958), "Imbalance in the world wheat economy", *The Journal of Political Economy*, Vol.66, No.1 (February), pp.1-23.

Farrell, M. J. (1966), "Profitable speculation", *Economica*, Vol.33, No.130 (May), pp.183-193.

Feige, E. L. and K. Ott (eds) (1999), *Underground Economies in Transition: Unrecorded Activity, Tax Evasion, Corruption and Organized Crime*, Hampshire, Ashgate Publishing.

Felbur, S. (1996), "Developments in production and economic efficiency", IRiSS, *Transforming Polish Economy 1995*, Warsaw, Institute of Development and Strategic Studies, pp.50-68.

Fleck, Hans-Georg and R. Lawniczak (eds) (1993), *Alternatywne Modele Gospodarki Rynkowej dla Krajow Transformacji (Alternative Models of Market Economy for Transition Economies)*, Poznan, Sorus Press.

Frank, G. A. (1967), *Capitalism and Underdevelopment in Latin America*, New York, Monthly Review Press.

Frey, B. S. (1984), *International Political Economics*, Oxford, Basil Blackwell.

Friedman, M. (1967), *Price Theory: A Provisional Text*, 5th ed., Chicago, Aldine.

Gemmil, G. (1985), "Forward contracts or international buffer stocks? A study of their relative efficiencies in stabilising commodity export earnings", *Economic Journal*, Vol.95 (June), pp.400-417.

Gilbert, C. L. (1985), "Futures trading and the welfare evaluation of commodity price stabilization", *Economic Journal*, Vol. 95 (September), pp.637-661.

Gilbert, C. L. (1986), "Testing the efficient markets hypothesis on averaged data",

Applied Economics, Vol.18, No.11 (November), pp.1149-1166.

Gilbert, C. L. (1990), "Primary commodity prices and inflation", *Oxford Review of Economic Policy*, Vol.6, No.4 (Winter), pp.77-99.

Gilbert, C. L. (1996), "International commodity agreements: An obituary notice", *World Development*, Vol.24, No.1, pp.1-19.

Goodwin, G. and J. Mayall (eds) (1979), *A New International Commodity Regime*, London, Croom Helm.

Gordon, B. and L. Rittenberg (1995), "The Warsaw stock exchange: A test of market efficiency", *Comparative Economic Studies*, Vol.37, No.2 (Summer), pp.1-27.

Goss, B. A. and B. S. Yamey (eds) (1976), *The Economics of Futures Trading*, London, The MacMillan Press.

Greenaway, D. and C. W. Morgan (eds) (1999), *The Economics of Commodity Markets*, Cheltenham, Edward Elgar.

Grubel, H.G (1966), "The Anatomy of Classical and Modern Infant Industry Arguments", *Weltwirtschaftliches Archiv*, 97, pp.325-344.

Glowny Urzad Statystyczny (GUS) (Central Statistical Office), *Rocznik Statystyczny (Statistical Yearbook)*, Warsaw, Annual.

Hare, P. G. (ed) (1999), *Systemic Change in Post-communist Economies*, London, The MacMillan Press.

Harris, S., M. Salmon and B. Smith (1978), *Analysis of Commodity Markets for Policy Purposes*, Thames Essay No.17, London, Trade Policy Research Center.

Hemmi, K. (1963), *Sekai Nousanbutsu Shijyo no kadai (Problems in the World Market of Agricultural Products)*, Tokyo, Taimeido.

Hemmi, K. (1967), *Daiichijishohin Mondai I (Primary Commodity Problem I)*, Tokyo, Institute of Developing Economies.

Hemmi, K. (1975-76), "Kokusai Komugi kyoutei no Rekishi" ("History of the International Wheat Agreement"), *Kanzei Chosa Geppou (Monthly Bulletin on Tariff Policy Research)*, Vol.29, No.1, pp.31-46.

Hicks, J. R. (1946), *Value and Capital: An Inquiry into Some Fundamental Principles of Economic Theory*, 2nd ed., Oxford, The Clarendon Press.

Hicks, J. R. (1956), *A Revision of Demand Theory*, Oxford, The Clarendon Press.

Hieronymus, T. A. (1971), *Economics of Futures Trading*, New York, Commodity Research Bureau Inc.

Irie, S. (1978), *Shijyo Keizai to Shohin Kakaku (Market Economy and Commodity Prices)*, Osaka, Investment Journal.

Itoh, M., K. Kiyono, M. Okuno, and K. Suzumura (eds) (1988), *Sangyoseisaku no Keizaibunseki (Economic Analyses of Industrial Policy)*, Tokyo, Tokyo University Press.

Japan External Trade Organization (JETRO), *Sekai to Nihon no Kaigai Chokusetsu Toshi (Foreign Direct Investment of the World and Japan)*, Tokyo, JETRO, Annual.

Jodkowski, A., D. Stuglik, and K. Zukrowska (1996), "East-West joint ventures in the transformation process", International research within the ACE PHARE project.

Johnson, H. G. (1967), *Economic Policies Towards Less Developed Countries*, Washington DC, The Brookings Institution.

Kaldor, N. (1952), *A Reconsideration of the Economics of International Wheat Agreement*, Rome, FAO.

Karpinska-Mizielinska,Wanda and T. Smuga (1996), "Ownership transformation process in Poland", IRiSS, *Transforming Polish Economy 1995*, Warsaw, Institute of Development and Strategic Studies, pp.153-168.

Kawagoe, T. (1993), "Land Reform in Postwar Japan", J. Teranishi, and Y. Kousai (eds) (1993) , chapter 8, pp.178-204.

Keohane, R. O. (1983), "The demand for international regimes", Krasner (ed) (1983a), pp.141-171.

Keohane, R. O. (1984), *After Hegemony*, Princeton, Princeton University Press.

Keynes, J. M. (1936), *The General Theory of Employment, Interest and Money*, London, The MacMillan Press.

Keynes, J. M. (1938), "The policy of government storage of food-Stuffs and raw materials", *Economic Journal*, Vol. XLVIII (September), pp.449-460.

Kiminami, A. and R. Kiminami (1995), "Chugoku ni okeru Kokumotsu Sakimono Torihiki ni Kansuru Kenkyu" ("A study of grain futures market in China"), *Sakimono Torihiki Kenkyu (Journal of Futures Market)*, Vol.1, No.1 (June), pp.41-50.

Kiss, K. (1993), *Western Prescriptions for Eastern Transition*, Budapest, Hungarian Scientific Council for World Economy.

Kolodko, G. W. (1992), "Polish hyperinflation and stabilization 1989-1991", Kolodko and others (eds)(1992), pp.70-113.

Kolodko, G. W., D. Gotz-Kozierkiewicz and E. Skrzeszewska-Paczek (eds) (1992), *Hyperinflation and Stabilization in Postsocialist Economies*, Dordrecht, Kluwer Academic Publishers.

Komiya, R. (1972), "Chokusetsu toshi no riron" ("A theory of foreign direct investment"), S. Sumita, R. Komiya and Y. Watanabe (eds) (1972), pp.166-192.

Komiya, R. (1975a), *Gendai Nihonkeizai Kenkyu (Study of Contemporary Japanese Economy)*, Tokyo, Tokyo University Press.

Komiya, R. (1975b), "Sengo Nihon no shihon chikusekiritsu" ("Capital accumulation ratio in Postwar Japan"), Komiya (ed) (1975a), pp.3-32.

Komiya, R. (1975c), "Kojin chochiku no kyokyu" ("Supply of individual savings"), Komiya (1975a), pp. 33-58.

Komiya, R. (1984), "Jyosho"("Introduction"), Komiya and others (eds) (1984), pp. 1- 22.

Komiya, R. (1988), *Gendai Nihonkeizai (Contemporary Japanese Economy)*, Tokyo, Tokyo University Press.

Komiya, R. and A. Amano (1972), *Kokusai Keizaigaku (International Economics)*, Tokyo, Iwanami.

Komiya, R. and M. Suda (1983), *Gendai Kokusai Kinyuron: Riron hen (Modern International Finance: Theory)*, Tokyo, Nihon Keizai Shimbun.

Komiya, R., M. Okuno and K. Suzumura (eds) (1984), *Nihon no Sangyo Seisaku (Industrial Policies in Japan)*, Tokyo, Tokyo University Press.

Kornai, J. (1993), "Transzformacios visszaeses (Transformational crisis)", *Kozgazdasagi Szemle (Economic Review)*, No.7-8, pp.569-599

Kousai, Y. (1995), *Yen no Sengoshi (Postwar History of Yen)*, Tokyo, Nihon Hoso Shuppan Kyokai.

Kousaka, M., and S. Kumon (eds.) (1983), *Kokusai Seijigaku no Kisochishiki (Grounding in International Politics)*, Tokyo, Yuhikaku.

Krasner, S. D. (ed) (1983a), *International Regimes,* Ithaca, Cornell University Press.

Krasner, S. D. (1983b), "Structural cause and regime consequences: Regimes as intervening variables", Krasner (ed) (1983a), pp.1-21.

Krause, L.B. (1976), "Cartels or cooperation: Current proposals for handling primary commodities", US House of Representatives, Committee on International Relations, Washington, DC.

Krugman, P. (1994), "The myth of Asia's miracle, a cautionary fable", *Foreign Affairs*, No.73 (November/December), pp.62-78.

Krugman, P. (1996), "Are currency crisis self-fulfilling?", *NBER Macroeconomics Annual*, Cambridge, MA, the MIT press.

Krugman, P. (1998), "Saving Asia: It's time to get radical", *Fortune*, No.7 (September), pp.74-80.

Kulikowski, R., Z. Nahorski, and Jan W. Owsinski (eds) (2001), *Modelling of Economic Transition Phenomena,* Warsaw, University of Information Technology and Management.

Labys, W. C. (1974), "Speculation and price instability on international commodity futures markets", UNCTAD, TD/B/C. 1/171 (December).

Lampe, J. R (1992), *Creating Capital Markets in Eastern Europe*, Baltimore, The Johns Hopkins University Press.

Lavigne, M. (1995), *The Economics of Transition: From Socialist Economy to Market Economy,* London, The Macmillan Press.

Lerner, A. P. (1944), *The Economics of Control*, London, The Macmillan Press.

Leybourne, S. J., T. A. Lloyd and G. V. Reed (1994), "The excess comovement of commodity prices revisited", *World Development*, Vol.22, No.11, pp.1747-1758.

Lipton, D. and J. Sachs (1990), "Creating a market economy in Eastern Europe: The case of Poland", Brookings Papers on Economic Activity 1, pp.75-147.

Lipton, D. and J. Sachs (1990), "Privatization in Eastern Europe: The Case of Poland", Brookings Papers on Economic Activity 2, pp.293-341.

Los, M. (ed) (1990), *The Second Economy in Marxist States*, London, The Macmillan Press.

Macbean, A, I. (1966), *Export Instability and Economic Development*, London, Allen and Unwin.

Mase, T. (1978), "Nihon no shohin torihikijyo <14> Tokyo Gomu Torihikijyo" ("Commodity exchanges in Japan <14> Tokyo Rubber Exchange"), *Shohin Sakimono Shijyo (Commodity Futures Markets)*, Vol.2, No.2 (February), pp. 24-25.

McCalla, A. F. (1966), "A duopoly model of world wheat pricing", *Journal of Farm Economics,* Vol.48, No.3 (August), pp. 711-727.

McKinnon, R. I. (1967), "Futures markets, buffer stocks, and income stability for primary producers", *The Journal of Political Economy*, Vol.75, No.6 (December), pp.844-861.

McKinnon, R. I. (1991), *The Order of Economic Liberalization*, Baltimore, The Johns Hopkins University Press.

McMillan, C. H. (1993), "The role of foreign direct investment in the transition from planned to market economies", *Transnational Corporations*, Vol.2, No.3 (December), pp.97-120.

McMillan, C. H. and M. Hakogi (1998), "Foreign direct investment and economic transition: Assessing the impacts on the hungarian economy", *Journal of the Graduate School of International Cultural Studies (Tohoku University)*, Vol.6, pp.101-116.

McMillan, C. H. and K. Morita (2000), "Attracting foreign direct investment in the first decade of transition : Assessing the successes", Paper presented at the VI ICCEES World Congress, Tampere, Finland, 29 July- 3 August.

Meade, J. E. (1949-50), "Degrees of competitive speculation", *Review of Economic Studies*, Vol.17, No.44, pp.159-167.

Meade, J. E. (1964), "International commodity agreements", *Lloyds Bank Review*, No.73 (July), pp.28-42.

Meyer, K. E. (1995), "Foreign direct investment in the early years of economic transition: A survey", European Bank for Reconstruction and Development (ed), *The Economics of Transition*, Vol.3.

Ministry of Finance (1978), *Showa Zaisei Shi (Showa History of Japanese Finance)*, Tokyo, Toyo Keizai Shimpou.

Ministry of International Trade and Industry (MITI), *Tsusho Hakusho (White Paper: Japanese International trade and industry)*, Tokyo, MITI, Annual.

Miwa, Y. (1993), "Economic effects of the anti-monopoly and other deconcentration policies in postwar Japan", J. Teranishi and Y. Kousai (eds) (1993), pp.129-152.

Miyazaki, Y. and M. Itho (1961), *Komentaru Keynes Ippan Riron (Commentary on Keynes General Theory)*, Tokyo, Nihon Hyoron.

Morita, K. (1978), "Kokusai Shohinkyotei no Keizaibunseki (An economic analysis of the international commodity agreement)", *Ajia Keizai (Developing Economies)*, Vol.19, No.9 (September), pp.2-25.

Morita, K. (1980), "Kokusai Shohinkyotei no Keizaishakaigaku (A sociological study of the international commodity agreement)", *Ajia Keizai (Developing Economies)*, Vol.21, No.12 (December), pp.2-19.

Morita, K. (1981), "Kansho Zaiko to Shotoku Hosho no Kikai Hiyo ni Tsuite (On opportunity costs of Buffer Stock and Income Compensation)", *Ajia Keizai (Developing Economies)*, Vol.22, No.2 (February), pp.61-68.

Morita, K. (1986), "Poland ni okeru Dainikeizai" ("On a second economy in Poland"), *Ajia Keizai (Developing Economies)*, Vol.27, No.2 (February), pp.2-14.

Morita, K. (1989), "Daihatsu-FSO keisu no Keizai Bunseki (An economic analysis of the Daihatsu-FSO case)", *Shogaku Tokyu (The Economic Review)*, Vol.40,

No.2 (October), pp.1-29.

Morita, K. (1992), "On an inefficiency of adjustment mechanisms in centralized economies", *Acta Slavica Iaponica*, Tomus X, pp.115-129.

Morita, K. (1993a), "Economic relations of Japan with East European Countries: International regime approach", paper presented at the 34th ISA Annual Meetings in Acapulco, Mexico, 23-27 March.

Morita, K. (1993b), "Analiza porownawcza powojennych japonskich reform Gospodarczych oraz w spolczesnych polskich reform ekonomicznych (A comparative analysis between postwar Japanese economic reforms and current Polish economic reforms)", Hans-Georg Fleck and R. Lawniczak (eds) (1993), pp.165-185.

Morita, K. (1994a), "On an economic analysis of foreign direct investment into Poland", paper presented at the 35th ISA Annual Meetings in Washington DC, 28 March-1 April.

Morita, K. (1994b), "Japonskie Doswiadczenia (Japanese experiences)", *Zycie Gospodarcze (Economic Life)* 2.

Morita, K. (1994c), "Common anticompetitive obstacles to development and transition: Poland and the Philippines", paper presented at the 26th AAASS Annual Meetings, Philadelphia, 17-20 November.

Morita, K. (1995), "Japan's foreign direct investment in East European Countries", Zloch (ed) (1995), pp.183-195.

Morita, K. (1996a), "Reformy w powojennej Japonii a reformy w Polsce (Reforms in postwar Japan and reforms in Poland)", *Gospodarka i Przyszlosc (Economy and future)*, 1/4, pp.62-66

Morita, K. (1996b), "Japanese foreign economic relations with Eastern Europe: Is Japan's FDI into Poland in underpresence?", paper presented at AAASS 28th National Convention, Boston, MA, 14-17 November.

Morita, K. (ed) (1996c), *Funsochiiki Gendaishi 4 - Chu-Toou (Modern History of Conflict Regions 4 - Central and Eastern Europe)*, Tokyo, Dobunkan.

Morita, K. (1997a), "Poland no shijyokeizai ikou: Balcerowicz Program wo megutte" ("Polish transition to the market economy: On the Balcerowicz Program"), *Kokusai Kyoryoku Kenkyushi (Journal of International Development and Cooperation)*, Vol.3, No.1 (March), pp.137-149.

Morita, K. (1997b), "On an analysis of Japan's FDI into Eastern Europe: A case of risky FDI into Poland", paper presented at the 38th ISA Annual Meetings, Toronto, 18-22 March.

Morita, K. (1997c), "An economic analysis of foreign direct investment into Eastern Europe: A case of Japan's FDI into Poland", paper presented at the Conference on Transition to Advanced Market Institutions and Economies, Warsaw, 18-21 June.

Morita, K. (1997d), "On the necessity of commodity exchange in transition economies: A case of Poland", paper presented at the Conference on the Socioeconomic Problems of Transitional Economies, 30-31 July, Nagoya, United Nations Centre for Regional Development.

Morita, K. (1997e), "On a weakness of Japan's FDI into East European countries", *South East European Monitor*, Vol.4, pp.3-16.

Morita, K. (1998), "On determinants of Japan's foreign direct investment in East Europe: The case of Poland", *Journal of East-West Business*, Vol.4, pp.141-148.

Morita, K. (1999), "Polish Economic Reforms in Japanese Historical Perspectives", Hare, P. G. (ed) (1999), pp.135 -146.

Morita, K (2001), "An analysis of foreign direct investment in Eastern Europe: a case of Japan's FDI in Poland", R. Kulikowski, Z. Nahorski and J. W. Owsinski (eds), pp.285-303.

Morita, K. and S. S. Rosefielde (1994), "Post Kyosanshugi Roshia no Keizai Hatten: Gerschenkron Kasetsu no Saikentoa" ("Russian post communist redevelopment in historical perspective: The Gerschenkron hypothesis reconsidered"), *Keizai Ronso (The Hiroshima Economic Review)*, Vol.18, No.3 (November), pp.1-15.

Morita, K. and P. Bozyk (1997), "Kaikaku no seiji keizaigaku (Political economy of reforms)", *Keizai Ronso (The Hiroshima Economic Review)*, Vol.20, No.2-3 (February), pp.1-15.

Morita, K. and D. Stuglik (1998), "Nihon no tai Poland chokusetsu toshi: Genjyo to kettei youin" ("Japan's foreign direct investment into Poland: Current situation and determinants"), *Keizai Ronso (The Hiroshima Economic Review)*, Vol.21, No.4 (March), pp.21- 40.

Mundell, R. A. (1969), "The crisis problem", Mundell R. A. and A. K. Swoboda (eds) (1969), pp.343-349.

Mundell, R. A. and A. K. Swoboda (eds) (1969), *Monetary Problems of the International Economy*, Chicago, The University of Chicago Press.

Nakamura, T. (1978), *Nihon Keizai - Sono Seicho to Kouzou (Japanese Economy - The Growth and Structure)*, Tokyo, Tokyo University Press.

National Bank of Poland (1990), *Annual Report 1990*, Warsaw, Office of the President.

Nishibe, S. (1975), *Soshio Ekonomikusu(Socio Economics)*, Tokyo, Chuo Koron sha.

Nuti, D. M. and R. Portes (1993), "Central Europe: The Way Forward", R. Portes (ed) *Economic Transformation in Central Europe: A Progress Report*, London, CEPR and Commission of the European Communities, pp12-14.

Panstwowa Agencja Investycji Zagranicznych (PAIZ) (Polish Agency for Foreign Investment), *Foreign Investments in Poland*, Warsaw, Annual.

Parsons, T. and N. J. Smelser (1956), *Economy and Society : A Study in the Integration of Economic and Social Theory*, Routledge and Kegan Paul Ltd.

Penrose, E. T. (1956), "Foreign investment and the growth of the firm", *Economic Journal*, Vol.66 (June), pp.220-235.

Polanyi, K (1977), *The Livelihood of Man*, H. W. Pearson (ed.), New York, Academic Press.

Polanyi, K., C. M. Arensberg and H. W. Pearson (ed) (1957), *Trade and Market in the Early Empires*, New York, The Free Press.

Poole, W. (1970), "McKinnon on futures markets and buffer Stocks", *The Journal of Political Economy*, Vol.78, No.5 (September/October), pp.1185-1190.

Praetz, P. D. (1976), "Testing the efficient markets theory on the Sydney Wool

Futures Exchange", B. A. Goss and B. S. Yamey (eds) (1976), pp.205-216.

Roberts, H. (1967), "Statistical versus clinical prediction of the stock market", unpublished manuscript, CRSP, University of Chicago, May.

Rosefielde, S. S. (ed) (1980), *World Communism at the Crossroads Military Ascendancy, Political Economy & Human Welfare*, Dortrecht, Kluwer Academic Publishers.

Rosefielde, S. S. (1998), *Efficiency and Russia's Recovery Potential to the Year 2000 and Beyond*, Hampshire, Ashgate Publishing.

Rotyis, M. R. (1992), "The Budapest Stock Exchange: Lessons and challenges", John R. Lampe (ed.) (1992), pp.47-55.

Rowe, J. W. F. (1965), *Primary Commodities in International Trade*, Cambridge, Cambridge University Press.

Ruggie, J. G. (1975), "International responses to technology: concepts and trends," *International Organization*, Vol.29, No.3 (Summer), pp.557-583.

Rugman, A. M. (1985), "Internalization is still a general theory of foreign direct investment", *Weltwirtschaftliches Archiv*, Vol.121, pp.570-575.

Sachs, J. (1994), *Poland's Jump to the Market Economy*, Cambridge, MA, The MIT Press.

Sajkiewicz, B. (1995), "Poland's price policy", IPiSS, *Social Policy in 1993-1994 : Main Problems in Transition Period*, Warsaw, Institute of Labour and Social Studies, pp.53-61.

Sakai, H. (1979), "Ichijisanpin kakaku no tanki fuanteisei" ("Short-term instability of primary commodity prices"), *Ajia Keizai (Developing Economies)*, Vol.20, No.10 (October), pp. 123-141.

Samonis, V. (ed) (1998), *Enterprise Restructuring and Foreign Investment in the Transforming East: The Impact of Privatization*, New York, The Haworth Press.

Santiso, J. (1997), *Wall Street Face à la Crise Mexicaine*, CEPII Working Paper, Paris, Centre d'Etudes Prospectives et d'Information Internationales.

Scherer, F. M. (1970), *Industrial Market Structure and Economic Performance*, Chicago, Rand McNally College Publishing Company.

Schiller, R. J. (1991), *Market Volatility*, Cambridge, MA, The MIT Press.

Sekino, I. (1976), "Long-term import contract", *MITI Primary Commodity Committee Report (Volume 1)*.

Sephton, P. S. and D. K. Cochrane (1991), "The efficiency of the London Metal Exchange: Another look at the evidence", *Applied Economics*, Vol.23, No.4A (April), pp.669-674.

Serletis, A. and D. Scowcroft (1991), "Informational efficiency of commodity futures prices", *Applied Financial Economics*, Vol.1, No.4 (December), pp.185-192.

Shiobara, T., H. Matsubara and M. Ohashi (eds.) (1969), *Shakaigaku no Kisochishiki (Grounding in Sociology)*, Tokyo, Yuhikaku.

Smelser, N. J. (1959), "A comparative view of exchange systems", *Economic Development and Cultural Change*, Vol.7, No.2, pp.173-182.

Smith, G. and G. R. Schink (1976), "The International Tin Agreement: a Reassessment," *Economic Journal*, Vo.86, pp.715-728.

Sohmen, E. (1966), *The Theory of Forward Exchange*, Princeton Studies in International Finance, No.17.

Stein, A. A. (1983), "Coordination and collaboration: regimes in an anarchic world", Krasner, S. D. (ed) (1983a), pp.115-140.

Stein, J. (1986), *The Economics of Futures Markets*, Oxford, Basil Blackwell.

Stiglitz, J. E. (1994), *Whither Socialism?* Cambridge, MA, The MIT Press.

Stiglitz, J. E. and A. Weiss (1981), "Credit rationing in markets with imperfect information", *The American Economic Review*, Vol.71 (June), pp.393-410.

Strange, S. (1983), "Cave! hic dragons: a critique of regime analysis", Krasner (ed) (1983a), pp.337-354.

Strange, S. (1986), *Casino Capitalism*, Oxford, Basil Blackwell.

Strange, S. (1998), *Mad Money*, Manchester, Manchester University Press.

Sueuchi, K. (1990), "Kokusai seiji keizai kenkyu no doukou to kadai (Studies of international political economy: Their evolution and limitations)", *Kokusai Seiji 93:Kokusai Seiji Keizaigaku no Mosaku (International Relations Vol.93:In Search of International Political Economy)*, The Japan Association of International Relations, pp.43-55.

Sumita, S., R. Komiya and Y. Watanabe (eds) (1972), *Takokuseki kigyo no jittai (Economic Analysis of Multinational Corporations)*, Tokyo, Nihon Keizai Shimbun.

Szanyi, M. (1997), "Experience with foreign direct investment in Eastern Europe: Advantages and disadvantages", Working Paper No. 85, Institute of World Economy, Budapest, November.

Szanyi, M. and T. Szemler (1997), "Investment patterns in Hungary 1989-95", Working Paper No. 79, Institute of World Economy, Budapest, May.

Szekeres, V. (1999), "Comparative studies of foreign and indigenous enterprises in the Hungarian manufacturing industries", paper presented at the 40th Annual Convention of the International Studies Association, Washington, DC, 20 February.

Telser, L. G. and H. N. Higinbotham (1977), "Organized futures markets: Costs and benefits", *The Journal of Political Economy*, Vol.85, No.6 (October), pp.969-1000.

Teranishi, J. and Y. Kousai (eds) (1993), *The Japanese Experience of Economic Reform*, London, The Macmillan Press.

Tokyo Rubber Exchange (1975), *Tokyo Gomu Torihikijyo 20 Nen Shi (20 Years History of Tokyo Rubber Exchange)*, Tokyo, Tokyo Gomu Torihikijyo.

Tominaga, K. (1965), *Shakai Hendou no Riron (Theory of Social Change)*, Tokyo, Iwanami.

Tominaga, K. (1999), *Shakaigaku Kougi (Lectures of Sociology)*, Tokyo, Chuo Koron Shinsha.

Tyszynski, H. (1949), "Economics of the wheat agreement", *Economica*, Vol.16, No.61 (February), pp.27-39.

UNCRD (United Nations Centre for Regional Development)(1998), *Transition of Asian, African and European Economies to the Market and Socioeconomic Dislocations*, UNCRD Proceedings Series, No.24.

United Nations (1954), *Commodity Trade and Economic Development*, Geneva, United Nations.

United Nations (1999), *World Investment Report 1999*, Geneva, United Nations.

United Nations, *Yearbook of International Trade Statistics*, Annual, United Nations.

Vaga, T. (1994), *Profiting from Chaos*, New York, McGraw-Hill.

Wallerstein, I. (1974), *The Modern World-System: Capitalist Agriculture and the Origins of the European World-Economy in the Sixteenth Century*, New York, Academic Press.

Wallerstein, I. (1980), *The Modern World-System II: Mercantilism and the Consolidation of the European World-Economy, 1600-1750*, New York, Academic Press.

WERI (World Economy Research Institute), *Poland: International Economic Report*, Warsaw, Warsaw School of Economics, Annual.

WERI (1993), *Transforming the Polish Economy*, Warsaw, Warsaw School of Economics.

WERI (1994), *Transforming the Polish Economy II*, Warsaw, Warsaw School of Economics.

Winiecki, J. (1988), *The Distorted World of Soviet-Type Economies*, London, Routledge.

Witkowska, J. (1997), "Foreign direct investment as a factor of structural change in the Polish economy", *Osteuropa Wirtschaft*, Vol 42 (December), pp.418-36.

World Bank (1993), *The East Asian Miracle*, New York, Oxford University Press.

World Bank (1996), *World Development Report 1996: From Plan To Market*, New York, Oxford University Press.

Yamazaki, T. (1989), "'Boueki Regime' e no shiten (Viewpoints towards a 'trade regime')," *Sekai Keizai Hyouron (World Economic Review)*, Vol.33, No.1, pp.74-78.

Zdebel, M. (1995), *Ustawa o Narodowych Funduszach Inwestycyjnych i Ich Prywatyzacji (National Investment Fund and Privatization Act)*, Bielsko-Biala, Studio STO.

Zecchini, S. (ed) (1999), *Lessons from the Economic Transition: Central and Eastern Europe in the 1990s*, Dordrecht, Kluwer Academic Publishers.

Zloch-Christy, I. (ed) (1995), *Privatization and Foreign Investments in Eastern Europe*, London, Praeger.

Zloch-Christy, I. (1996), "Industrial policy: Does Eastern Europe need one?", paper presented at the ISA-JAIR joint conference, Makuhari, 20-22 September.

Index

Printed in the United States
by Baker & Taylor Publisher Services